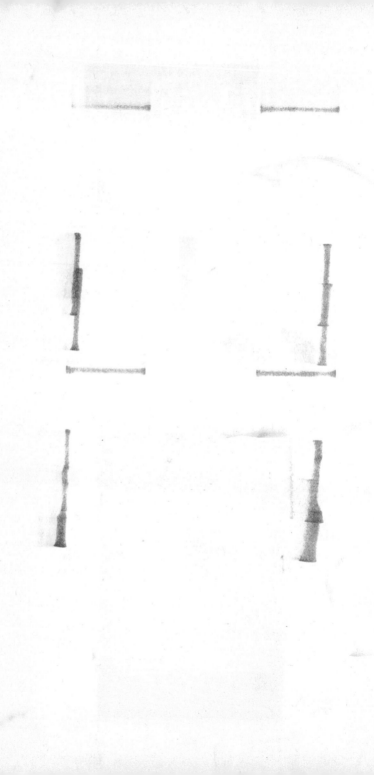

The Logic of the Law

THE
LOGIC OF
THE LAW

GORDON TULLOCK

Basic Books, Inc., Publishers

NEW YORK   LONDON

Preface

Not long ago a British barrister told me that we should have drastic overhauls of the law, and completely re-examine legal procedures, only about every two hundred years. Normally, he felt the law should proceed by gradual development without any effort to return to first principles. I pointed out to him that the two-hundredth anniversary of the year when Jeremy Bentham first began to press for law reform was rapidly approaching, and that if any of the changes now proposed took as long to implement as the Benthamite changes, we would have another two-hundred year interval until the time they come to pass if we started thinking about radical revision now. Since he had intended his argument essentially as a protest against any basic reconsideration of the law, my remark rather took him unawares. However, being one of the most rational of men, he conceded that upon his own premises it was time to begin to consider legal reform.

This volume is an effort to start such a basic reconsideration. At most times and, for that matter, at the present time, there is a great deal of public dissatisfaction with the law and a good many proposals are being canvassed for reform. In general, however, this dissatisfaction and these proposals for reform take most of the law for granted and merely propose to change minor details.

Bentham, of course, attempted to go back to basic principles and examine the law in its entirety. Although the changes Bentham eventually succeeded in implementing were fairly drastic, the foundations of the law are much the same as they were before he was born. It seems likely that any rethinking of the law will conclude that the law is fundamentally rational, and changes, even those as drastic as the Benthamite reforms, will leave a great deal of the basic legal structure intact.

A great many changes have occurred since Bentham's day, such as the great development of social science. Since we now have a vast collection of tools that was not available to Bentham, it is possible for us to improve on his work. Another modern advantage is the existence of a large community of scholars. The most desirable effect of this book would be to start a scientific discussion of the foundations of the law. Hopefully this discussion, together with empirical research, will lead to significant reforms. In any event, it is reasonable to look at the law *de novo*—to go back to basic principles and attempt to develop a logical structure. The conventional legal scholar will no doubt regard my methods as a radical departure from those to which he is accustomed. He will be correct. In a sense, my book is an attack upon the traditional methods of legal scholarship, which takes the form, however, not of direct criticism but of a presentation of a different procedure that I believe to be superior.

My own formal education was in the law (D. J., University of Chicago, 1947), but the methods used in this book are those of modern welfare economics. A few legal scholars—Calabrese, Blum, and Kalven come immediately to mind—have begun applying similar methods to various aspects of the law, but most law professors have never even thought of using them. This book makes no moral assumptions, and it is strictly utilitarian in its approach to legal institutions. In this I follow Bentham, but I have an advantage over him: that of modern welfare economics. As the reader will discover in Chapter 1, I even have a modification of welfare economics to suggest. It seems to me that these tools give us an advantage. Hopefully, this book will merely be a first step in the application of modern welfare economics to an analysis of legal problems. Our present legal system cries out for reform, and improved knowledge is a necessary prerequisite for genuine reform. It is my hope that many other scholars will push forward along the lines that I have followed.

This book is intended to begin discussion in a new field; it applies the latest tools of the social sciences to the law and to legal institutions. Eventually, after a number of other scholars have added their work to mine, it should be possible to improve our present legal institutions and our law. The substantive improvements, however, will probably not be gigantic. Although there are areas in which, if I am correct, our present law is far from optimal, the changes I propose in general are not of a revolutionary nature. In many cases, in fact, all I propose is that what we say be made to conform to what we actually do. To repeat, if the actual changes that I suggest are relatively modest, the foundations of my reasoning are radically different from the tradition.

Still, I feel confident that, at the very least, it is worthwhile to experiment with new techniques. The law is an important area and deserves every bit of light that can be shed upon it. Even those who think my light faint and flickering should agree that it will do at least some good. Economists are likely to feel that the tools I am using are correct. Indeed it is partly my own economic experience and partly my desire to attract economists into the field that has led me to use these tools in an extremely strict way. Actually, it is possible to achieve most of the conclusions of this book without such a rigorous adherence to the welfare economics schemata. People who are antagonistic to formal welfare economics could, strictly speaking, skip the first two chapters of the book and still find that they were able to agree with much of the rest of it.

Before closing this preface, I should like to explain why the institution of property is not thoroughly examined in the book, and why there is very little discussion of externality. The reason for leaving out externality is quite simple: I have written another book in this general field.* The reason for not discussing property is somewhat more complicated but basically similar. This is an extremely complex area in which welfare economics has a major

---

* Gordon Tullock, *Private Wants, Public Means* (New York: Basic Books, Inc., 1970).

role. Unfortunately, the complexities are so great that they would take another book to discuss them properly.

I should like to thank Donald Dewey for his thorough and penetrating criticism of an earlier draft of this book. I feel I should also thank Irving Kristol and Martin Kessler of Basic Books, Inc., for their willingness to publish a book that is fairly certain to receive vigorous, not to say acerbic, criticism.

Contents

PART IV
ETHICS

PART I

FUNDAMENTAL ASSUMPTIONS

1

Law Without Ethics

In recent years, "ethical science" has fallen into disrepute, not because we are necessarily less moral now or because we worry about ethical problems less, but because of the obvious flaws in the "scientific" treatises on the subject. From Plato and Aristotle to St. Thomas Aquinas and William James, numerous books of all degrees of profundity have been produced that purport to deduce an ethical system from a few basic postulates. The dearth of current books on the subject reflects neither disrespect for the great minds who have labored in the field nor a belief that they have solved the problem, but is merely an indication of simple skepticism. Any critical examination of these works indicates that their authors have made mistakes in logic that escaped their notice because they were morally convinced of the truth of their results. A man who firmly believes murder to be undesirable is not likely to be critical of a line of reasoning that leads to this conclusion.

In a way the modern skepticism about these classics, or about a modern attempt to repeat them, stems from our interest in different cultures. The knowledge that other people have different moral systems, although not really fully integrated into the reasoning of many students, has resulted in a more critical approach to the moral philosophers, and hence has contributed to the present lack of courses in "ethical science." In partial compensation, anthropologists have undertaken genuinely scientific studies of the ethical systems of different peoples and modern philosophers also study ethics in a more cautious and less sweeping way.

The philosophy of law is normally based on ethics. Although exceptions have occurred, most justifications of law are built upon an ethical base. These, until recently, were in much the same category as "ethical science," since they normally tried to justify the ethics. The more modern examples of legal philosophy simply assume an ethical system, either explicitly or implicitly, and then go on from there. Beginning in the 1930's, a school of legal positivists argued that the law was simply what the state decreed, and morals were not involved. The history of this movement would appear to indicate, however, that the positivists were unconsciously applying notions of natural law; they thought that the state was only going to enact laws of which they approved. The realization that states might enact laws that they violently disliked resulted in a fairly complete, albeit not necessarily publicly admitted, return to the natural law. Whatever else may be said about the Nuremberg trials, they marked the burial of legal positivism.

Recently legal positivism has had a limited and partial revival in the form of the view that the "Constitution is what the Supreme Court says it is." An analysis of the writing of the proponents of this view, however, will always uncover examples of Supreme Court decisions that they regard as incorrect. According to their strict argument, of course, this is impossible, and some higher standard is necessary. Again, the higher standard is simply a rather cloudy version of the natural law. In fact, it is more or less true that the whole present upsurge of apparent respect for the Supreme Court as a law-making body is based upon the fact that the decisions of the Court have recently tended closely to approximate the views on ethics held by a number of very articulate students.

This desperately brief and overcondensed discussion of recent developments in the field of legal and moral philosophy is intended to put the present study in perspective. In this book I intend to return to the approach of the nineteenth century, albeit with so many changes that Mill and Bentham might not recognize it. If the efforts to develop a science of norms were all unsuccessful, they were at least attempts to do something worthwhile. A system of behavioral rules deduced from a few realistic assumptions would be of great value. The men who tried to find it can be criticized for erroneously believing they had found it when they had not, but they were right to look.

This book, then, continues the quest. I am using radically different methods, but my goal is the same. Unfortunately, I cannot promise that I will find the grail. A set of general rules is "justified" by reasoning from basic principles, but they do not cover all of law and ethics. In part the limitation is self-imposed and is motivated by a desire not to bore either myself or the reader. I carry certain chains of reasoning only far enough to indicate their general direction without working out all of the details. In a more important part, however, the limitations on my reasoning are not matters of choice. The method that I propose as "the logical foundation of law and ethics" may eventually lead to a solution of many important legal and ethical problems or, then again, it may not. Be that as it may, at present it is merely a start. For some whole fields the method only gives the most feeble results. Thus, I present my method, apply it in the areas in which I can make it work, and hope that others will extend the reasoning to cover the areas that I must forego.

My first radical departure from that used in earlier studies is that it starts with law and then proceeds to ethics. Instead of deducing the law from previously deduced ethics, I shall attempt to deduce legal principles that are not based upon ethics, and then use these principles to produce a justification of ethics. This may seem an attempt to be paradoxical, but the procedure is not merely an effort to be clever. It is a different basic approach which, I feel, may avoid many of the difficulties that have stultified previous work.

The history of discussion of the law indicates that it is extremely difficult to avoid the unconscious use of ethical premises. I cannot, therefore, promise that I will not make such a mistake. All I can do is to say that I honestly tried to avoid it. The basic tools used in this book will be those of welfare economics. Like most welfare economists, I have always used the basic Paretian tools and have always felt a little unhappy about them.[1] In this book, I not only use the Paretian apparatus, but I should like to suggest a

---

[1] Cf. James M. Buchanan and Gordon Tullock, *The Calculus of Consent* (Ann Arbor: University of Michigan Press, 1962), especially pp. 85–99.

rather modest improvement in it; a somewhat simpler set of basic assumptions from which both welfare economics and the specific conclusions of this book can be deduced.

If we consider all possible changes in the state of the world, there will be some subset of those changes that is to my advantage. Furthermore, within this subset of possible changes is a further subset of changes that will also be to the advantage of you, the reader of this book. Last, but not least, within this second subset there is or at least may be another subset of possible changes that would be to the advantage of any person to whom you are talking. If this last subset is not an empty set, clearly I can argue that you should adopt it because it would be to your advantage and you can then argue with other people that they should adopt

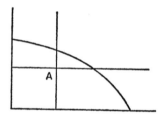

FIGURE 1–1 Conditional Public Welfare Diagram

it because it would be to their advantage. Since I have put the matter in a perfectly general way, this amounts to saying that there may be some changes in the state of the world that are to everyone's advantage and that I can reasonably argue for them in terms of the advantage to other people, although my motive for doing so is self-interest. If such changes are possible, then we have an extremely elementary criterion for suggesting change. A proposed change within this set cannot be objectionable to anyone because if it is objectionable to anyone, it is not in the set.

Note that the converse is also true. In traditional discussion of Pareto optimality, changes that are desirable have been the principal theme and there has been little mention of changes that are clearly undesirable. Nevertheless, the traditional Paretian diagram shown in Figure 1–1 can be used to indicate undesirable changes.

It is assumed that society is now at point A. The area of Pareto optimal changes shown by the triangle between the two lines through point A and the possibility frontier is, of course, the traditional area for desirable changes. The rectangle below and to the left of the point A, however, is an area of inefficient changes. Changes from point A to any point in that area injure at least one person and benefit no one. The two other areas, the second and fourth quadrants around point A, are areas of ambiguity. Strictly speaking, the economist cannot say anything about changes that will move into these two areas.

But if we have here a logically perfect method of selecting certain desirable policy changes, we still must ask if there are any possible policies that lie within the set. I think there are and I am willing to argue that the policy of always undertaking Pareto optimal changes is an example. Suppose some change in the status quo is proposed and we discover by careful examination that it will injure no person and benefit at least one. Clearly my criteria do not indicate that everyone should favor it, although we could say that no one would be against it. Consider, however, a "constitutional" decision to adopt all changes that may be suggested that are Pareto optimal. Clearly each person would be guaranteed against harm by any such change and would have some finite probability of being benefited by one of these changes in the future; therefore, this policy would be in the self-interest of each of us. Thus the traditional Pareto optimal criteria can be "justified" by the new and more primitive criteria that I have suggested.

The converse of this situation is also easily dealt with. We can imagine a possible change in the status quo that injures me. It might be part of the set of those changes that also injures you and some of the joint members of these two sets that would injure substantially everyone. I can argue against such a change for the same reasons I can argue for generally beneficial changes. If we consider possible changes in the real world, clearly not all changes would fall either in that set of changes that benefits substantially everyone or in that set of changes that injures practically everyone. The possibility of compensation, however, convinces most economists that the set that falls in one or the other of these categories is sizable. In this book, we will devote ourselves mainly to discussing

changes that are either in the subset of those that benefit everyone
or in the subset of those that injure everyone.

However, I may have not yet convinced my readers that the set
of all changes that meets my present criteria is not an empty one.
There are people who believe that there is no such thing as a truly
Pareto optimal change. It should be noted, then, that the criteria
that I have proposed would also indicate that some changes that
are not Pareto optimal should be made. Suppose we consider not
an individual change but a policy for making changes in the future.
Such a policy might well offer to every person a positive present
discounted value *ex ante* while at the same time injure people in
specific instances *ex post*. This type of Pareto optimality in the large
was used as a foundation for *The Calculus of Consent* by James
M. Buchanan and myself.[2] It can be used, however, for purposes
other than developing a rationale for political institutions. One can
imagine specific policies that would meet these criteria.

Martin Bailey once suggested that the federal government appoint an impartial board of cost-benefit analysts, which would
then examine all proposals for public improvement in the United
States. Those that the board found had a payoff higher than cost
would be undertaken, and those in which the opposite relationship
was found would not. Granting Bailey his implied assumptions
about the ability of this committee to accurately analyze costs and
benefits and to be free of bias, it is clear that an institution of this
sort would provide a positive discounted value for all of the
citizens of the United States except possibly (and I emphasize possibly) some people who presently have a high prospect of obtaining
a sizable gain from a project that is on the verge of implementa-
tion. Even this group, however, would be benefited if the proposal
were to put Bailey's reform into operation ten years from today
while permitting the present system to continue for ten years. I
am sure that we could produce many further examples of general
policies for making decisions in specific instances that would meet
the criteria proposed.

It will, of course, be noted that these criteria carry within them
a justification for welfare economics. If a proof has been developed
that some particular change is Pareto optimal, then we can dem-

[2] *Ibid.*

onstrate, on the basis of our criteria, that this change should be adopted without any ethical presuppositions at all. In any event, this is the basic methodological tool that I shall use throughout the book. If, however, I am going to argue that any specific policy change or (as will be true in many cases in this book) a retention of our present policy is desirable for me, for you, and for any random person to whom you may speak, I must have some way of convincing you that this change is in accord with other people's preferences. This means, in a sense, that I must make some statement about everybody's ordering of preferences. These statements are contained in Chapter 2 and, in a sense, the theoretical work contained in the rest of the book is a development of these assumptions as to what people want. Explicit assumptions as to the shape of individual preference curves have not played much of a part in economic thought. I think, however, that a set of assumptions as simple and relatively obvious as the ones I propose to use has been implicit in much of the thinking that has gone on in this field.

2

Fundamental Assumptions

A scientific theory consists of a logical structure proceeding from certain assumptions to certain conclusions. We hope that both the assumptions and the conclusions may be checked by comparing them with the real world; the more highly testable the theory, the better. Normally, however, certain parts of the theory are difficult to test. We are not unduly disturbed by this, since if parts of it survive tests we assume that the untestable remainder is also true. The theory contained in this book raises exceptional problems in testing. Unfortunately, many of its implications are normative; that is, they simply indicate what people should do. This is an extraordinarily hard-to-test type of implication. I hope that it will turn out that these implications are difficult, but not impossible, to test; but I must confess that for many of them I can, at the moment, propose no tests. Of necessity, if I cannot propose many direct tests for the implications of my theory, I am rather more concerned with its assumptions than I would be were they more testable.

The three major assumptions upon which I base my discussion are fairly simple and should raise relatively few difficulties. Their content is so slight and so much in accord with ordinary experience that they are reasonably invulnerable. The reader should note that two of these assumptions are assumptions about *his* preferences.

The fact that these assumptions are assumptions about the reader may seem surprising. Certainly if I am to make assumptions about any random reader of the book, these assumptions must be extremely general and primitive. Otherwise, they would not fit all possible readers. In fact, I shall occasionally point out special groups who might find that certain assumptions will not fit them in certain circumstances. In general, however, I think most of the readers will indeed find these assumptions are characteristic of their own situation.

In a sense, my argument for a given legal standard will be an appeal to the reader and will also be an argument that he could use in talking to other people. The other people, or, for that matter, the reader, could be drawn more or less at random from the entire population. The argument for the use of general standards instead of special laws for each individual person is simply that such laws can be urged in general debate. I cannot depend upon convincing anyone else that a special law giving me special powers is likely to be in his interest. If there is, however, some change in the law that would benefit substantially everyone, then it should be easier for me to argue for it. The person to whom I am speaking may have difficulty following a long train of reasoning, but at least no conflict of interest will result.

My first general assumption is that the reader is not in a position to assure himself of special legal treatment. That is, if I argue that you, the reader, should favor a law against theft, one of the basic assumptions is that you do not have a real opportunity to have a law enacted that prohibits theft by everyone else but leaves you free to steal. I am quite prepared to agree that such a law, with its special privilege for you, would be more to your advantage than general prohibition of theft. My argument applies only if you are in a position (as most of us are) wherein you have no real chance of securing such a special privilege. Dictators and kings would be differently placed, and the use of my logical system might lead them to enact such special laws. In point of fact, that "the law does not bind the sovereign" is a very old principle. In recent years, with the decline of the powers of kings and rulers in the English-speaking world, the rule has been modified to a very large extent. Still, even the most radical egalitarian of today would agree that the

Supreme Court cannot bind itself. It can be argued, of course, that it should act as if it were bound. But these are special cases that do not include most readers.

For most readers, a rule that everyone except X should be prohibited from stealing would be worse than a rule prohibiting everyone from stealing because most readers would have no possibility of being X.[1] The reader should favor *general* standards simply because a set of individually categorized standards is not likely to put him in a very favorable category. If he has a real chance of being put into a high category, such as a member of a legally privileged nobility, then I cannot argue that he should turn it down. In fact, my line of reasoning would suggest that the nobles have normally been sensible in trying to retain their privileges, just as the commonalty has been sensible in trying to reduce them.

While I can offer no argument for a set of general standards as against a set of special rules carefully designed to benefit the reader himself, I can warn him that historical evidence indicates that such systems have sometimes worked very badly. Furthermore, they sometimes turn out to be fraudulent. Often people have favored systems that they believed would give them a special position, only to later discover that they were deceived. The Bolsheviks, for example, promised the Russian proletariat a very special position in the state that they proposed to construct. At least some of the proletariat presumably supported the Bolsheviks for this reason. It turned out that the special position that was valuable in the "new society" was that of Bolshevik, not proletarian. The system did, of course, discriminate against some nonproletarians, but that can hardly have been much consolation to the proletarians themselves.

But this is merely an historic example. Basically the argument for *general* standards must turn on the fact that the probability of being in a privileged minority is low. Parenthetically, it is also hard to propagandize for a system of special privilege. If you wish to publicly argue for a certain set of laws, you must either argue for laws that are, or appear to be, in the general interest, or that concentrate on a powerful group that can override the majority. The only other alternative is the Bolshevik one of a secret conspiracy,

[1] See "A and B," *The Mikado*, William Gilbert and Arthur Sullivan.

but this will seldom be effective. For most people this set of alternatives is unreal, and they must thus argue for general standards, not a set of categorized norms.

It should be noted that in one area special groups seem to be able to obtain special legislation *ad infinitum*. This is what we may call "economic legislation." The old common law was, in general, binding on all people and intended to control everyone's activity. Modern legal codes are filled with special economic privileges for special groups. I cannot, for example, become a barber without the permission of other barbers, who are permitted to manipulate this permission in such a way as to obtain cartel gains. As a professor, I cannot be fired because of pressures that university professors in general have succeeded in applying to the university structure. We could go on and on with such examples. The "protective" tariff system, the regulatory agencies—all are examples of special privileges for special groups that are part of the law.

As I stated previously, it is not possible for me to criticize special groups for favoring laws that give them special privileges. It is possible however, to prove fairly readily that no one who is *not* a member of these special groups should favor these special privileges, and that probably most of the members of these special groups would be better off than they are now if *all* privileges— their own and the others that now exist—were abolished. The real question is how political systems permit certain small groups to obtain special economic legislation that discriminates in their favor. Since I have written a good deal on this subject, I will only briefly discuss it here.[2] I would argue for a general rule prohibiting this type of special legislation. My argument clearly has not been accepted by any present-day government, but that does not mean it is incorrect.

If the first assumption indicates that most people should favor general legal standards, it does little to tell us what these standards should be. This situational assumption then plays only a minor explicit role in the discussion of specific laws that make up the re-

[2] See James M. Buchanan and Gordon Tullock, *The Calculus of Consent* (Ann Arbor: University of Michigan Press, 1962) and Gordon Tullock, *Toward a Mathematics of Politics* (Ann Arbor: University of Michigan Press, 1967).

mainder of the book. It will, however, underlie all of the proposals made herein because without it there would be no argument for general laws at all. The two remaining major assumptions are about the preference schedule of the reader (any reader) of this book. In order to make use of the preference schedule of an unselected individual, I must obviously use only certain highly general aspects of the individual preference schedule, and must believe that these aspects are universal. The reader can check my basic assumptions very simply by considering introspectively whether they do or do not describe his own preferences. If they do not, then in my opinion he has either not understood what I have said or he needs help badly. In his opinion I would be wrong.

Proceeding, then, I assume that the reader normally chooses what he prefers; that is, if he is presented the right to take either A or B and he prefers A, he will take A. This seems obvious, but it is sometimes alleged that an individual may want to take A, but, for reasons of ethics or duty, he actually takes B. I do not doubt the observation upon which this denial is based, but I contest its interpretation. The difference really concerns the word "prefer." My hypothetical critic believes that the word covers only part of the reasons why a man may do something. Thus a child seeing a candy bar may "prefer" to eat it but refrains from doing so because it is not his and he has been taught not to steal. This is, I think, a legitimate usage of the word "prefer," but I am employing another usage that is equally legitimate.[3] In this second use, "prefer" is much broader and takes in all influences upon a decision. The child "prefers" not to take the candy bar because the pleasure of eating it would not compensate him for breaking a rule of conduct. The distinction, of course, is familiar to economists. By a preferred action I mean one that lifts the individual to a higher indifference surface, regardless of the reasons for the "preference."

I should perhaps pause at this point in order to remove a possible suspicion that may be forming in the reader's mind. Since I am including moral drives in the individual's preference schedule, may I not, therefore, be sneaking them into my reasoning? May

[3] Paul A. Samuelson, *Economics*, 3rd ed. (New York: McGraw-Hill, Inc., 1955), pp. 432–435.

I not urge that stealing should be made illegal because all people want it to be illegal? To set the reader's mind at rest, I do not use such preference for moral action in deducing my laws. Such a preference may turn up occasionally, but in a manner that is, I think, free from this criticism. If my system is to be realistic, I must recognize that real men have such drives, but I do not need to use them as the foundation of my theory.

My third basic postulate is that the individual normally prefers a choice to a lack of a choice. This principle, which is almost deducible from the prior one, is that an individual would prefer to be permitted to choose.[4] Given his choice between simply receiving A or being permitted to select either A or B, he will choose to select. It should be noted that, for the principle to apply, A and B must be different. If the individual knows that they are identical, he will not care. Furthermore, if A and B are not identical, the difference between them may still be less than the effort involved in making the choice. In this case, also, the individual will choose not to choose, not because he values the choice at zero, but because he values it less than the cost.

An example may clarify the matter. Suppose an oriental monarch tells one of his subjects (in a kingdom from the Arabian Nights) that he may go to a room in the royal treasury and take the contents. Surely the subject would be gratified, but he would be even more gratified if told that he could inspect the contents of two rooms, and then take whichever one he wanted. Given the choice between simply taking the contents of the first room or choosing between it and a second room, he would surely prefer the second choice. Note, however, the necessity of efficient sets. For our assumption to apply, the larger collection of alternatives must include the smaller.

If, of course, the individual knew that he preferred the contents of the first room over that of the second, he would be com-

---

[4] Trout Rader argues quite strongly that, in fact, my third basic postulate is deducible from the second. "[The individual's] preference should be for final outcomes. If he is uncertain before making investigation, then he prefers a choice only because the expected outcome is thereby increased. Thusly interpreted, there is no logical problem and assumption three is implied by assumption two and the definition of choice." (From private communication.)

pletely indifferent; but in this case he has already chosen between the two rooms. For our purposes he must choose between having freedom of choice or not before making up his mind on the ultimate question. This is a simple logical requirement, since making up his mind on the ultimate question involves the choice under discussion. If he has already chosen between A and B, he must first have chosen to consider the matter and then made his choice.

Our basic principle that individuals prefer choice, however, raises an apparent logical problem. Would an individual prefer to be given a choice between getting a choice and not getting a choice? The individual prefers being given a choice between A and B to simply receiving A. This means that he has chosen an alternative, let us call it X, which involves a choice between A and B over another alternative, let us call it Y, which involves only receiving A. Would the individual prefer a choice between X and Y to simply receiving X? At our present level of generality the answer is "yes." This appears to involve a contradiction, but it is merely an apparent one. If the individual has already in fact chosen between X and Y, then he may not wish to bother to repeat the operation. If, however, he actually has not chosen, he would prefer to do so. Once he has chosen X, then he becomes indifferent between simply receiving X or choosing it, but prior to his making the choice he should prefer freedom to coercion. The fact that we as outsiders can predict what choice he will make at every stage is irrelevant.

If we wish, we can easily construct an infinite series of choices for our individual. Thus M and N represent, respectively, a choice between X and Y or simply receiving X; would the individual prefer freedom of choice between them to simply receiving M? Clearly the series can be extended infinitely. This infinite regress, however, is something that we artificially construct, not something that impedes the individual's choice processes. At any stage we can give the long series of choices to the individual and he will quickly work his way down to a definite final choice between A and B. The infinite series is infinite in an opposite direction from that in which the choosing individual would travel, and hence the possibility of infinite regression need not trouble him or us.

But would an individual continue to desire multiplication of his choices no matter how many there were? In our example, it is clear that the courtier would prefer to choose one out of two rooms full of treasure to being given one, but would he necessarily prefer to choose one out of 1,000 treasure rooms to one out of 999? The problem, obviously, is that a random sample of 999 is very similar to one of 1,000. Whether the choosing individual would regard the difference between these two alternatives as being great enough to justify the expenditure of energy used in making a choice would appear to be a matter upon which we cannot make any *a priori* judgment.

In order to analyze the situation, however, let us turn to the traditional probability apparatus of an urn filled with balls. Let us suppose that each ball has a number inside it and a wealthy man agrees to let a friend reach into the urn and remove a ball, the wealthy man being willing to pay the friend the amount of the number on the chosen ball in dollars. Clearly this would be a very advantageous proposition for the friend. Equally clearly, permission to select two, three, or more balls and collect the money for whichever had the largest number would be even more advantageous.

As the number of balls drawn increases, however, the likely gain from each one drawn goes down. The best of seven is likely to be greater than the best of six, but the probable gain is much smaller than between the best of two or the best of three. Thus, the net expected gain from the operation of drawing another ball out of the urn, opening it, and determining whether the number it contains is higher than any previously drawn ball declines steadily as the number of balls drawn increases. The actual work involved in drawing the balls, small though it is, does not decline. In fact, if the man who is drawing the balls is normal, the disutility of making the additional drawings will actually slowly increase. It is thus clear that eventually the friend will stop drawing the balls from the urn even if his wealthy benefactor tells him he may draw as many as he wants. This occurs not because he prefers a choice between 2,316 alternatives to a choice between 2,317 (which contain the original 2,316) but because he thinks the difference between a set of 2,316 and a set of 2,317 is trivial. He does not wish to draw one more ball from the urn because the tiny disutility associated with the act of drawing is greater than the anticipated profit.

Even if the person who was to be permitted to draw the balls out of the urn thought that he was likely to stop after drawing 2,316 balls, this would not mean that he would be indifferent if the wealthy man proposed to restrict him to that amount. Firstly, he could not be certain when he would tire to the point of wishing to stop. Secondly, before he began drawing, he would not know anything about the distribution of the numbers on the balls. They might be distributed in such a way as to offer considerable inducements to continue much beyond 2,316 draws. If, for example, there were 1,000,000 balls in the urn and each of the numbers between 1 and 1,000,000 appeared on one of them, he might stop at 2,316. If, however, 99.9 percent of the balls had $1.00 on them and the remaining balls had one of the numbers 1,000, 2,000, 3,000, . . . , 1,000,000 on it, he might be motivated to continue on beyond 2,316 in spite of his ennui.[5]

Although the individual might not exhaust his opportunities, he would normally want no external restrictions on the area in which he can make choices. There is, however, one situation (and, practically, a most important one) in which he might choose a less extensive range of choices over a larger one. If the choices in the smaller range are preselected so that they are more favorable than those in the larger range, he might prefer the smaller area. Thus, if our wealthy man gave his friend the choice of drawing 1,000 balls out of his urn or of drawing 900 balls out of an urn that contained duplicates of the best half of the balls in the first urn, he would choose the second. The choice of 1,000 is not strictly comparable to the choice of 900, because the set of 900 is not contained in the set of 1,000.

The same line of reasoning indicates that the individual would not choose to extend his range of choice if the additional choices made it less likely that his final choice would be a high value ball. Thus, a proposal to put another 100 balls into the urn, each of them with a sum between zero and $1.00 on it, would not be regarded as an improvement even though it does widen the apparent realm of choice. There might seem to be some contradiction between our basic assumption that an individual will always prefer to have his range of choice widened and our listing of areas where

[5] In this case he might stop after eight or nine drawings unless he was somehow informed of the high value 0.1 percent.

he will not choose to select from the widest possible assortment. In fact, he always prefers a wider choice, but this preference is limited; he can be paid to give it up. These payments can take the form of direct gifts, change in the structure of the alternatives, or simply the avoidance of the time-consuming task of making up one's mind between two substantially identical alternatives. In each case, the individual accepts a restriction on his choices in one area, but the "payment" he receives permits him to increase his area of choice somewhere else.

In order to explore this matter further, let us assume that the man in the Arabian Nights tale looking at rooms full of jewels is able to predict that, after looking at exactly 1,000 rooms, he will be unwilling to continue the search. He feels that the difference between the best of 1,001 and the best of a 1,000 is small enough so that the time cost to him of examining the additional room would not be worth the benefit. Would he be perfectly happy if the Sultan specified 1,000 rooms? I do not think so. However, in this case the matter is somewhat dubious; it would depend upon the motives of the Sultan.

If the Sultan simply selected a collection of 1,000 rooms at random, my subject would presumably be indifferent between this and his own choice, although the possibility of perhaps simplifying his search by selecting rooms that were close together should also be considered. If, however, the subject suspected that the Sultan was beginning to regret his initial offer and that perhaps the 1,000 rooms pointed out were a negatively biased sample, he presumably would object strenuously to the change in conditions. On the other hand, if he felt confident that the Sultan was actually pointing out the 1,000 best rooms, he presumably would be very grateful.

We may consider it as a general rule that we would not wish to have our freedom of choice restricted by someone whose interests are contrary to ours. A restriction exactly the same as one we ourselves would impose (if this could somehow be worked out) would be something to which we would be indifferent, but anyone who claimed that he intended to do this would be suspect. A restriction that gave us a superior sample, however, might well be an improvement. Here our reasoning leads us to step back. If the Sultan pointed out 1,000 rooms to which his choice would be restricted, the individual would prefer to be given a choice between selecting his own 1,000 to accepting those pointed out by the Sultan. Thus, once again we move to a larger choice field from a narrower one. If he decided to accept the Sultan's 1,000 rooms, this would not contradict our general principle of wider choice being desired because this set is not contained within the alternative set.

This general principle has wide application to society in general. We frequently choose to patronize an establishment where a number of possible assortments of goods and services have been excluded by the management. Restaurants, for example, commonly are not purely à la carte, but have menus in which the entire meal is at least partially specified. In part this is the result of certain mechanical efficiencies that the restaurant can achieve with this type of organization, but in part it also proceeds from the desire of the restaurant keeper to provide superior food for his customers and his customers' knowledge that he is so motivated. Customers are willing to permit him to restrict their choice because they assume that he will restrict them, on the whole, in a favorable manner.

Similarly, wealthy people frequently patronize stores that have a smaller variety of goods on display than the ones patronized by the less wealthy—not because they want their choice restricted in a pure sense, but because this smaller selection contains goods of a higher average quality than those available in the larger stores catering to the middle class. The wealthy man's advantage is that he has a choice between going to the large store dealing in a large range of goods or going to the smaller store with a superior selection. A movement toward greater wealth is thus a movement toward a wider range of choice.

The similarity between the statement that people want more freedom, more choices, and the common economic principle that people prefer more to less is of broad significance. In general, the structure of preferences that economists normally assume people to have can be deduced from our very general proposition. In particular, the view that an individual will always choose—assuming that he considers the matter carefully—that alternative that maximizes the present discounted value of his income stream is deducible from our premises.[6] Thus, frequently in the latter part of this book we prove something to be desirable simply by proving that it does increase the present discounted value of the lifetime income stream.

Our procedure, however, has an advantage over the standard economic approach; it can be applied in nonmarket areas. Increased political power may also bring a wider range of choice. What we normally refer to as personal freedom will usually, although not always, increase the total range of choice, and here again we can use the present discounted value technique. It must be admitted, however, that most of the applications of our greater freedom hypothesis are in areas customarily discussed in a study of economics and come down to choosing more rather than less.

The relationship of these propositions to the set of intersecting sets in the first chapter is, I presume, obvious. If my statements about individual preferences are correct, then the type of polity that meets our greater freedom hypothesis, or "the-more-rather-than-less-than" hypothesis of conventional economics, is within the set of propositions favored by everyone. Changes may also exist that are opposed by everyone and that would therefore be in a converse set. By starting with a general specification of the type of change in society that would be "sellable," we have pointed out that if there are changes in society from which substantially everyone would benefit, we may be able to convince people to make these changes. Then by specifying several very weak restrictions on individual preference functions, we find that there are indeed some cases within this set of desirable changes. The remainder of the book largely consists of exploring cases that fall within these categories.

Before closing our discussion of this particular subject it is necessary to point out a minor, more or less obvious but extremely important, corollary. Suppose an individual prefers a class of choices that we shall call A to another class of choices that we shall call B. As a normal rule, he would be willing to pay something,

---

[6] There are, of course, the problems of risk aversion here as in other economic reasoning. Fortunately, in most of the succeeding reasoning the choice that maximizes present discounted value also reduces risk. In those cases where it does not, special arrangements are proposed to take risk aversion into account.

perhaps only a little, in order to receive class A instead of class B. In the marginal case this would not be so, but the marginal case is not a common phenomenon. Mainly, he will be willing to receive A minus some small payment in preference to B if he prefers A to B. This is of great importance to our later discussion because in general we demonstrate that the individual will be well advised to participate in the establishment of a social organization that guarantees him the receipt of some particular class of choices. Thus, he will have to pay for it. In general, we will not discuss the size of this payment, mainly because we lack empirical evidence in the field, but obviously this would also be a relevant matter.

In addition to these three major assumptions about individual preferences, three far less important assumptions should be dealt with before we turn to the law itself. These assumptions are much more dubious than the three we have discussed thus far, and it is fortunate that they are of less importance. A reader disagreeing with any one of them can disregard the portion of the book in which it is used and still accept most of our conclusions. The first is quite complicated and requires a fairly lengthy explanation. It is simplest to start with an example. When I taught at the University of South Carolina, the summer school was drastically reorganized. Among the new regulations was one that provided that any member of the teaching staff could have an appointment to teach in one of the two summer sessions, but that no one could teach in two sessions. I was rather critical of this provision, arguing that it simply reduced the freedom of choice of the professors. Instead of being given a free choice between no summer teaching, teaching in one session, or teaching in two sessions, professors were restricted to the first two alternatives.

Several of my colleagues disagreed with me quite vigorously, offering arguments that at the time I thought were stupid, but that now seem to me to have been quite sensible. They stated that they did not want to teach through the whole summer but that they feared that if the option of teaching two sessions were left open to them they would find the money for the second session too attractive, and hence would teach two sessions, which they did not want to do. Although I thought this just indicated intellectual confusion at the time, there is an assumption that makes their position defensible, and explains many provisions of both law and contracts.

Consider an alcoholic. Some alcoholics are sober for considerable periods and only fall "off the wagon" occasionally. These people, when sober, normally are strongly opposed to their behavior when drunk, and will take precautions (usually unsuccessful) to prevent their next binge. Suppose we offered such people a commercial service, which, in return for an advance payment, provided a large, tough man to follow them around and physically stop them from drinking. I suspect that such a service would be quite popular if alcoholics could pay the price. In any event, surely some alcoholics would be interested.

This, however, appears to contradict our basic theorems. The individual is willing to undergo a reduction of his freedom of choice now, *i.e.*, pay a fee, for the purpose of reducing his future freedom of choice. How do we explain this if individuals always prefer an increase in their freedom of choice? There does not appear to be an off-setting side-payment. The alcoholic's freedom is reduced both now and in the future. It could, of course, be argued that the alcoholic is being "forced" to do something that he does not want to do by the alcohol, and the bodyguard merely counterbalances that force, thus leaving him free. This argument is not very appealing, however, and in any event it does not account for my colleagues who did not want to be permitted to teach two terms in the summer.

A better solution can be developed from a consideration of the discounting of future events. Economically, discounting appears simple. We simply apply market interest rates together with some allowance for the relative risk, which takes the form of a mark-up of the interest rate, and then compare the present value of the future events. For our present purposes, however, I would like to present normal economic discounting in a rather unusual way. Figure 2–1 is a graphic representation of the theory. The vertical axis drawn on a (logarithmic) scale represents the utility units to be obtained from any given action. The horizontal axis represents time with the origin at "now."

If the individual is contemplating immediate action X, he draws a line from the point representing the utility value of X on the vertical axis slanting upward at an angle determined by the appropriate rate of interest. Action X, if taken, will prevent the individual from performing some other action, say Z, in the future. He is, for example, buying a house, and if he puts his money into that, he will not have the money available to invest in a business opportunity in the fall. We plot action Z at its proper time and with the number of utility units it will produce at that time. If it is below the line originating at X units, then the individual should take action X. If, on the other hand, the second action were above the line, such as Y, the individual would logically refrain from

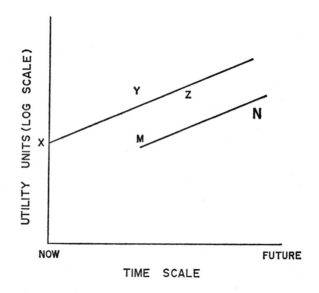

FIGURE 2–1 Classical Time Discounting

action X and take action Y when the time was propitious. Suppose, however, that the individual is called upon now to make up his mind between two actions, M and N, both being in the future. We can deduce his decision quite simply. We simply plot the two points on our graph and draw a line from M at the slope of the rate of interest rate. If N is below this line, the individual will choose action M; if N is above the line, he will choose N.

All of this, however, assumes that we have an appropriate rate of interest. Since we are making our judgments in utility units, this would seldom be the case. The active businessman, interested in monetary matters, whose utility is highly correlated with his income, can easily use our model. He can simply take the market rate of interest for his discount rate and he will come out ahead if he follows the rules we have shown. The market rate of interest, however, is the result of the interactions of a number of people and is not the subjective discounting factor of any individual. The businessman adjusts his actions so that his own margins match on this rate of interest, which is a given phenomenon to him. The fact that the choosing individual has a choice between X and Y on our diagram can be taken as evidence that, for at least some other person, the subjective values of these acts are sufficiently different so that this other person would prefer the present X to the distant Y.

In real life, very few people have access to short-term loans at the same rate of interest as longer-term loans. Thus, the part of our line that approaches the vertical axis is theoretical rather than real. In those cases where no actual market transaction is possible —and we shall turn to a number of such cases in Chapter 3—the individual must make his decisions in terms of his own subjective discounting formula. That is, he must weigh present against future gains by use of his own judgment. It seems likely that, for most people, the subjective time discounting schedule would not follow the straight line of Figure 2–1, but a curve of the type shown at X, in Figure 2–2. The axes of this graph are the same as those of 2–1, but it is assumed that the individual has no market rate of interest at which he can discount the particular transactions he is contemplating.

Being unable to use the money market, he is forced to make his own judgments. The curve shown simply indicates that the individual's time discounting is not of the simple straight line sort that we find in the commercial market. Roughly, I have assumed that the individual discounts small differences in time more sharply when they are immediate than when they are far away. The individual would pay more to advance some pleasure from tomorrow to today than he would to advance it one day five years from now.

This assumption about the individual's preference schedule seems reasonable, and I shall shortly offer some arguments for its validity, but it plays a relatively minor role in the rest of the book. Its invalidity would result in destroying the proof of only a small minority of the propositions that are presented shortly. Thus, the reader who feels that his particular preference function does not have this shape can disagree with the propositions built upon it while accepting those in which it plays no part.[7] Most readers,

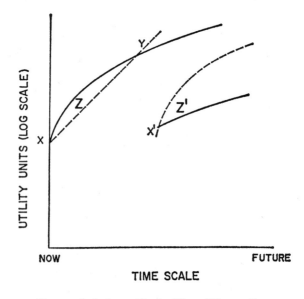

FIGURE 2–2 Logarithmic Time Discounting

however, will probably find that they do have a subjective time anticipation function of about this shape.

Given this sort of preference schedule, the individual will prefer the present satisfaction X to the near future satisfaction Z, but he will prefer the satisfaction Y in the more distant future to both of them in spite of the fact that a straight line connecting

---

[7] I have no strong feelings about the exact shape of the curve I have drawn. Presumably, it varies somewhat from individual to individual, and may be much more complicated than this one. My basic assumption is simply the greater steepness of the early section.

point X on the vertical axis and point Y (the dashed line) passes below point Z. I am not alleging any irrationality on the part of the individual, only that he regards the delay in the next few hours as being more significant than the delay of a few hours in the distant future. In a sense, the individual views future time on something like a logarithmic scale. For the individual, this may be very rational, but the market smooths individual preferences out to produce the straight line discounting function of Figure 2–1.[8] The market function is not more rational than the individual function hypothesized—it is merely the result of aggregating a large number of such functions.

This type of function, however, has a very real effect upon decisions about future choices. Suppose an individual at the "now" point of our diagram is contemplating the choice between X at the same time and Z a little later. Let us assume that X is the pleasure of taking one more drink and Z the pleasure of not having a hangover the next morning.[9] The individual will choose the extra drink. Suppose, however, that the individual is able to contemplate the desirability of taking a fourth cocktail at a party to be held next Saturday night (X′ on Figure 2–2) as compared with the pleasure of avoiding the hangover next Sunday morning (Z′). We construct another discounting function parallel to the one originating at X and running through X′ and observe that Z′ lies above it. The individual now prefers Z′ to X′.

If, however, we consider the individual at time X′, then his discounting curve would follow the dotted line, and he would prefer X′ to Z′. Thus, he now feels that he should not have the fourth cocktail next Saturday night; but he realizes that when the choice comes up, he will drink another. Clearly, he should be

[8] The difference between the discounting line in Figures 2–1 and 2–2 is mostly in the first segment. Since very short-term loans are more or less unobtainable in the real world, this segment in Figure 2–1 does not represent the real market situation.

[9] It seems probable that one of the effects of drink, or any form of excitement, is to bend the discounting line even more sharply than its normal shape. Thus, it may be that the additional drink would not appear worth it in any event if the man were sober. It also seems possible that conduct referred to as "irrational" quite frequently is simply the result of a more sharply bent discounting curve than that possessed by the normal individual.

willing to make at least some sacrifice now to prevent himself from getting X–Z'. Thus, he should now be willing to reduce his freedom in order to put restraints on his freedom of choice at some time in the future. If he is successful in putting some restraint on his freedom of choice at time X', then he will be unhappy about the restraint when the time comes. It does, however, increase the present discounted value of his future and probably will also seem like a good decision from time Z'.

This permits us to explain both the alcoholic who hires a man to stop him from drinking and my colleagues who did not want to be given a free choice as to how much of their summer they would spend teaching. In both cases, the individual now has a preference as to which choice he should make between two alternatives, both lying in the future. He can also predict that the change in perspective that will occur when the future becomes the present will change his preferences. He maximizes his present satisfaction by taking action that prevents him from obtaining his preference in the future.[10]

Our second minor assumption is that people are risk avoiders. This proposition has given economists a great deal of difficulty, because it would appear that people are also risk seekers.[11] The same person who buys insurance on his home also goes to Las Vegas and spends an evening gambling. Although attempting to reconcile these two behavioral patterns into one preference function has caused a great deal of trouble to many economists, for us, the problem is fortunately simpler. We can take the minimal assumption that some people are sometimes risk averters. Surely, no one will question that. The reason that we can use this modest assumption is that the institutional changes that we propose make it possible for people to reduce the risk if they choose. These changes will not make it impossible for them to increase the risk if that is their desire. Our objective is simply to separate the decision as to how much risk one will run from the decision on other matters.

[10] See Robert H. Strotz, "Myopia and Inconsistency in Dynamic Utility Maximization," *Review of Economics and Statistics* 23, No. 3 (1956): 165–180.

[11] Cf. Leonard J. Savage and Milton Friedman, "The Expected Utility Hypothesis and the Measurability of Utility," *Journal of Political Economy* 60 (December 1952): 463–474.

As an example, at the present time when I drive I run a real danger that some other car will collide with me. If I am a risk avoider, I would like to have this risk reduced. If, on the other hand, I like risk, there is no reason why I cannot place near my bed a bomb with a random device that may or may not set it off. By suitable choice of the parameters of the random device, I can obtain any risk to life and limb that I desire without injuring or endangering anyone else.[12] Thus, reducing the likelihood of accidents would lower the risk for the risk averters but would still leave it open to the risk seekers to obtain whatever amount of risk they feel is best.

This assumption would seem to be fairly invulnerable to attack. Nevertheless, any individual who feels that it is not descriptive of the real world, who feels that all human beings always seek additional risk, will find it possible to modify the reasoning that follows by leaving this assumption out and still accepting many conclusions in the book.

Our third minor assumption is also one that the reader may disbelieve without rejecting the bulk of the conclusions in the book. It simply states that people do not get greater amounts of pleasure from inflicting injury or observing injury inflicted on others than the pain that they would suffer themselves if they were the victim. To clarify, let me give an imaginary example. Assume roughly, that you would be unwilling to enter into a gambling agreement under which each of ten people drew a straw out of a hat and the short straw was subject to physical harm by the others. It seems to me that this is a fairly modest assumption and, indeed, a great many people receive pain rather than pleasure from observing injury inflicted on other people or from inflicting it themselves. Still, once again, this assumption is needed only for a small part of the reasoning of the latter part of the book.

As we proceed, various other special minor assumptions are used in the reasoning, which normally concern the situation covered by a particular law. In general, these should cause no great difficulty, but it is possible that one or more of them is incorrect and in that event, of course, a particular theorem is false. Running through

12 It might be wise to require individuals seeking this type of risk to either live in isolated areas or armor-plate their bedrooms.

this part of the assumption set, however, is a complete set of assumptions mainly *im*plicit rather than *ex*plicit of very minor nature and having a considerable family resemblance. I doubt that they will upset any practical man, but conceivably some theorist may raise questions about them. Basically, these will be assumptions that people do not positively value certain types of activity to such a great extent that their practical inconveniences are overridden. More specifically, individuals do not get enough of a thrill from being robbed so that it more than compensates them for the loss of their money.

A person might favor making theft legal for several reasons, including the thought that he would gain from making theft legal because he would be able to commit more thefts on other people than would be committed on him. This one is discussed in the body of the book. I ignore the second possibility that he would get such a thrill out of being robbed that he would enjoy the process and would rather have it legally possible for people to steal from him. With respect to this particular possible preference ordering, however, there is no logical reason why the existence of some people who had this particular preference ordering could not be dealt with by a simple institutional change. Since I regard this as a highly unlikely preference set and the whole issue as unimportant, I have placed the demonstration of this point in an Appendix. Thus, in the body of the book I assume that there is no one who has this particular preference ordering.

The third possibility, the existence of someone for whom a large number of thefts (not committed on him or by him) is a source of positive pleasure, is also ruled out. This pleasure would have to be sufficiently strong that he would be willing to accept a substantial reduction in his living standards in other respects in order to obtain this amount of theft. This type of preference ordering would cause very great difficulties for the reasoning in the book, and I shall assume there is no one of this sort around. In the real world, people like this would be disregarded, so their possible existence would have very little effect upon the application of my reasoning.

It would be possible to specify various other quasilunatic preference orderings that individuals might have that would conflict with the conclusions reached in this book. It is not possible for me to compile a list of all possible wildly deviant preference orderings and discuss them one at a time. Hence, I shall simply assume that they do not exist. This, as I said before, should cause no great difficulty for the practical man, but the purist may object. I am sorry in this respect that I am not able to demonstrate my point regardless of the preference orderings. It should be noted, however, that very, very few things can be demonstrated to be desirable if one assumes a complete and totally uncontrolled range of preferences. The oldest chestnut in economics is the demonstration that tariffs on the whole are undesirable. If we assume that there is one person in the world who positively likes tariffs *qua* tariffs, and whose liking for tariffs is so high that no possible payment would compensate him for eliminating them, this proof fails in pure welfare terms. Economists implicitly ignore the possible existence of such people. I see no reason why I should not behave similarly.

PART II

CIVIL LAW

3

Contracts, Substantive Law

A simple contract involves a promise by A to do something tomorrow in return for B's doing something today. A promise, however, can be broken. Would it be sensible to favor the establishment of a system for enforcing selected promises? Simply from our assumption that the individual will choose to extend his range of choice, it follows that it would. If confronted with the choice between situation A, in which promises are not "enforced" and situation B in which promises may either be "enforced" or not, as the maker chooses, it would be rational to take the latter. It does not, after all, compel you to make enforceable promises, it only makes it possible. Situation A, on the other hand, limits you to unenforceable promises. Situation B is, of course, the existing law.

The fact that most legal codes permit the making of unenforceable promises is, for some reason, normally overlooked in discussions of the law. Since courts are largely engaged in dealing with enforceable contracts, the fact that not all promises are enforceable at law or in equity tends to be ignored. In fact, it is very easy to make an unenforceable promise. It seems likely that most promises that are made in day-to-day life are lacking in the technical characteristics that would give a court power to enforce them. If a promise might be enforceable, a simple statement that it is not to be legally binding will normally make it unenforceable.

Thus we have demonstrated that people should favor the establishment of a mechanism to make it possible for them to make enforceable promises. It is clear that situations in which making such an enforceable promise is desirable are fairly frequent. I wish to buy a house and do not have enough money to do so. Borrowing the money will improve my satisfaction, but in order to borrow I have to convince the lender that I will repay. Perhaps I can get away with an unenforceable promise, but for most people such loans are only possible if there is some mechanism to enforce the repayment.

At first glance, it would appear that we would favor a complete freedom to make any promise we wish under any conditions that we wish and, indeed, the early utilitarians argued just that. A more careful examination of the problem indicates that there are possibly desirable limitations, and limitations and restrictions are contained in the present contract law. I do not wish to argue that the present body of contract law is ideal, but some limitations on unfettered freedom of contract are, as we shall see, sensible. The "optimum" restrictions, furthermore, would follow somewhat the same lines as those now in existence. On the other hand, it is clear that some of the existing contract rules are irrational, the results not of careful thought but of obscurantism and emotion.

As an example, once I have bought my house, I will obviously be better off if I can somehow avoid paying, or at least get better terms. If I have the normal human attitudes, I can easily convince myself that these desires are morally right, and that the mortgage holder is wicked. In recent times, the technical discussions of mortgages have normally been dominated by a sympathy for those mortgagees who have difficulty paying. Thus, a climate of opinion in which modifications of the mortgage contract by law in such a way as to benefit the mortgagee has arisen. Since the number of people who are currently paying off the mortgage on their houses is always much larger than the number who are in the business of lending money for such mortgages, or those who are currently contemplating borrowing, the possibility of modifying the contract for the benefit of the mortgagee is always present in a democracy.

This is, of course, not irrational. While it is sensible for me to want to be able to make an enforceable promise to repay the money loaned to me, once it is in my hands it is equally sensible for me to approve modifications in the contract in my favor. Once again our expansion of choice hypothesis is useful. Having the choice of repaying or not is obviously a superior position to not having this choice. Thus, the people who are now paying off their mortgages are likely to favor measures that reduce the security of the holders of the mortgages. The result has been the development of a set of laws that "protects" the debtor. These laws, however, do not compel people to issue mortgages. Naturally, they refrain from granting mortgages unless the interest rate compensates them for the additional risk. A full discussion of this problem requires tools that are introduced in Chapter 4, but the net result is that people who want to borrow money to buy houses have to pay higher interest rates to compensate the lenders for the additional risk imposed by rules supposed to help the borrowers. No doubt those who were paying off mortgages when the new regulations were enacted gained, but those who now try to borrow money would be better off if they had the choice of giving the lender better security at a lower rate.

In discussing limitations on freedom of contract, one of the first things to remember is that judges make mistakes. Since the problem of judicial procedure is the subject of several later chapters, serious discussion of this issue is deferred. An appreciation of the fact of such mistakes is, however, necessary. Most traditional institutions are surrounded with what anthropologists call "magic." They are thought of in unrealistic terms, the lack of realism having the effect of making us more satisfied with our environment by convincing us that it is better than it really is.[1] The courts are no exception. The view that the outcome of judicial process is "true" is widely held. Thus, I have been criticized for expressing the opinion that a person who has not been tried is guilty of a defalcation, the criticism taking the form of saying that he is not guilty until found so by a court. I may, of course, have been wrong, but the reason given for the criticism is irrational.

Most people do not really feel that the court's decision is always

[1] The psychological phenomenon of "reduction of cognitive dissonance" is closely connected to this social effect.

right. Neither the decision in the Sacco-Vanzetti case nor the Hiss case was regarded as settling the matter by large and articulate groups in our intellectual community. On the other side, Judge Youngdahl's release of Owen Lattimore was not regarded as "clearing" the Johns Hopkins professor by a quite different group of persons. Regardless of what we may think of the specific facts in these cases, the refusal to accept the court's decision as necessarily determining the truth of the matter was clearly right. Courts do make mistakes, and the Supreme Court no less than others. We should hope for improvements in this regard, but we should not have any illusions about either the present (or likely future) efficiency and ability of our judges.

The judge and/or jury in a case have heard the case. They are in possession of more information, therefore, than most casual observers. The judge, furthermore, will normally be of above average intelligence. It must be assumed that the responsibilities connected with their decisions normally result in the judge's thinking seriously about the case. Their judgment, therefore, should be regarded with respect, and in easy cases (which make up the vast majority), we can accept their opinions as probably true. Furthermore, it is socially necessary to have some end to litigation. The fact that a given case has been settled in a given way legally ends it, regardless of the real rights and wrongs. But I have a perfect right to believe that a judicial decision is wrong. If I have made a careful study of the matter, my opinion may well be more authoritative than that of the court. Almost everyone can think of at least one decision that he regards as wrong, and his judgment in the matter may well be correct.

When I was in law school, our professor of Procedure related the following case. A wealthy woman saw an advertisement for an antique dining room set in the morning paper. She decided to buy it and mentioned that fact to her maid. When she arrived at the store and inspected the set, she changed her mind; but she spent the rest of the day shopping. During the afternoon, the set was delivered to her house and the maid signed a receipt. The store refused to take the set back and sued for the price. The law firm with which the wealthy lady normally dealt looked over the evidence and suggested settlement out of court on the basis of a partial payment. Righteously indignant, the lady turned to another lawyer and, by some coincidence, came into the hands of a shyster. When the case came to trial, the attorneys for the store put the salesman on the witness stand who testified that the woman had bought the set. The truck driver testified that it had been delivered and that the maid had expected it.

The woman thought she had been double-crossed by her attorney, who didn't even cross-examine these witnesses. When his turn came, however, he put three witnesses on the stand who testified that they had seen the defendant pay for the set. Having a great deal of experience in such matters, the three trained witnesses were able to defend themselves under vigorous, if rather confused, cross-examination. The jury found for the defendant; the lawyer took the dining room set for his fee, and (I suppose) substantial justice was done. But, clearly, this is not the type of court proceeding in which we can have high confidence. We must recognize, however, that it may be impossible to design courts so that this type of thing cannot and does not happen.

The possibility of erroneous court decisions must be taken into account in any discussion of the desirability of "enforcing" contracts. Someone must decide that the contract has been violated and take steps to enforce it. If that "someone" should be prone to frequent mistakes, then this fact must be taken into account when deciding whether or not contracts should be "enforced," and the extent to which that enforcement should be carried. Since judges are human, they will always make mistakes, although the number of these mistakes may possibly be reduced. What effect will this have on the desirability of making "enforcements" of contracts possible?

We can distinguish two main classes of error into which judges may fall in "enforcing" contracts. They may negatively fail to enforce a clause of a contract, or (positively) they may enforce a nonexistent clause. Thus, suppose A pays B a sum of money for some future act by B, and B refuses to carry out his promise. A goes to court and the court errs by agreeing with B that he has no legal liability. This is a negative error. For an example of a positive error, assume that A demands that B perform some additional act not provided for in the contract. The court errs by ordering B to carry out his nonexistent contractual obligation. Placed in this schematic form, these errors do not seem very likely. In fact, of course, contracts may be almost impossibly involved and the occurrence of errors is certain. Simple cases are likely to be decided correctly, but not all cases are simple.

Positive errors are considerably less likely than negative ones simply because it is more likely that an individual will try to get out of an existing obligation than that he will create a convincing obligation of someone else.[2] Note that the errors do not cancel out. A classic piece of legal wisdom holds that "you will lose some cases which you should have won, but, on the other hand, you will win some cases you should have lost." For the lawyer it cancels out, but what about the clients? For the client who only goes to court a few times in his life it is statistically unlikely that the errors will cancel. Even for those in continual litigation, however, the errors do not really cancel.

Imagine an importer who is engaged in commercial dealings, and for whom disagreements with other parties are frequent enough so that he can expect to become involved in 1,000 lawsuits during the course of his life. Suppose, furthermore, that courts dealing with cases of the degree of complexity represented by his litigation normally make errors 10 percent of the time. It might seem that with about 100 erroneous decisions, the likelihood that they will balance out would be fairly good. Assuming that the man is honest, this would not be so. If he never sues another man or forces someone else to sue him, except when his cause is just, then all of the errors will be against him.[3] It is only the man who sues when he has no case or refuses to carry out a contract until he is sued who can hope to profit from miscarriages of justice. Between the just and the unjust, court errors always favor the "wrong" side.

This naturally raises the question of whether some institutional modification might not be helpful. Clearly, improving the efficiency of the courts is such an institutional modification, but a discussion

---

[2] Third parties, *e.g.,* legislators, may think of additional obligations and enact them into law.

[3] Much the same general conclusions can be reached on less restrictive assumptions. If we assume that the man misjudges his own case as often as the judge does, or even twice as often, then the results are reached by more complicated chains of reasoning, but they are fundamentally the same.

of this must be deferred. Consideration of other possible modifications, such as making it harder to take a man's last dollar than his millionth should also be deferred to some possible future occasion. This latter problem is really no different when the hardship is imposed as the result of an incorrect decision than in the case of a correct decision, and there are many reasons why decisions may fall in a gray area between the two extremes.

Suppose that I contract with a builder to add an extension to my house. After agreement on the plans and formal signature of the contract, a flood sweeps the town and, in addition to doing other damage, it destroys my house. On re-examining the architectural drawings, I realize that by simply closing off the end of the "addition," which would normally face my house with a few sheets of plywood, I will have housing that will serve to at least keep me warm until my house is rebuilt. I, therefore, appear in court and ask that the builder be forced to proceed with the contract. As a result of the flood, the builder, on the other hand, faces much higher costs because of the shortage of labor and materials, the changes of the topography of the site, the unavoidable delay in starting; hence, he can only finish by the contract date through the use of expensive overtime labor. He has also lost his own machinery in the flood and will have to buy or rent the necessary equipment.

He, therefore, argues that the contract called for the construction of an "addition," and that there is now nothing to be added to. I argue that I want him to produce the structure shown in the architect's drawings, and that the fact that there is now no longer a building located directly adjacent is irrelevant. Obviously, the judge is presented with a difficult problem.[4] The two parties certainly were not thinking about the flood when they entered into the original contract. There are no specific provisions in the contract that clearly cover the problem in dispute.

Any decision of the court will contain an element of arbitrariness, and it would be more or less impossible to say that any

[4] All of this assumes that the addition can stand by itself. Many additions, of course, could not be built by themselves because they depend upon the basic building for their support. Anyone who thinks that he sees an obvious solution should present the case to two or three other persons and see if they also reach the same conclusion.

decision was, in the eyes of God, right or wrong. The court must somehow or other supplement the original contract. For this purpose it is likely, in the real world, to turn to some general rule for such cases. The rule chosen would depend mainly upon the nationality of the court. Let us, however, examine some of the possible rules.

The simplest rule would be to flip a coin, and there is an element of this in all other rules. No modern legal system, however, openly adopts this expedient. A second rule would be to say that if the contract did not directly refer to the circumstances that arose, it has no present effect. This would lead the court to give a decision in favor of the defendant. In this particular case, such an outcome does not seem to be bad, but in most cases of this sort the difference between the situation that actually occurred and the one anticipated by the parties at the time the contract was signed is less extreme. Invalidating the contract because there is some minor difference does not seem very sensible.

A third possibility is to try to get some hint from the contract itself as to what the parties would have decided if the flood came (if they had any thought of it when they were making the original contract). Technically, this is "resolution by analogy." Thus, if the contract contained a provision canceling the entire arrangement if the house burned down, it would seem reasonable to assume that the parties would have put in a similar clause regarding floods if they had thought of it. Here again, we would get a decision for the defendant. Again, however, the relative ease of such a decision is a result of the simplicity of the case. Normally, no clause is as close to the contingency that actually occurs as fire is to flood. Courts trying to apply this general approach are frequently driven into the most extreme contortions in their attempts to find something in the contract that can be extended to cover the new situation.

A fourth possibility would be to try to find other evidence of the parties' intent. If, for example, in looking over the diagrams, I had said, "Gee, if the house burned down, I could actually live in the addition," and the contractor had replied, "You sure could," it would seem likely that the court would decide to force the contractor to build the addition. Once again, however, there is normally no such clear evidence of intent.[5] Lastly, the rule actually followed by most courts in the world is simply to apply general legal norms to the matter. Stated more simply, this approach assumes that the written contract between the two parties is only a part of their agreement. A body of legal decisions, statutes, and codes that provides a set of rules for what should be done in cases where there are no specific provisions in the contract will be in existence. Thus, the court assumes that the contract was drawn up with the parties in actual, if not express, agreement that in any contingency not specifically covered by the contract, the rules provided by law will apply.

This approach also has the drawback that the contingency that arises may not be at all clearly covered by the existing laws. Thus, here again considerable contortions may be necessary to apply the procedure. The problem, however, is not as significant with this general approach. The contracting parties to the innumerable contracts that do exist tend to forget somewhat the same possible contingencies, with the result that rules originally developed for contracts of the past may very well fit. This procedure, of course, relieves the court from having to make up its mind on a difficult problem, which probably accounts for its popularity with judges.

Another advantage of this way of interpreting contracts when there is nothing in the text covering a contingency that has arisen is that it permits great economies in drawing up the contracts. The law of bills and notes, for example, is an extremely elaborate set of rules that fills many volumes. The contracts with which these rules deal may well take the form of one or two sentences printed on one side of a small piece of paper. If it were necessary to put into the actual contract all of the conditions that the law implies, no bill would be less than 100 pages long. Thus, the present situation provides a simple and quick contract, but it also provides definite rules that in effect elaborate that quick contract into a lengthy and complicated one.

The disadvantage of this method of interpreting contracts if

[5] Modification of a contract by testimony about verbal statements of the parties raises a series of difficult problems considered under the title of "Parole" in our legal system. The difficulty is that permitting such testimony is practically an invitation to perjury, particularly since courts, like other people, are not terribly good at detecting liars.

some unprovided for contingency arises is that it results in the contract, in effect, being quite different from what the men have agreed to. If the contractor and I were not experts in the law and there was a large body of interpretive rules that would be applied by the courts, we might end up with a contract that surprised both of us. It might be, for example, that the rule in that jurisdiction was that, unless otherwise provided in the contract, a builder was responsible only for the structure itself, but not for the foundation. The court might thus rule that the contractor was not required to build the addition because I had not provided him with a foundation in proper time. This would please the contractor, but also would surprise him if he were not aware of the rule. Such ignorance on the part of the contractor would, of course, be unlikely, but the law of contracts has innumerable interpretive rules and no one can possibly know all of them. Thus, the application of such rules must, at least occasionally, result in surprises.

  What is perhaps more important, they may result in surprises for one party to the contract. Given the complexity of the rules surrounding contracts and the fact that they vary greatly from field to field, it is not unlikely that one party to a contract will know them fairly well and the other not at all. The second party, of course, may get legal advice, but this is expensive. The contractor, for example, would no doubt know about the rule on foundations hypothesized in the last example, but the purchaser might well not know this. Thus, this procedure encourages sharp practice. A and B enter into a contract that seems reasonable to A, who knows little of the specialized legal rules surrounding such a contract, but which is actually heavily weighted in favor of B. B has drawn the contract so that, when the standard legal interpretative rules are used, it is highly in his favor. In practice, the courts normally lean over backward to interpret rules in favor of whichever party seems to know the least about them. Still, the formal rule is that the "ignorance of the law is no excuse" and a good deal of sharp practice must be perpetuated under that rule.

But this has been a discussion of the situation as it now exists. Let us try to consider the problem in a more rigorous form. The judge, when he comes to a part of the contract that is not plain on its face, must make a decision according to some rule. As suggested previously, this rule might be flipping a coin, or it could be the application of some general rule dealing with all contracts of this sort. The difference between these two different techniques may not be significant from the standpoint of the litigants. Suppose Smith and I enter into a contract and we agree that Jones will decide any contractual disputes that may occur. Unknown to us, Jones has already decided with respect to one particular type of dispute how he will shape his verdict. From the standpoint of Smith and myself in making up the original contract, this decision is essentially unpredictable since we did not know what Jones planned to do. Therefore, at the time we drew up the contract we were essentially facing the same situation we would have faced had the rule for this contingency been decided by flipping a coin.

It might, of course, have been possible for us to have predicted in some way the decision Jones would make. Even more likely, it might have been possible for us to feel that it was probable that he would decide in one particular way. We might feel, for example, that his decision on this matter would tend to be very similar to one we ourselves would make. We could hardly be certain of this, however, and in a sense, we would be making a guess that has a stochastic element. We might feel, for example, that the odds were three to one for the plaintiff. Although this would still be a stochastic model, it would require more than a single flip of a coin. Let us, however, ignore these intermediate stages between certainty and uncertainty because they are simply a mixture of the two conditions, and confine our discussion entirely to those cases in which we can predict what the judge will do or in which we are totally uncertain. Real world situations in which these two conditions are mixed can then be dealt with by mixing our two models.

With this model, we can now address ourselves to the question of how detailed the legal provisions for "interpreting" contracts should be. Note that we need say nothing, at this stage, about the substantive content of these provisions because the parties to the contract can always avoid any particular substantive provision by simply putting an appropriate clause into their contract. Later in this chapter, we discuss limitations on freedom of contract that might well be part of our law, but at the moment we can confine ourselves to those areas where the contracting parties may reach any bargain that they wish. In this case, the substantive rules may perhaps be more efficient in one form than in another; that is, one particular set of legal rules as to what is done in the case of a contract that does not specifically cover a matter may lead more contracting parties to shorten their contracts than another set of rules. This is obvious, but I have nothing to add to the point and, hence, will turn to another matter—the optimal degree of detail for the law.

In order to approach this problem rationally let us begin by considering the amount of detail that the contracting parties should put into their contract in a situation in which everything that they clearly express in the contract will be carried out; those things that the contract clearly does not cover but in fact occur are dealt with in a stochastic manner that we may represent by the image of the flipped coin, and those issues that are related to the language but are not clearly covered by it will be dealt with by a mixture of certain and stochastic elements.

Suppose that I am buying a house and the seller and I have agreed on the price and a few other general matters, but have not completely and totally exhausted the possible items we could put into the contract of sale. Under these circumstances, I can weigh, on the one hand, the possibility that if some contingency not now covered by the contract occurs, I will lose in the essentially stochastical decision against the advantages and disadvantages of continuing the negotiations to get an additional clause covering the given contingency. The first thing to note, of course, is that the time spent in negotiations is a cost and clearly if the contingency is unlikely enough, I would be well advised to leave the matter in the lap of the gods. Furthermore, it is by no means obvious that if I negotiate with my bargaining partner the certain clause that we end up with will be more to my advantage than flipping the coin. This might or might not be true, depending on whether there is some mutually advantageous way of dealing with this particular problem. If there is some provision that could be reached with respect to this particular problem that will be to both of us *ex ante* better than flipping a coin, we would, of course, do it; but there is no intrinsic reason to believe that this would be so for all the details of a contract. Furthermore, even if such a possibility for profit did exist, it might also exist after the contingency itself had occurred and, therefore, we could make an agreement at that time rather than using the coin-flipping process.

This line of reasoning could, of course, be put in a highly rigorous form. It seems to me, however, that we have no great need to go further than the analysis thus far presented. The two parties under these circumstances would thus determine the length of the contract in full knowledge that some things were not covered. They would expect that those things would be determined by some process over which they had no control because the cost of extending their joint control is greater than the present discounted value of the injury they might or, then again, might not suffer from the lack of control.

The same line of reasoning may be used to decide in general the proper degree of detail in the interpretive part of the law of contracts. The only real point of this part of the law is to save the parties the inconvenience of making their own contracts very long. Thus, it permits them to leave certain provisions out of their contract because they are covered by the law. Furthermore, since this technique in and of itself is more efficient than actually negotiating each contract clause step by step, one would assume that the parties would count it as a lower-cost way of obtaining certainty and, therefore, would prefer more details in this legally specified portion of the contract than in the part they actually negotiate between themselves. Still, it does seem likely that the amount of details they would require is not terribly high.

In particular, there is no reason why the parties should be concerned about the certainty or uncertainty of that part of the law that they do not know about. If there is a definite legal principle providing for the interpretation of a certain clause in a certain contingency, but this interpretation is not known to the parties, they are no better off than they would have been in my earlier example in which Jones had a secret rule. Only if the parties know and take into account the provision of the law is it of any advantage to them in reducing the hazard to which they are exposed. It is, in fact, true that many men engaged in practical activity know a great deal about the legal effects of contracts in their particular line of business. Thus, in these lines of business a rather long and detailed code would be reasonable.

Although we now have a set of principles for determining the
desirable amount of detail in the interpretative portion of the
law of contracts, there is no reason to believe that this set of principles has been applied in real life. Certainly, it has not been
characteristic of the Common Law. Under the Common Law, each
case that reaches an appellate court adds an additional bit of
detail into the law. There is no effort on the part of anyone to
decide how detailed the law should be. The result is a situation in
which the person more learned in the law has the distinct advantage over the person less learned. In particular, it gives a
major advantage to the lawyers. It is also helpful to the ego of the
judges who are permitted to make the law for future contracts.
Nevertheless, it cannot be said that it works any vast amount
of harm. Substituting flipping coins for the details of our present
interpretative law would be somewhat more efficient, but the
difference would be minimal.

There is, however, something that can be said about the degree
of detail in the law that should be of interest to the reader of this
book (whom, I presume, is an intellectual). Looking at the matter
from our purely pragmatic, nonethical approach, obviously each
reader should simply try to decide the degree of detail that would
be best for him. The question really is which degree, over a period
of time, will give him the widest range of choice. This means that
he must consider the likelihood of his becoming involved in suits
to enforce contracts in the future and then decide what rule will
best suit him. Most readers will be people of above average intelligence, with literary and scholarly interests, and, probably, having
research skills. For such people a maze of legal rules has decided
advantages. If the system of interpreting contracts that do not
clearly cover the given situation is to turn to a large body of legal
rules containing a provision for a mass of such cases, then the
average individual of normal intelligence, little patience for reading, and a complete lack of experience in library research is apt
to be at a loss. He most assuredly will not find out what the rules
are until it is too late. The intellectual, on the other hand, is much
more likely to know what the rules are.[6]

[6] This last statement is not necessarily true in the United States. It is
one of the more remarkable characteristics of our law that a good deal

This means, of course, that the intellectual has a real material interest in a detailed and complex set of rules. Since most of his contracts will be with nonintellectuals, this gives him a significant advantage. From this we could deduce that the intellectual should favor more detail than the common man. Furthermore, a system of written laws is something the intellectual can argue for openly. It does not appear on the surface to give a specific class an advantage, although it is in fact in the interest of the more intelligent and scholarly members of the community. In practice the common man sometimes realizes this, and has a considerable distrust both of the law and of lawyers.[7] Individuals who are trapped by provisions of the law of which they were ignorant are common in our fiction, and they are always treated sympathetically. The court may say "ignorance of the law is no excuse," but the novelists do not agree. The frequent pleas for settling cases on the "facts," "on the merits," or "by common sense" may also be efforts on the part of common men to avoid entering an arena in which the intellectuals have an obvious advantage. It is not at all apparent what decision would be made in our flood case on the "facts," "merits," or "by common sense," but it is clear that such a rule would give the intellectuals less advantage over the nonintellectuals.

Since, on the other hand, the intellectual normally dominates public debate, the long-run odds would appear to favor him in this clear-cut class difference. The judges, too, are intellectuals, who have the further advantage of being trained in the law. In his private contracts, the judge or any other lawyer who really knows the law of contracts has an advantage over almost anyone with whom he deals if contracts are interpreted by a complex set of legal rules. Further, this knowledge is a valuable piece of "capital." The judge can, therefore, be said to have a real interest in a detailed and complex system of interpretation.

of it is almost undiscoverable. Trained legal advice is frequently necessary and even experienced lawyers are frequently wrong. In countries with civilized legal institutions, however, the problem is not so difficult. It is, doubtlessly, impossible to draw up the law in such a way that an untrained man can discover it easily, but we don't even make the attempt. In those countries in which a serious effort to state the law simply and concisely is made, the situation is far different from that in the United States.

[7] William Shakespeare, *Richard II,* "First, let's kill all the lawyers."

Since we have not yet reached the portion of this book in which ethics are discussed, and since it seems fairly certain that we have here an area in which the individual reader might favor certain rules because they would benefit him, we might pause here to reconsider our first basic assumption. This assumption, it will be recalled, is that the individual reader is not in a situation whereby he can gain from rules designed to benefit a single class in society. It is only when this assumption is fulfilled that everyone can be expected to agree to a general rule. Rules that classify society and then give special privileges to some classes are obviously beneficial only to the favored class. These rules should thus be favored by members of the favored class, and opposed by members of other classes. In such an open and obvious situation, it is unlikely that such rules can be imposed unless the benefited class is, for some reason, stronger than the injured class or classes. The whites in South Africa, for example, are constitutionally in complete control of the government and are well armed and organized. They can, therefore, impose their rule on the blacks.

In addition to such overt class legislation, however, rules that appear to be general may, in fact, benefit special groups. Thus, a set of rules that has general application but that gives an advantage to the better educated as opposed to the less educated may be class legislation. The recent expansion of government-financed fellowships has been largely discussed in terms of general benefit, although it is obvious that only a tiny minority of the population can directly gain from them. Furthermore, this tiny minority is composed of people who, because of their intelligence, family background, and primary education, are likely to do very well in life anyway. More indirectly, the working man who has no plans to send his son to college is much less likely to benefit from a lavish provision of scholarship help than is the middle-class parent who is willing, if necessary, to make great sacrifices to see that his son receives a good education.[8]

[8] In this discussion, I do not wish to deny the possible indirect benefits for the poorer classes of having the brighter members of society educated well. The public advocates of subsidization of higher education for a small, gifted minority, however, are almost all professional educators, who will benefit from an expansion of the educational system, or middle- and upper-class intellectuals.

But all of this merely illustrates the general problem. We have assumed that the individual does not have much of a chance of obtaining special "class" legislation that benefits him. For the average man, this is no doubt true. Furthermore, even the most influential people have little or no possibility of arranging for legislation that openly aims at their benefit. Deception, however, is possible. It is possible for people who have exceptional access to channels of influence and communication to benefit themselves to some extent. The father of an intelligent boy who would rather not pay his son's tuition in college can hardly hope to have a special bill passed. It is possible, however, that he, together with others similarly placed, can have a general bill passed that will reach the same end. Note, however, that the margin for this type of maneuver is narrow. Only if the special bill comports with generally held (if vague) ideas of proper governmental activity, and only if it does not appear to be specially geared to the interests of some group, can the trick be pulled off.[9]

Thus, the gains to be made from this sort of deception are quite limited. The intellectuals are best situated to get special legislation, but it is difficult even for them. They must, furthermore, work without overt coordination. All public references to the aid to education bill must be in terms of its general benefit. The fact that it is of special interest to the intellectuals and the upper class must not be mentioned. Still, for this particular type of problem, the first of our basic assumptions is probably not true for most potential readers of this book. They can, to some extent, give themselves an advantage by arguing for legal rules that appear to be general, but that in fact favor intellectuals. Nevertheless, the advantage to be gained would normally be small.

Is full freedom of contract desirable? Should it be possible to enter into any contract? It might appear that any reduction in the area of free contract would contravene our basic assumptions, but there are some situations where this is not true. We can begin by inquiring if there are any types of contracts that should simply

[9] Strictly selfish legislation is also possible. This, however, requires that the beneficiaries pay for their advantage by logrolling, and the total outcome, whatever else may be said about it, will not necessarily benefit a minority.

be denied all enforcement. In our law no contract of enslavement is legal—is this provision desirable? At first glance it would appear to be a perfectly clear and unambiguous contravention of our basic principle. The individual who wishes to sell himself into slavery is prevented from doing so, and his freedom is thus restricted. This would seem to lead us into a direct conflict between two forms of freedom, but, fortunately, the conflict can be avoided.

Firstly, an individual desiring to sell himself into slavery would obviously be very rare. Once he is a slave, his new master could take back the price. In practical fact, most systems of slavery depend upon people's being sold into slavery by other persons. A will not regard a legal provision preventing B from selling him (A) into slavery as a restriction on his freedom of choice. This is equally true when B is an ancestor of A as when he is not. The right of an individual to sell himself into slavery may be argued for in terms of increasing his freedom of choice. His right to sell his children, including his unborn children, into slavery clearly reduces the freedom of choice of the children.[10] It is sometimes said that the Chinese may sell themselves into slavery during famines in order to obtain food for their families.[11] Clearly, this should be permitted. If a man has a choice between seeing his family starve or selling himself into slavery to feed them and chooses the latter, we should not impede his freedom of choice. A society in which a man confronts such a dilemma, however, is obviously one that is seriously ill. No one should ever be confronted with this dilemma. It seems dubious, in any event, that this ever really was a factor in the development of slavery. Real slaves were always born slaves, captured, or the victims of another process.

Readers of Romantic literature about the Roman Empire are familiar with the character who had been "sold into slavery." In

[10] The issue of minors, morons, the insane, and other people who are not thought fully capable of handling their own affairs is a most difficult one, and I have substantially no suggestions for handling it. The guardian system, used in one form or another, has obvious defects, but nothing better has been suggested.

[11] As far as I am aware, this factual allegation is incorrect. It arises out of the difficulties encountered in trying to understand an alien civilization. What actually happens is quite complicated and not really relevant for our present discussion. The case, however, is theoretically interesting even if it never happens in the real world.

fact, this could happen under Roman law as the result of a voluntary contract, although it was probably less frequent than the novels imply. A man could borrow money and then post himself as part of the security; that is, he could agree that if a certain loan was not repaid, the creditor could not only proceed against the debtor's material assets he could foreclose on the debtor himself. Why should we ban such contracts in which the individual pledges himself as part of the security for a loan? If we do not wish to take the risk ourselves, we need not do so, and the individual is likely to be the best judge of his own circumstances. Legally banning this form of contract clearly reduces the freedom of individuals to make choices and, hence, would appear to be decreasing freedom of choice. The freedom to decide now, in return for adequate compensation, to restrict my freedom in the future is a freedom, and we have deduced that its limitation would be a genuine reduction in the freedom of choice. Thus, it would appear that we should opt to retain the freedom to pledge ourselves as security for a loan.

The reason why we might decide to restrict our freedom to enter into such a loan contract in the future comes from our first minor assumption—that we discount future events in a manner that is not a linear function of time. Consider a businessman who is getting started in a retailing operation. He has begun well but is in what he feels confident is a temporary bind. A little more time, he believes, which means a little more money, will carry him over until the business really begins to prosper. This stage is familiar to anyone who has studied the history of successful or unsuccessful businesses. In this situation, the businessman is likely to go to great extremes to obtain money. He will mortgage his house, his car, and anything else since he feels fairly certain that prosperity is "just around the corner." If he were given the opportunity to mortgage himself, he would probably do it.

Here, however, we have an example of the different rates of discounting that the same man may apply to the same situation at different times. The individual who would be willing to pledge himself in order to obtain additional capital the following year may this year think that it would be unwise. He knows that next year he would be likely to take a course of action which considered from this distant perspective of the present, seems undesirable. Under the circumstances, he would like to bind himself today not to make such a mortgage agreement in the future. Hence, he would, if he had the assumed preference schedule, favor laws prohibiting such mortgages. The situation is the same as that of a compulsive drunkard who hires private detectives to forcibly prevent him from taking a drink. When considered calmly, most of us would agree that we should not take the risk of enslavement and also that we might make a fatal mistake some time in the future. Thus, a prohibition on contracts containing clauses involving enslavement is similar to voting for prohibition because we feel that we are too subject to temptation.

The same line of reasoning can be used to support bankruptcy laws and laws against imprisonment for debt. Surely, if I were in financial difficulties, I could get loans on better terms if I could agree not to avail myself of the benefits of bankruptcy. The bankruptcy laws, however, prohibit this and, hence, prevent me from committing possibly unwise acts in the future. Similarly, giving my creditor the option of having me sent to prison will surely make it easier to borrow money.[12] A determination now that I would rather pay a somewhat higher rate of interest in future transactions than take these risks is not necessarily irrational.

Limitations can be placed on the application of this line of reasoning. In many areas I might suspect that my judgment of the future would be erroneous. A law prohibiting me from making decisions in these areas, if we considered no other aspect of the matter, would appear to be rational. In practice, of course, the costs must be offset against the advantages. Little can be said in general about this subject, but I doubt that the problem would be particularly difficult in any specific situation.

In the past, contracts of employment sometimes contained

[12] It should be stressed that imprisonment for debt was always at the option of the creditor. The argument against such imprisonment so often seen in textbooks, *i.e.,* that a man in prison can hardly earn any money to pay back his debts and, hence, the creditor does not gain by the right of imprisonment, is incorrect. The threat of imprisonment was a most potent debt-collecting device. An individual in prison because he could not pay his debts would not be able to earn money, but he would serve *pour l'encouragement des autres.*

clauses under which the employee discharged his employer of liability in the case of injury to the employee. These clauses are now normally illegal. If we assume that an individual thinks that the risks are real, but also thinks that at the time he was about to be hired he might tend to estimate them differently than he does now, he would be sensible to favor such legislation. It is interesting that normally very dangerous activities are exempted. I cannot agree with my employer that he will not be liable for injuries I sustain as a lathe operator, but I can waive all claims for injuries received while driving a racing car. This would seem to support our line of reasoning since the risks of driving a racing car are less likely to be overdiscounted—they are too obvious.

Thus, it is possible to argue that numerous types of contracts should be prohibited. Again, costs are involved. Surely interest rates will be higher if bankruptcy is permitted and contracts calling for imprisonment for debt banned, and this may be a disadvantage that outweighs the gain. It will be more difficult for the man trying to get started in business, but failure will not be quite so final. These considerations must be weighed against each other in deciding which rule to choose. The conclusion in any given case is far from obvious, and it is fairly clear that different people could reach different conclusions, but this is a problem of judging likely future actions, not of principle.

Our discussion of contract law is now brought to a close. It has been lengthy, perhaps too lengthy, but it has hardly scratched the surface of the subject. What I have been trying to do is to demonstrate that it would be possible to draw up a law of contracts on the basis of our basic assumptions and without any ethical assumptions. From maxims of pure self-interest (in the sense that that term is understood by economists), we can deduce that a rather complex and detailed law of contracts, complete with enforcement agencies, is desirable. I think that I have carried the line of reasoning sufficiently far so that it is obvious that it could be used to formulate a complete law of contracts.

4

Enforcement of Contracts

Chapter 3 ignored the problems of enforcement of a contract; these problems are discussed fully in this chapter. One point must be clarified at the outset—certain restrictions on freedom of contract in the existing law are discussed under the rubric of "lack of enforceability." We assume here that certain types of contract—involving enslavement or imprisonment for nonperformance—are banned, and only discuss the enforcement of contracts that do not fall into these categories. Secondly, we do not explicitly discuss degrees of enforcement. It might, for example, be provided that the court would only enforce nine out of ten contracts brought before it or that it would not enforce contracts where the alleged defaulter was very poor or a clergyman or a member of the local aristocracy. It might also be that the measures taken in enforcement will vary according to the status of the defendant, the code of Hammurabi provides quite different penalties for persons of different status who have performed the same prohibited acts.

Enforcement of contracts can be divided into two grand divisions. Suppose that A alleges that he has a contract with B under which B has agreed to do act X. A further alleges that B has not done act X and asks enforcement. The first problem is deciding whether A's double allegation is correct, and the second is compelling B to perform. The second part, the actual application of compulsion, is not very interesting or complicated and we need not linger over it.

The first problem in the other aspect of the problem of enforcement is the certainty of error. Any "judicial" system is certain to decide sometimes that B does not have to perform act X when he really should and decide sometimes that he should perform it, even though, in the eyes of God, he has no obligation to do so. In addition there are numerous cases in which it is most uncertain what "carrying out the contract" means. The intrinsic tendency to error can be reduced, but it cannot be completely eliminated and must be borne in mind in considering any judicial system. This fact, although perfectly obvious, tends to be ignored in most discussions of the problem. Theoretical discussion in which it is implicitly assumed that the court will always reach a correct decision are not at all uncommon. The view that appellate courts are less likely to err than courts of original jurisdiction is also widely held, although I have never seen any discussion of why this should be so.[1]

Our basic assumptions about human behavior do not directly help us in deciding what sort of judicial mechanism would be best. Clearly, individuals would normally prefer to be left a choice of judiciaries when they make their contracts. Such agreements would be subject to the restrictions outlined in Chapter 3, but the desirability of permitting individuals to freely contract and to include in their contract provisions for the enforcement of those contracts seems clear. This in itself, however, does not get us very far. Before trying to do more, let me diverge again from the main course of the argument to deal with an essentially false issue that might enter the minds of some readers. It is commonly stated that governments must have a monopoly on the legitimate use of force and here we are discussing the establishment of a set of competing enforcement mechanisms, with the individuals who sign contracts deciding the ones they will patronize.

[1] Appellate courts probably reduce the number of completely ridiculous decisions, since it is not likely that two different courts will have identical ridiculous ideas. The whole problem of appeal will be discussed in Chapter 10.

In fact, the problem is unreal. A government need not really have a "monopoly" on force. All that is necessary is that its forces be strong enough to enforce a reasonable degree of public order. I suspect that in New York City there are far more private police-men than publicly hired ones. Certainly the private guard forces are more conspicuous. Las Vegas, of course, is the extreme case in which the individual casino guard forces are larger than the city police force. Normally these private guard forces are nominally in-corporated into the official government police force; all of the Las Vegas guards are deputy sheriffs, but this is mere lip service to the principle of governmental monopoly of force.

In any event, the physical enforcement of the contract—which is what is involved in the "monopoly of force"—is not our present subject. We are discussing who or what organization decides whether a man shall be compelled to perform a certain act. It is quite possible for this decision to be taken by some private citizen while the actual compulsion remains a governmental function. In much of the world arbitration is a private "court" whose decision is enforced by the government. The Jurisconsults, whose decisions shaped Roman law, were private citizens whose rulings were en-forced by government officials. Whatever else one may think about these procedures, they clearly left "force" completely in government hands.

Thus, we return to our basic finding that the parties to contracts would wish to be permitted to choose the judicial mechanism that would enforce their contract. Can we say anything about the gen-eral characteristics of the judicial procedures that would be chosen? The answer to this question is "yes," but it requires a rather lengthy digression into high school algebra in order to make the issues clear. Assuming that we have some method of enforcing contracts, the payoff that an individual would obtain from entering into a sym-metric contract is shown in Equation (4.1).

$$(4.1) \quad P_1 = B_{c_1}(1 - L_{b_1} - L_{b_2}) + L_{b_1}\{B_{b_1}L_{ns_1} + (1 - L_{ns_1})$$
$$[B_{b_1}L_e + (1 - L_e)B_{c_1} - C_{c_1}]\} - L_{b_2}\{C_{b_1}L_{ns_2} + (1 - L_{ns_2})$$
$$[C_{b_1}L_e - (1 - L_e)B_{c_1} + C_{c_1}]\}$$

This equation requires some explanation in addition to the table of symbols, but I think I should begin by explaining what I mean by a symmetric contract. A symmetric contract is a contract in which each of the parties has about the same likelihood of breaching the contract as the other, and the benefits that each party will gain from the contract are the same. In other words, it is a contract for something to happen in the future with both parties making promises that they will perform in the future; both parties, therefore, are capable of breaching the contract. For the sake of simplicity I have made the symmetry perfect. We will shortly be dealing with asymmetric contracts.

TABLE OF SYMBOLS 4–1

B_{b_1}	=	Benefit obtained by Party One from successfully breaching the contract
B_{b_2}	=	Benefit obtained by Party Two from successfully breaching the contract
B_{c_1}	=	Benefit derived by Party One from the completion of the contract
B_{c_2}	=	Benefit derived by Party Two from the completion of the contract
C_{b_1}	=	Cost to Party One of the successful breach of contract by Party Two
C_{b_2}	=	Cost to Party Two of the successful breach of contract by Party One
C_c	=	Total court costs to both parties
C_{c_1}	=	Cost to Party One of court proceedings
C_{c_2}	=	Cost to Party Two of court proceedings
I	=	Insurance payment
L_e	=	Likelihood that court will make an erroneous decision
L_{b_1}	=	Likelihood Party One will attempt to breach the contract. Note this attempt may be successful, then again it may not
L_{b_2}	=	Likelihood Party Two will attempt to breach the contract. Note this attempt may be successful, then again it may not
L_{ns_1}	=	Likelihood that if Party One breaches the contract, Party Two will refrain from suing him
L_{ns_2}	=	Likelihood that if Party Two breaches the contract, Party One will refrain from suing him
P	=	Procedural function
P_1	=	Payoff of contract to Party One
P_2	=	Payoff of contract to Party Two
P_{b_1}	=	Payoff to Party One of breaching the contract
P_{b_2}	=	Payoff to Party Two of breaching the contract

P_1 is the net expected payoff to Party One. The benefit received by Party One from the contract continuing without any breach or attempted breach by either party times the probability that this will in fact occur is shown by the portion of the equation before the plus sign. The possible profit that Party One might obtain from breaking the contract himself or attempting to break it, which must be computed in terms of the probability he will do so, is shown by the portion of the equation within the first set of braces, together with the probability multiplier attached to it. If Party One chooses to breach the contract, he may obtain a profit from that breach, which is particularly likely if Party Two chooses not to sue him. Therefore, the probability of his not being sued is the first item inside the brace. However, if the other party sues him, he may nevertheless be in a better position than without having attempted to breach, and this is shown by the portion of the equation within the square brackets, together with its probability. If the other party chooses to sue, the court may erroneously decide in favor of Party One despite the fact that he is in breach of contract; the probability of judicial error is shown at the beginning of the brace. On the other hand, the court may decide in favor of Party Two, which would mean that the court is reaching a correct decision; again a probability is attached. In this event the contract continues as if it had not originally been breached. In any event, if Party One does decide to break the contract and Party Two decides to sue him, Party One would incur a court cost, which is also shown within the brackets.

Although Party One may obtain advantages from the contract, he obviously can suffer losses if Party Two breaches the contract. These losses are shown in the second set of braces together with the probability that they will happen, and they are basically the converse of the advantages that I have already described in connection with the first set of braces. In this symmetric case, all of the probabilities of Party One's doing something are the same as the probabilities of Party Two's doing it. Furthermore, the cost of a breach of contract to one party is the same as the benefit of the cost of that breach of contract to the other. This is not a necessary characteristic of the real world, and it is introduced here primarily to simplify the equation. As another simplification, I have left out negotiated settlements.

With these symmetries, Equation (4.1) simplifies to Equation (4.2) and, by collapsing the probabilities, to Equation (4.3).

$$(4.2) \quad P_1 = B_{c_1} (1 - L_{b_1} - L_{b_2}) - (L_{b_1} + L_{b_2})(1 - L_{ns_1} - L_{ns_2}) C_{c_1}$$

$$(4.3) \quad P_1 = B_{c_1} (1 - 2L_{b_1}) - 2L_{b_1}(1 - 2L_{ns_1}) C_{c_1}$$

Party One and, by symmetry, Party Two will enter into a contract only if the payoff is greater than zero. Note from Equation (4.3) that this amounts to saying that the benefit to be obtained from the contract together with the probability that the contract will be carried out quietly—without lawsuits or threats of lawsuits—must exceed the cost of court action times its probability. In general, the lower the value of $2L_{b_1}(1 - 2L_{ns_1}) C_{c_1}$, the greater the payoff will be. Furthermore, the lower the value of this expression, the lower is the benefit from the quiet continuation of the contract (B_{c_1}) while still making the contract profitable. We can thus tentatively draw the conclusion that the individual would prefer a system that minimized the value of $2L_{b_1}(1 - 2L_{ns_1}) C_{c_1}$.

But why would anyone want to breach a contract? At the time of contracting, the parties, naturally, do not, but as time goes on further information accumulates and one party or the other may decide he would like to breach the contract. Suppose, for example, that one of the parties is a wholesaler who has contracted for the regular delivery of certain goods to a retailer for resale. After a period of time the goods are no longer salable at the original price and the retailer wants to stop future deliveries. Would he be wise to allege that the goods are substandard?

The payoff for the breach of the contract by Party One is shown by Expression (4.4).

$$(4.4) \quad P_{b_1} = B_{b_1} L_{ns} + (1 - L_{ns_1})[B_{b_1} L_e + (1 - L_e) B_c - C_{c_1}]$$

If this expression (the right side of which is simply a portion of Equation (4.1)) is greater than zero, he will be well advised to breach the contract. One of the important things that he must determine in deciding whether or not to breach is the likelihood that

Party Two will sue. The expression for the desirability of suing is
shown in Inequality (4.5).

$$(4.5) \qquad\qquad -C_{b_2} < (1-L_e)\, B_{c_2} - C_{c_2}$$

If the left side of the equation is less than the right side, then Party
Two would be well advised to sue.

The decision whether to sue or not is greatly influenced by the
probability of error. This in turn (Equation (4.6)) is a negative
function of the investment of resources in court procedures that
we consider as court costs and a variable called P that stands for
the procedural routine of the court. This equation requires some explanation.

$$(4.6) \qquad\qquad L_e = -f(C_c, P)$$

When I say L is a negative function of something, I am using
verbiage that I have invented myself, which simply means that, in
general, as you increase each of the variables inside the parentheses
it will reduce the likelihood of error. A negative function means
that the thing to the left moves monotonically in the opposite direction from the things to the right. The fact that the percentage of
errors would go down as resource investment is increased is not
very surprising. It may be, however, that this reduction is very,
very slow. For example, if both parties hire more expensive lawyers, the increase in the resources put into that trial is very substantial; but the reduction in the likelihood of error may be extremely
small.

The procedural variable (P) is introduced because we have no
reason to believe that our courts are operating at maximum efficiency. Normally, economists assume that any institution they are
dealing with is efficient and, therefore, do not include a variable
for its efficiency. We have no reason for this assumption with
respect to courts. In fact, Chapter 5 presents an argument that the
Anglo-Saxon tradition inherited from the Middle Ages is a highly
inefficient method of organizing the courts. Thus, a change in procedure could significantly reduce the likelihood of error.

Our equations thus far will probably surprise no one, although they are perhaps more concrete than the usual discussion of the matter. We can, however, draw a most interesting conclusion from them. Let us suppose that we had a very great improvement in the efficiency of the courts in the sense that we were able to sharply reduce the court costs without changing the likelihood of error. The ironic result of the change is that the parties would more likely breach their contracts. In order to demonstrate this, let us first note that if the court costs were cut to zero, Inequality (4.5) would always be satisfied and, therefore, Party Two would always sue if there were a breach. On the other hand, Equation (4.4) with court costs equal to zero simplifies to Equation (4.7). Under these circumstances, the likelihood of a breach of contract would be very high. Whenever B_{b_1} became positive, there would be a breach. This may provide the best "social" justification for laws against barratry, *i.e.*, "unauthorized" practice of law.

$$(4.7) \qquad P_{b_1} = B_{b_1} L_e + (1 - L_e) B_c$$

Thus, court costs assume a new and rather surprising role. They are a basic reason why contracts are maintained. This does not mean, however, that we must compel parties to waste resources. If nothing else, a tax on the use of the courts could solve this problem.[2] Secondly, a reduction of legal error running *au pair* with a reduction in cost would be a more reasonable way of "using" improvements in efficiency. Note that, strictly speaking, the argument applies only on the assumption that only one party is willing to breach the contract. If the party who was injured by the breach would make a false claim against the party who had breached the contract, *i.e.*, demand more than his true damages, and there were a finite chance of the judge's awarding this excess amount of damage, then there would still be some cost of breach, but probably less than the gain.

From our set of equations we can isolate the effect of the social control variables that are in essence the court proceedings them-

[2] See my "Excess Benefit," *Water Resources Research* 3 (2d Quarter, 1967): 643–644.

selves. By choosing between a more or less efficient procedural routine and reducing or increasing the amount of resources that are put into the court proceedings, parties can change the amount of legal error. Other things being equal, reducing legal error causes a reduction in the net waste in society. Thus, if I am setting up a contract, I have motives for choosing that court procedure that is least likely to make errors. There are essentially two types of errors a court can make in enforcing a contract—either a mistake in its interpretation of the contract or a mistake about the real world. We have already discussed writing contracts in order to obtain the optimal amount of error in court interpretation. Little else can be said about this in discussing court procedure except, of course, that on the whole the more intelligent the person who decides the outcome, the less likely he is to make such an error. Turning to the facts, however, the problem is essentially a new one.

The difficulty in determining what the facts are is that simple problems seldom turn up in court proceedings. Both parties will normally be arguing that what they have done is quite proper. In part, their arguments may depend upon interpretations of contract but, in part, they involve statements about what has happened in the real world. For example, suppose that A is a retailer who has entered into a contract to purchase a certain quantity of goods each month from B, a wholesaler. A alleges that the goods delivered to him were not up to specifications and, therefore, he is relieved from his obligation to purchase them. B, of course, says the goods were up to specifications. The court now is presented with the factual question of the quality of the goods. Furthermore, it is likely to be more interested in what the quality of the goods was at the time they were delivered to the party than now, several months later. In other words, it is attempting to make a historical reconstruction. The court is attempting to find out what happened in the past in order to apply the provisions of the contract to this version of the facts.

Such historical reconstruction is often extremely difficult. Furthermore, there is no reason to believe that the courts are much better at it than are the historians. We would normally hope that the courts would use those techniques that are most likely to produce the truth from any given resource investment, but let us temporarily leave that question aside. The use of specific procedural techniques and their relative efficiency is discussed in detail in a later chapter. Let us presently assume simply that the courts make efficient uses of the resources presented to them and discuss solely the problem of the amount of resources that should be invested.

In order to discuss this problem we require a little bit in the way of formal theory. In Figure 4–1, from right to left I have drawn in the amount of evidence that one finds against the defendant in various cases. All cases can be put on this axis in a location corresponding to the weight of the evidence. On the vertical axis, I have put the percentage of people in each evidence category who have in fact, violated the contract. Thus, there will be many people

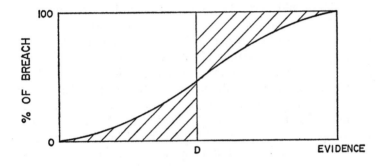

FIGURE 4–1 Evidence and Decisions

at the far left who are accused of breach of contract but who are not so guilty. There will be some, also, on the left who have breached the contract but who do not have much evidence against them. As we move to the right and the evidence against the person accused of breach of contract increases, the percentage of people who, in fact, have breached the contract will also increase. The court must make up its mind in terms of the evidence not through some sort of absolute knowledge of who has breached the contract and who has not.

The court follows a simple rule. When the evidence is stronger for the plaintiff than for the defendant, it finds the defendant guilty of breach. When the evidence is stronger for the defendant than for the plaintiff, it finds the defendant not guilty of breach. This rule is represented by the vertical line (D) at the middle of our diagram. Naturally, there will be some miscarriages of justice (shaded in Figure 4–1). In some cases the evidence appears to indicate something that is not true. I have drawn in the curves showing this effect in a logistic form that seems reasonable.

Anything that increases the efficiency of the court in effect increases the accuracy of the evidence. Although we are now discussing the commitment of more resources, the point is perhaps easier to discuss if we consider an increase in scientific knowledge. Let us suppose that Puddin'head Wilson discovers that fingerprints are unique to each individual. The result of this would be that the S curve after this discovery would be somewhat steeper than before. This would occur because as the result of this improved knowledge, the amount of evidence against certain defendants would appear to be greater and less against other defendants. This would shift the location of these cases on our horizontal axis, thus making the S curve somewhat steeper. Ideally, we would like to have the S curve actually merge with the vertical line, but we are not likely to reach this goal.

The court's efficiency in judging evidence and, hence, the steepness of the S curve in our figure is affected by the resources invested. Longer periods of time spent questioning the witnesses, seeking out less obvious witnesses, using additional technical methods—all take time and add to cost. Improving the quality of the personnel is also an expensive process. Every time the efficiency of the court is increased and every time we increase the investment of resources in this improvement and reduction of error, we reduce L_e. Presumably, however, investments in resources in improving courts would be subject to declining returns as are all other resources. This would mean that if we compute the payoff of a given contract with a number of different amounts of resource invested in court activity, we would find a curve such as Line A in Figure 4–2.

The parties would rationally choose the high point of this curve (D) as the optimum. Note that under some court arrangements they would not be interested in entering into the contract at all and there would be many court arrangements under which they would enter into the contract, but which they would not regard as optimal. Note also that as the total benefit of peaceful continuance of the contract $(B_{c_1} + B_{c_2})$ is reduced, the curve rotates toward line B. As a consequence, the optimal amount of resources to be invested in court proceedings declines; D′ is optimal for the contract represented by B. This is, of course, what we observe in the real world. There are numerous quick and inexpensive judicial procedures that give low accuracy results for small claims. When we have a major issue at trial, however, we use elaborate procedures (normally including appeals) that we hope have a lower error content. Today people normally make decisions as to the court after the

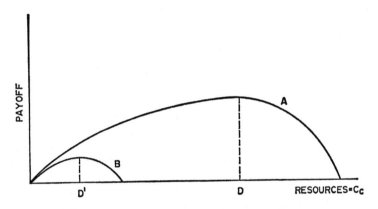

FIGURE 4–2 Optimal Investment of Resources

contract has been breached, although, of course, the small claims court is not available to everyone; but the parties would reach somewhat similar decisions if they were permitted to choose the courts beforehand.

In actual practice, in arbitration contracts there are sometimes arrangements for more complex arbitration if the problem is an expensive one than where the problem is minor. In any event, the arbitrators themselves are normally selected in such a way that the better ones are given the large cases and, for that matter, the larger fees, and the poorer ones take the small cases. In labor arbitration, for example, the Department of Labor keeps a list of arbitrators. Each arbitrator specifies his fee and the parties to labor contracts simply select one from the list. All of this is in accord with our model and in accord, also, with common sense.

Risk aversion might have some effect on the calculation. If losing a lawsuit could be very expensive for the parties and the parties only very rarely are engaged in such lawsuits, they might be interested in "buying insurance" by putting more resources into court proceedings than otherwise. Conversely, if the parties are frequently engaged in litigation and each of the contracts that is litigated involves only a very small part of their resources, they might well be interested in minimizing court costs. A very interesting case is the situation in which one of the parties, let us say an insurance company, engages in a great deal of litigation about suits that are relatively minor to it, while the other party, perhaps a customer of the insurance company, is engaged in litigation very rarely and the amounts concerned are to him very major. This, one would anticipate, would lead to differential risk avoidance on the part of the two parties.

This is all that we can learn from the symmetric case—the case where the two parties are essentially identical. Let us now turn to the asymmetric case and, in order to keep the discussion simple, let us go to a completely asymmetric example. Suppose that Party One loans Party Two money. The contract, then, is a contract by Party Two to repay Party One. Clearly, under these circumstances it is physically impossible for Party One to breach the contract, and all breaches must be breaches by Party Two. It is clear that we must have two equations—one for each party. Furthermore, these equations can be written easily as simplifications of Equation (4.1). In each case, one of the expressions in the braces vanishes because all the values in it are equal to zero. The two equations are presented as (4.8) and (4.9).

$$(4.8) \qquad P_1 = B_{c_1}(1 - L_{b_2}) - L_{b_2}\{C_{b_1}L_{ns_2} + (1 - L_{ns_2})$$
$$[C_{b_1}L_e - (1 - L_e)B_{c_1} + C_{c_1}]\} + I$$

$$(4.9) \qquad P_2 = B_{c_2}(1 - L_{b_2}) + L_{b_2}\{B_{b_2}L_{ns_2} + (1 - L_{ns_2})$$
$$[B_{b_2}L_e + (1 - L_e)B_{c_2} - C_{c_2}]\} - I$$

In Equations (4.8) and (4.9), however, I have added something—
an Insurance payment, "*I*." With the possibility of breach entirely
on one side, it is possible that one party may find it necessary to
make a payment to the other party in order to induce him to enter
into the contract. Needless to say, this is simply a possibility. "*I*"
could have a value of zero or even a negative value. Let us continue with our assumption that breaches of contract involve simple
transfers from one party to another since any other assumption
adds unnecessary elements of complication. Therefore, C_{b_1} is equal
to B_{b_2}. For the contract to be entered into, it is necessary that both
P_1 and P_2 be greater than zero. For this to be true, the double Inequality must also be true. (4.10)

$$(4.10) \qquad L_{b_2}[\ldots] - B_{c_1}(1-L_{b_2}) < I < L_{b_2}[\ldots] + B_{c_2}(1-L_{b_2})$$

Certain limitations are placed on *I*, although these limitations are
not necessarily very narrow. If, for example, $B_{c_1} + B_{c_2}$ were very
large, and L_{b_2} fairly small, *I* could well be a negative number.

It might seem that Party Two, the only person who can breach
the contract, would have strong motives for favoring an inefficient
court system. If it were not for the "Insurance payment," this would
clearly be true if Party Two could get Party One to enter into the
contract with him. Note, however, that for Party Two to borrow
the money from Party One, he must offer to Party One a positive
value of P_1, which means that if the likelihood of legal error is high
and, hence, L_{b_2} is great, the payment that Party Two must make
to Party One under the insurance rubric is also large. There is,
however, another matter. Let us suppose that we have a contract,
which, in net, if it is quietly carried out, will produce a gain of \$5;
that is, $B_{c_1} + B_{c_2} = \$5$. The cost of breach, however, might be
much larger than that. If the loan were at 5 percent, nonrepayment
inflicts \$100 cost on the lender. Thus, C_{b_1} and B_{b_2} might be as much
as \$100. If, under these circumstances, L_{b_2} is greater than .05, *I*
will necessarily be greater than \$5.

This would mean that the contract is impossible because Party

Two cannot make enough by performing his obligations, no matter how much of the total gain he obtains, to make the payment to Party One that is necessary to induce Party One to enter into the contract. Party One, on the other hand, is unlikely to be willing to enter into the contract if he knows that the borrower will surely lose unless he succeeds in avoiding repayment.[3] Thus, if the courts are inefficient, there is no gain for Party One or Party Two. On the other hand, the more inefficient the courts and, hence, the higher the likelihood of error, the higher the net benefit of the contract must be before it becomes possible to enter into an agreement. In

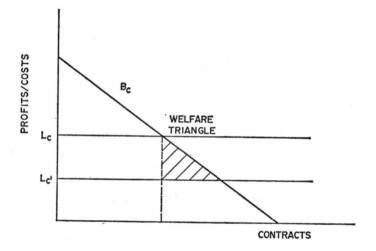

FIGURE 4–3 Gains from Improved Court Procedures

essence, the parties are charged a tax by the inefficiency of the courts, and this eliminates many agreements that would be desirable with a more efficient court system.

In the traditional Dupuit welfare diagram (Figure 4–3) all contracts are arranged on the horizontal axis in order of potential profitability. The ones with the highest net profit are at the left.

---

[3] Special cases in which agreements of this sort are possible can be thought up. They have little or nothing to do with normal contractual situations, however.

The profits from various contracts are shown by the slanting line B_c. The horizontal line L_c represents the costs inflicted by a relatively inefficient court system. If we switch to a more efficient court system as represented by $L_{c'}$, not only do we pick up the traditional welfare triangle but the rectangle to the left of the welfare triangle is obtained by the parties through a reduction in waste, *i.e.*, the inefficient court system. In both the symmetric and asymmetric cases, then, the parties have strong reasons for hoping that the courts will make relatively few errors and that the costs of legal proceedings will be relatively low. They have, of course, a motive for keeping the cost of legal proceedings always great enough so that the discounted value of the errors does not lead to continuous litigation, but this should be fairly simple to arrange.

I have used only the two rather pure cases for reasons of simplicity. We could easily extend our equation to five or six lines instead of the present two and obtain a general expression that would deal with varying degrees of asymmetry. We could similarly drop our assumption that the cost and benefits of a breach of contract involve simple transfers, where in the real world they probably normally do not, and produce an even more complicated equation —further "realistic" changes could be made. I do not think, however, this would give us any particular new information and it would certainly make our exercise in high school algebra even more tedious.

Our conclusion that efficiency in the court decision process is desirable from the standpoint of all parties who are contemplating entrance into contracts would not be modified. Note, however, that this conclusion is an *ex ante* conclusion. Once I have entered into a contract with you, I have very strong motives to want that contract modified in my favor, and such modification may take the form of either injuring or improving the efficiency of the court's enforcement of the contract. Since most of us are likely to enter into far more contracts in the future than the number we are involved in now, it is likely that the value we obtain from generally efficient enforcement procedures is greater than the value we would obtain from making enforcement procedures less efficient.

As noted previously, a situation might arise in which one of the parties was engaged in a great deal of litigation and the other party was engaged in relatively little. In these cases the individual suit for the first party may be a relatively small matter and for the second party a relatively large matter. Since differential risk aversion would occur, it should, therefore, be possible to set up an arrangement whereby one party pays the other a small fee for reducing his risk. If the risk is that the courts will decide incorrectly, then straightforward insurance against that risk is impossible. Since the courts are unlikely to admit that they are wrong in a given case, it would not be possible, if I lost a lawsuit, for me to successfully

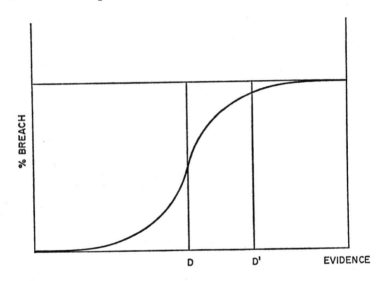

FIGURE 4-4 Biased Court Procedures

sue my insurance company alleging that I lost the suit unjustly. An insurance policy that insured me against the cost of losing lawsuits in all contracts would be equally difficult because I always have it in my power to simply breach the contract and, thus, put myself in a situation where I could profit. Thus, the moral risk would be overwhelming and the insurance companies would not be willing to offer this type of insurance.

If, however, we cannot actually make a direct insurance contract of this sort, perhaps an arrangement between the two parties may serve something of the same end. Let us suppose that we have the situation shown in Figure 4–4, that the defendant is rarely likely to be involved in lawsuits, and these lawsuits are, for him, quite major. The plaintiff is in the opposite position with respect to these matters. For example, consider a bank that has a great many mortgages outstanding and an individual who will only undertake a few mortgages during his lifetime. Under these circumstances, we can provide something in the way of insurance for the potential defendant by biasing the proceedings. Instead of simply trying to follow the fair preponderance of the evidence and using decision rule D, the court might take the view that it will decide for the defendant unless the evidence is much stronger for the plaintiff as at the line D'. The number of errors the court makes, then, will be increased, but the number of errors against the defendant will be reduced. Individuals interested in risk reduction would presumably be willing to enter into contracts in which they paid a fee for this type of service. Similarly, the party on the other side would be willing to do this, if the fee was large enough.

In the real world, a number of organizations do offer this kind of treatment to their customers. Insurance companies normally make quite a play in their advertisement and sales techniques of the generous way in which they settle claims against them by the people who have been insured.[4] Thus, it would appear that an insurance company sets up its own little court system—its claims adjustment office. This court system is under instruction to insure that any errors it makes are more likely to be against the insurance company than against the client. Needless to say, the cost of this bias is actuarially computable and the insurance company adds the amount to its premiums. The net effect from the standpoint of the customer of the insurance company is that he is buying insurance in two different ways: he is buying insurance from the insurance company against fire by direct payment of premiums, and he is buying insurance from the insurance company against the contingency that

[4] Note that, in automobile accident cases, the person who has the claim is not normally the insurance company's customer. He is someone who is threatening to sue the insurance company's customer. The insurance company's customer wishes to be protected against the suit, but he has no particular concern as to how this is done or how generously the insurance company pays off the person who is suing him.

the insurance company will erroneously refuse to pay him, again by paying a small premium to the insurance company. The same thing can be done by the courts. It is by no means obvious, however, that we would expect this phenomenon very often in a law of contracts. Later when we turn to the criminal law, we will find it almost omnipresent.

We may pause profitably to briefly discuss out-of-court settlements. In Figure 4–5 we have a situation that confronts an attorney, who is, let us say, representing one of the parties in a case at "C." From the standpoint of the court that will reach eventual decisions, the outcome appears to be a simple application of a decision rule

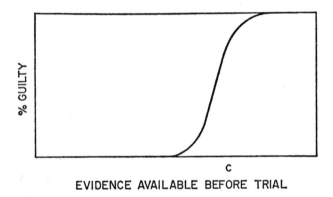

EVIDENCE AVAILABLE BEFORE TRIAL

FIGURE 4–5 Negotiated Settlements

taking into account the amount of evidence. To the lawyer before the trial, it is not so simple. Firstly, he does not have access to all the evidence that will come out at the trial. Secondly, he cannot be certain exactly what will happen at the trial in such matters as good and bad impressions made by the witnesses. Thirdly, he cannot perfectly foretell the decision makers' reactions. Thus, the vertical line that is seen by the judge as describing his behavior appears as an S curve to the lawyers. In our case, from the standpoint of the lawyer, at point C the defendant has about three chances out of four of being found liable for breach of contract. If the attorneys for both sides are in general agreement as to these odds, then risk aversion would indicate that they should reach an agreement outside of court that properly discounts this predicted behavior of the court. If there is disagreement, which takes the form of the lawyer for the defendant's feeling that it is more likely that his client will be found guilty of breaching the contract than does the lawyer for the plaintiff, then again, an agreement is likely. If the lawyer for the plaintiff thinks that the decision of the court is more likely to go in his favor than does the lawyer for the defendant, then the matter will proceed to trial.

An element of bargaining and game theory, however, is involved in settlements, and occasionally the matter will go to trial even though a suitable bargain could be reached. This will occur in those cases in which the attorney on one side or the other (or, for that matter, the client on one side or the other) feels it important to develop a reputation for being tough. This raises no particular theoretical difficulty. Note that the question of whether the judge is simply attempting to determine what happened as accurately as possible or whether he is biased toward one party or the other makes no major change in the role of the attorneys. They simply attempt to predict his decision. The S curve drawn in Figure 4–5 would move to the right or to the left in terms of the degree of bias that the judge is believed to have. Bargaining, however, would still continue under approximately the same conditions.

5

Anglo-Saxon Encumbrances

We shall begin discussion of the procedure used in court and the problems of its efficiency by considering how information is brought before the court for decision. Obviously, the simplest method of obtaining information is to choose as the person to make the decisions someone who already knows this procedure. That is, of course, what is done. The judge is customarily an expert in the law, which is a technical matter. In those cases where the law is not known to the judge—foreign law, for example—it is normally "proved" as any other "fact." Where there is some doubt in the minds of the parties as to whether the judge does or does not know the law in any given area, the discussion of this matter is very similar to that of a factual question. Evidence in the form of written briefs and affidavits is presented and arguments are made by the attorneys.

It is not, by any means, necessary that the judge be a technical expert on this particular matter. In the formative period of Roman law, an outsider, the Jurisconsult, was normally brought in as a technical expert to deal with any difficult problem of law. The Jurisconsult who stated the law was not a judge—he was a private citizen. In our law when the jury is called upon to make ultimate decisions, it must also obtain information from the judge as to what the law is. Finally, in those innumerable cases in which the case proceeds to an arbitrator rather than a judge, the arbitrator may find it necessary to turn to an outside source of information on the law.

There is, however, no compelling reason why the special field of which the judge knows a great deal must be confined to the law or even be the law itself. In commercial arbitration, the arbitrator is very frequently an expert in some technical matter. If, for example, an importer alleges that a shipment of wool he receives is not up to the specified quality, the arbitrator selected for this matter will normally be a man who is capable of telling by inspection whether it is or is not up to that quality. Courts martial normally require that the officers on the court martial must be as high or higher in rank than the person subject to court martial. The official explanation for this is that such persons will be able to understand, from their own experience, the problems confronting the officer under trial and, hence, can bring some knowledge with them.

It is an oddity of our law that although in many areas we attempt to see to it that the decision maker is already possessed of a good deal of information, in other areas we do just the opposite. There are efforts, for example, to see to it that jurymen know nothing whatsoever about the case before they enter the jury box. It is of some interest that the *raison d'être* of the jury has been completely reversed over the years. The original justification was that the twelve local men knew *more* than the circuit judge. It would seem, on the whole, that it is more sensible to follow the rule of selecting judges who know something about the subject than people who know nothing. This is, however a subject on which two opinions are possible.

A second method of obtaining information for decisions in a court is to consult an expert who (himself) is not the judge. There are two ways of doing this: one is to have the judge select an expert; the other is to have the parties find (usually competing) experts who present their statements to the court. Once again, it would seem reasonable that the former is the better of the two procedures and, of course, it is the procedure used in most of the world. We in the Anglo-Saxon world, however, have a rather provincial and unusual form of procedure in which the two parties themselves provide the experts.

Regardless of who provides the experts, there is the problem of obtaining them; which is normally done by offering them a fee. The parties to a contract, if they are interested in reducing L_e, would normally be willing to include provisions for such fees in the contract. If the court, for example, is to select its own experts, then one would anticipate that the parties would provide that it could, in cases of trial, draw the funds from the parties. The provisions could, of course, be arranged so that large fees would be available in major disputes and small fees in minor ones, and, hence, the experts would be much more expert for large contracts. Where the two parties provide the experts (as is the normal Anglo-Saxon practice) they, of course, pay them; but it is by no means obvious that this is a major defect in our procedure. The experts, after all, must protect their reputations.

The fourth category of information that may be important at a trial is documents and written papers. The text of the contract would do as an example. Our procedure, in general, descends from the Middle Ages when illiteracy was common. It seems that this is the only available explanation for the fact that this procedure is primarily oral. It is frequently true that a written document, in order to be brought before a court in the United States or England, must be read aloud. In an attempt to be efficient in decision making, we would try to maximize the use of written rather than oral information. As much of the total volume of information as possible should be presented to the court in written form and should be circulated rather than compelling the parties to all get together at one time to receive it. This is, in general, the custom in commercial arbitration, although it must be said that in such cases the total volume of written documents may be small.

The fact that all the parties—the decision maker, the parties on both sides, the witnesses, and the attorneys—must all get together at the same time, causes a great deal of waste in our present procedure. The use of written testimony, including the use of testimony taken before referees and then presented to the decision maker, would greatly reduce the total investment of time by various people waiting for other people. It would particularly be an improvement in the use of the time of the professional decision makers whom we call judges. Today they must spend most of their time hearing cases and, as a consequence, sizable delays are imposed on other people who are waiting to have their issues decided. If judges could devote a greater part of their time to reading documents on cases, it would be possible to greatly improve the scheduling of that part of their time that is spent in hearing oral argument. There seems no reason why the formal speeches of the attorneys, for example, should not be replaced by written documents, or why a good deal of the testimony we now get should not be delivered in written form. Modern appellate procedure has moved in this direction.

It is, of course, true that under our present procedure the decision as to whether a witness is honest or not is made very largely by the technique of looking intently at his face while he testifies. This technique, in the present state of scientific knowledge, must be continued and this does mean (at least to some extent) that witnesses must testify before the decision maker. Development of better ways of detecting lying would seem desirable. Such better methods will, in fact, be discussed later in this chapter, but for the time being we can note that a good many of the witnesses who appear in the average court case are not suspected of lying. The police photographer who appears for the purpose of identifying certain photographs that he took during the investigation of some crime, the fingerprint expert who simply testifies that certain fingerprints are the prints of a certain person, or the professor of comparative law who appears to testify as to the provisions of the German code of inheritance, are all normally accepted by both parties as being completely honest witnesses. In those cases in which there is a question, of course, special arrangements should be made.

Thus far our problems with respect to obtaining information have been relatively easy. We now come to the difficult problems concerning evidence in the hands of people who would rather not present it to the court. The first and obvious case is found in the parties to the litigation themselves. A sues B for breach of contract. B would very much like to keep certain of his records out of the litigation because they will injure his case. Should he be compelled to produce them?

In the contract action we could, of course, simply provide an answer in the contract itself. It seems fairly certain that this would lead, in most cases, to a provision that both parties would be compelled (in the event of any dispute as to the enforcement of the contract) to present to whomever is to decide the dispute all the evidence in their possession. This would reduce L_e and, as we pointed out, would be to the advantage of both parties at the time the contract is entered into. The only exception would be cases whereby the presentation of this evidence might in and of itself be very expensive. We would, of course, weigh cost against benefit in this area, but it does not seem very likely that the cost would be sizable in many cases. The existing procedural law compels the parties to a litigation to produce their records; hence, it is unnecessary to include a special provision in the text of current agreements.

There is here, however, another problem. Suppose we are going to ask questions in court of the individual parties to the contract. They may well have strong motives to lie (or produce bogus documents). What should we do about this at the time we are drawing up the contract? If there were some perfect method of detecting lies, we could very easily incorporate the use of this method into the contract. Note that if we did so, there would be no need to place any particular restriction on lying when the matter came up for decision. The person who lied would normally find that (1) he prejudiced the decision maker against him; and (2) under some relatively ingenious questioning, his lies (each of which was properly detected) would, in fact, lead to the truth's being known to the decision maker. Unfortunately, we do not have such a certain method of determining whether or not people are telling the truth. The lie detector, which is discussed at somewhat greater length later, is an imperfect instrument. It is certainly better than staring at the man's face to detect lying, but that is feeble praise.

What then can we do? One procedure is to place a cost on lying. Thus, we can provide that, if one of the parties is called to testify and the decision maker thinks he is lying, some special cost will be imposed upon him. For example, suppose the contract provides that if Party A testifies falsely in a matter where the lie would profit him by the amount of $100 (if his testimony were believed) and his falsehood is discovered, he will be required to pay a fine of $500. If the probability of detection were greater than one in five, this would make lying unprofitable and the parties would seldom resort to it. Here, clearly, we are coming very close to the criminal law of perjury, but note that the present line of reasoning would indicate that the parties would be inclined to include such provisions in their contracts if the law of perjury did not exist. We can, in fact, regard the legal provisions as a time saver that makes it unnecessary for the parties to put such provisions into their contracts. A clause providing that testimony in any litigation arising out of a contract should not be under oath and, hence, not subject to prosecution for perjury would, I presume, be legally possible in present-day contracts. It seems unlikely that anyone will take advantage of this opportunity.

We now come, however, to the witness who is not directly concerned with the contract. It frequently happens that some factual information that would be of interest in determining whether or not a breach of contract has occurred is in the possession of an innocent bystander who is not a party to the contract or in any way connected with it. Note that what we are now discussing is not the expert witness. Expert witnesses are basically engaged in the competitive business of providing their expert knowledge for a fee. If one expert witness asks too much money for his services, the parties can turn to another. The individual who has seen something that is of importance to the trial, however, normally cannot easily be replaced.

Under these circumstances, if these outside witnesses (people not connected with the contract) are permitted to bargain for their fee, we can anticipate that they will attempt to extract the full economic value of their information in this bargaining process. Frequently, the economic value of their testimony is nearly as great as the total amount in dispute in the trial. Thus, permitting open bargaining would mean that the court costs would be so high that it would be very rare that contracts would be judicially enforced. This would be particularly true if there were several witnesses, each of whose evidence was of great importance to one or the other of the parties. Needless to say, the party against whom the witness was to testify would be willing to pay him not to testify. In Equation (4.5), $C_{b_2} - B_{c_2}$ would tend to equal C_{c_2}; hence, Party Two would not sue.

Obviously, since this type of witness is not a party to the contract, he cannot agree in advance to any specific treatment. Here all that can be done is to turn to broad social instrumentalities. Thus far, we have been able to discuss the law of contracts without any duties for the state. We have been able to demonstrate that agreements between the parties could lead to almost any outcome that was desired. The state has come in simply as the guardian of its own use of force and violence and as a labor saving device providing certain facilities that the parties could otherwise provide for themselves. The problem of the essential witness who is not a signatory of the contract is impossible to solve by provisions in the contract. We are thus forced to turn to a purely governmental technique that we first describe simply and then with regard to its relationship to our fundamental assumptions.

Suppose that a law is enacted providing that in civil suits the parties or the judge (depending upon how we arrange the acquisition of information) may order any person they wish to testify. Let us further suppose that the law provides for payment for the witnesses' time. Unless the payment is excessive, this would be highly desirable from the standpoint of the parties to the contract. But would it be desirable to a person who is not, at the moment, involved in the contract under litigation? I think the answer is "yes." Firstly, a general law of this sort would make all future contracts that a person might wish to enter into much more readily enforced. *Ex ante,* it is a tremendous improvement in the efficiency of the contracting system. As we have pointed out, this is to the benefit of people who are thinking of entering into contracts, and we all are thinking of entering into contracts. There is, it might be said, an additional advantage to such a law. Not only are we ourselves interested in entering into contracts in the future, but the efficient functioning of our economy requires that it be possible for other people to do so as well. There is something similar to an externality involved in the contract process in that the existence of an efficient contract procedure makes it possible for the economy to function at a higher level than it otherwise would and, thus, raises all of our living standards.

We need not, however, depend upon this. Clearly, the present discounted value to me of a very sharp reduction in the cost of enforcing any contracts that I may enter into in the future is greater than the disutility I might suffer from not being permitted to bargain for a fee in those cases in the future in which I might become a witness to a breach of contract action. If the compensation that I would receive for testifying is such that I suffer no positive loss (only the loss of possible profits that I might make from bargaining), this is particularly clear. It is quite possible, however, that my present discounted value might be improved by compelling such testimony, even if witnesses were not paid at all. The payment of the witnesses really is important, less in terms of compensating them for their time (if we look at the matter *ex ante*) than providing an incentive for the court or the parties to be economical in the use of witnesses. In this case, we are eliminating an externality by imposing upon the parties to the litigation the cost of one of the resources they are using—the time of the witnesses.

Naturally, however, if we are going to compel people who are not parties to a contract to testify, we cannot permit the parties to the contract to set the conditions of this compulsion. In other words, we cannot permit the parties to a contract, when they choose their own method by which the contract is to be enforced, to also choose who is to compel the third party witnesses and how much they are to be paid. For this purpose, we would need a social institution that represented the witnesses as much as it represented the parties to the contract. Thus, a court system that is established by the government would be necessary for this particular part of the process. Note that it would not be necessary for it to hear the witnesses; it could simply determine which witnesses should be called, what their compensation was to be, and the punishment (if any) if they were found to be lying in their testimony.[1]

This argument takes us back to the sets of possible institutions that benefit each person and their intersection discussed in Chapter 1. The present discounted value of compelling testimony with

[1] The argument for putting a "price" on telling lies in court is just as strong for these witnesses as it is for other witnesses. Normally witnesses of this sort have much weaker motives for telling lies than the interested parties and, therefore, perhaps it might be argued that we could get by with lower penalties.

compensation is positive for everyone and, hence, would benefit all persons. Similarly, its abolition would injure all persons. It might, of course, be true that some person would be injured by being compelled to testify in a case tomorrow, but surely if we put the establishment of this institution off for several years and made it apply only to contracts entered into in the future, we would find no one who could reasonably object to it.

We now turn to the pure procedural variable (P) in our equation; that is, to a discussion of what types of procedure are most efficient in a court system. We have already noted that reducing the number of legal errors is extremely desirable. If we can do so in an essentially costless way (that is, by simply improving the efficiency of the organization of the court), this would obviously be sensible. It is my own opinion that this is quite readily possible in our present court system. The reader, however, may not agree with me. The remainder of this chapter, in any event, discusses improvements in our court system, mainly involving a radical change from the traditional Anglo-Saxon procedure that we have inherited from the Middle Ages. In a sense, the discussion is inconclusive. Here, as in so many other areas, a good deal of further research, particularly experimental research, is needed before one can have much confidence in the superiority of any given system. Thus, my arguments for changes in our present system are really an attempt to demonstrate that there is a good case for a careful consideration of changes and extensive research in the area. Our present knowledge is simply not sufficient to permit placing any real confidence in our judgments of the efficiency of the various court systems.

I should like to begin by discussing two rather general issues that are, I think, normally the subject of a great deal of obscurantism and superstition. If we confine ourselves to the European legal tradition, we find two general ways of organizing legal procedure—the adversary and the inquisitorial system—and two methods of reaching ultimate decisions—judges and juries.[2] In both cases, the

2 A number of European countries use an interesting system that combines the jury and the judge system. Under this system, a group of people are appointed to decide cases, but some, and usually a majority of them, have had no legal training. Furthermore, these nonlawyer members

system used in the United States is the minority system. We use juries, whereas most Western countries use judges; [3] we use the adversary system, whereas most countries use the inquisitorial system. Since there are cases in which the inquisitorial system of organizing the courts is combined with juries [4] and the adversary system of organization is also not infrequently combined with judicial decision making,[5] we can regard these as two independent variables and discuss them separately. As a further word of warning to the readers, I agree with the foreigners. Patriots who strongly favor retaining our sacred institutions will be annoyed by my analysis.

Three valid arguments for the peculiar institution of the use of juries are: it makes tyranny impossible, it makes corruption difficult, and it makes it likely that the results of judicial proceedings will be in accord with the "popular will" regardless of the law in the matter. The first argument was, perhaps, of historic importance. With the jury system, kings simply could not plan on imprisoning anyone. The juries were not necessarily favorable to rebels or opponents of the crown, but they were unreliable. Furthermore, if the king chose to follow a policy that was genuinely unpopular, the jury might follow popular feeling and not the law when it came to trial. Thus, an unpopular law might not be enforced.

It is probable, although not certain, that our traditional devotion to "the right of trial by jury" is derived from these considerations. I have always wondered why it should be such a privilege to be tried by a group of complete amateurs who have not been

---

of the "judiciary" are not permanently assigned to this duty, but are periodically returned to their nonjudicial jobs and replaced by new untrained persons. The Courts Martial of most Western armies operate on somewhat the same basis, although in these cases the legally trained personnel are normally reduced to an advisory status.

[3] During the period of the French Revolution, most European countries adopted the jury. Basically, they have now abandoned it, but a few remnants remain. See Harry Kalven, Jr., and Hans Zeisel, *The American Jury* (Boston: Little, Brown and Company, 1966), especially footnote 3 on pages 13–14.

[4] For a few types of cases in Switzerland, for example.

[5] All chancery cases in the traditional common law and the bulk of all cases now tried in the United States under either chancery or common law rubrics are examples.

specially trained. In any event, the protection against despotism
by the use of juries particularly concerns the criminal law. It is
difficult to see any great danger to liberty in permitting contracts
to be litigated before judges. In England—the home of our jury
system—juries have been largely abolished for civil trials since
about 1870.

A second argument for jury trials is that it is fairly easy to
control juries so that bribery is unlikely. With reasonable care,
it will be impossible for the parties to a litigation to know before
the jury is finally impanelled who is going to be on it. Furthermore, once the jury is impanelled, it can quite easily be kept from
any contact with potential bribers. Thus, if one fears corruption,
the jury is more readily protected against bribery than is a judge.
It should be noted, however, that if we are convinced by this
particular argument, then a reform that has recently been much
mooted in England would be desirable. The English noted that the
unanimity requirement that is necessary in most cases in England,
although not in Scotland, meant that only one person must be
bribed in order to hang a jury. Therefore, they proposed reducing
the requirement from unanimity to ten out of twelve, which would
make it necessary to bribe three jurors and thus make it much
more difficult to corrupt the jury. In any event, this entire argument of corruption, like that of the tyranny of the government,
depends largely on other matters than the court procedure itself.
It surely is not impossible to arrange things in such a way that the
bribing of judges is extremely unlikely. If the likelihood of the
corruption of judges is very low, then the argument for a jury
under this head would be correspondingly weak.

The third argument for juries is "democracy." A judge is likely
to follow the law a good deal more than a jury. Firstly, the jury
does not know what the law is in any detail (and is likely to be
confused by the highly technical "directions" on the law that the
judge is required to give them). In addition, the jury is likely to
ignore the law if it "doesn't seem right." Judges do this, also, but
to a considerably lesser extent. Since the juries are an average
group of people, this means that the mores and moral ideas, the
emotions and sentiments of the average man are closely reflected
in their judgments. Whether it is more "democratic" to have the

cases decided in accord with rules which have been selected by democratic procedures, or to have them directly decided by a small random sample of the people is clearly an open question. Arguments for the latter procedure can be made, however, and they are clearly arguments for the use of juries.

Before turning to the arguments against the use of juries for the enforcement of contract, I should like to point out that I am not suggesting that jury trials for this purpose be outlawed. In terms of our initial assumptions, we should favor the widest field of choice, which would mean permitting the contracting parties to choose their own form of enforcement. If they chose a jury, that would be their prerogative. I am opposed to our present law, which makes it extremely difficult or impossible to draw a contract in such a way that a jury may not be involved in its enforcement. My basic argument, however, is that contracting parties should be given greater freedom than they now have, not that their "right" of jury trial should be taken away.

Under our present procedure, in contract actions, there will be no jury if the matter falls within the completely arbitrary limits of a "chancery" action. If, on the other hand, the litigation is a "law" action, the parties decide at the time of the litigation whether there will be a jury. Normally either party may ask for one and a provision in the original contract that barred a request for a jury would probably be void. The situation of the two parties at the time of litigation is quite different from that at the time the contract was originally signed. In particular, the party whose case is weaker is likely to feel that he would prefer to have the case heard by a group of untrained people of only average intelligence to having it heard by a trained expert on contract law who is of above average intelligence.

As evidence of real preferences, we can consider the real world situation in those contracts in which the parties are permitted to choose their own procedure. Those contracts in which the decision on enforcement will not be made by the regular courts are unusual in the United States, somewhat less so in England. Normally they are called "arbitration" contracts, but the word should not mislead us. They involve a private procedure for deciding who has broken the contract in the event of a dispute. In no case is this procedure the selection of a group of average and completely unqualified citizens who are then allowed to decide. In most cases an individual who is thought to be particularly well qualified is selected as the "judge" of the dispute, in some cases a board of such "judges" is established or, sometimes, there is an arrangement for the automatic selection of such a "judge" at the time of the dispute.

It seems likely that granting a general permission to individuals who enter into contracts to select their own method of enforcement would lead to the expansion of the methods now used in cases where this freedom exists. The nonuse of the jury system by people who have a choice at the time they write their contracts would appear to be strong evidence that juries are not something that contracting parties value highly. In any event, the experiment should be tried. Permitting people to choose judges to enforce their contracts instead of juries would surely not be likely to lead to despotism, particularly if they are also permitted a freedom in deciding which judge they will "hire."

The advantage that judges have over juries is fairly obvious. On one side is training and selection, on the other a tiny random sample. The random sample is a good way of finding out the characteristics of the universe from which it is drawn, but it is not a good way of attaining superior performance. In any event, the variance of a sample of twelve is great. The judge, even the rather poor judges that we often have in the United States, is likely to be considerably above average intelligence. Even if his background has been basically political rather than legal (and that is the case with many of our federal judges, particularly those on the appellate and supreme courts), he will quickly pick up at least some expertise by hearing large numbers of cases. If we selected and trained our judges more carefully, these arguments would apply with even more force. An obvious improvement in our judicial system would be simply raising the level of the personnel on the bench; permitting the parties to contract for their judge (or arbitrator) in advance would probably lead to such an improvement.

Not only is the judge more intelligent and better trained than the jury, the lawyers who appear before him are aware of this fact. Skill in influencing the common man, so well known on

Madison Avenue and at 1600 Pennsylvania Avenue, is also the secret of the success of any good trial lawyer. The experienced pleader before a jury knows that many of the jurors are not able to follow difficult lines of reasoning; he knows that the jury is likely to forget the details of the case, so he can rely on such convenient lapses of memory; he knows that the jury will either simply accept an expert's view or follow some vague idea of its own. With this idea of the average juror's ability, the jury lawyer does not make any real effort to present his case in a logical or coherent manner. He searches for slogans, simplifications, and emotional appeals. Since his opponent is doing the same thing, the presentation of the case is not likely to be highly coherent.[6]

The contrast between the attitude taken by lawyers toward juries and that taken toward judges is sharp. Of course, judges have emotions, and the lawyers try to appeal to them. Furthermore, some members of the bench are not intelligent or have prejudices that are known to and played upon by the lawyers. Nevertheless, the intellectual level of judge trials is normally higher. The judge normally can follow involved lines of reasoning, so that lawyers are willing to present them if they are relevant and serve their interests. The judge can understand the contract even if it is complicated. He has heard technical evidence before and probably has at least some idea of what it is about. Consequently, the attorneys present their case to the judge on a much higher level and the outcome is likely to be a better decision, not only because the judge is better qualified than the jury to make a decision, but also because the attorneys, knowing that he is not

[6] These strictures are of considerably greater importance in the United States than they are in England. Under the English procedure, juries are drawn from the upper class and the judge closes the case with a long, careful discussion of the case addressed to the jury. Since the juries are likely to be very, very heavily influenced by this performance on the part of the judge, the attorneys are almost as much concerned with influencing the judge as the jury. This leads to a more intellectual approach to the case. The reader who wishes to have an idea of the usual situation in the United States can do no better than to read *The Reader's Digest Murder Case.* This is very close to a verbatim record of the proceedings in a New York murder case that involved two employees of *The Reader's Digest* as victims. A reading of the opening and final statements of the attorneys involved is quite revealing. J. Fulton Oursler, *The Reader's Digest Murder Case* (New York: Collier Books, 1962).

as easily influenced by Madison Avenue techniques, make less use of them.

As a final matter, we might consider whether a single judge is better than a board of judges. A simple fact must be taken into account here. For a given amount of money, you can hire a single man of very high quality, three men of less quality, or five of even still less quality. Thus, in general, the board of judges will be individually less qualified than the single judge. This fact is not necessarily decisive, but it should always be remembered. Other than that, I do not think that we can say very much about the question of whether an individual judge is better than a board of judges. I, myself, tend to prefer the individual judge, but this may be simple prejudice. In continental Europe, boards of judges are used. The issue should receive further study, and any definitive outcome would probably be applicable to fields far outside that of jurisprudence.

Our second general problem is the choice between the adversary system of procedure and the inquisitorial system. The latter system has had a very bad press in the United States and England, possibly because of the resemblance between its name and that of the Inquisition. In fact, again, we are the ones who have a peculiar and unusual system, whereas the inquisitorial system is the norm of the Western world. Such countries as Sweden, Denmark, Switzerland, and the Netherlands all use the inquisitorial system; surely no one will argue that this results in any great loss in freedom for their citizens. The actual cause of the difference in procedure in the Anglo-Saxon world and the continental countries is an accident of history. The Roman law used an inquisitorial procedure. When the German tribes conquered the Western Empire, they replaced the Roman system with judicial chaos. In England, however, this chaos gradually developed into the distinctive Anglo-Saxon judicial procedure while on the continent there was a return to the Roman system. It should be noted that the judicial systems used in the non-European world are also mainly of an inquisitorial nature, although in many of them the courts should not be regarded as models.

Even in English procedure there are elements of inquisitorial proceedings. In particular, Chancery, or "equity," with its close connections to canon law and through it to the Roman legal system, has a number of inquisitorial features. Even in strict "law" cases, the British judge has a much freer hand with the witnesses than does the United States judge. Thus, the British original, from which we copied our system, is somewhat closer to the inquisitorial procedure than we are.

Basically, the difference between the two systems is simply a matter of who dominates the procedure, the lawyers or the judge.[7] In the inquisitorial system, the judge or judges institute an inquiry into the matter. They call such witnesses and ask them such questions as they think desirable. The parties, either in person or through their attorneys, are permitted to ask such further questions and call such additional witnesses as they wish, but the basic procedure consists of an inquiry into the matter by the judge or judges. In the Anglo-Saxon system, the judge plays little role in the actual presentation of the case.[8] The two lawyers dominate the proceedings. Normally the plaintiff's attorney first presents his case and the defendant's attorney tries to break it down. The judge may ask questions himself, but this is frowned upon in the United States. The argument offered for the Anglo-Saxon procedure is that the judge is more likely to be impartial if he plays little or no role in the case except as an auditor.

This argument has never been completely clear to me, but what I think it means is that the judge, when he begins asking questions, must have at least some "theory." As the philosophers of science are so fond of pointing out, no investigator can start out with a completely empty mind. He requires at least some elementary theories in order to ask his questions. The judge is in the same position. Thus, he will start out with an idea, however faint, of what the investigation is likely to produce. It is the nub of the argument against the inquisitorial procedure that he is likely to stick to this initial theory even if the evidence does not support it. Or, in a milder form, he will stick to his initial theory unless the evidence against it is substantially greater than the

[7] This is true even in those cases in which inquisitorial procedures are combined with a jury as the ultimate trier of the facts.

[8] Again, this is much more true of the American court system than of the British. The English judge plays a much more active role than does his American opposite number.

evidence for it. This argument is not completely without merit; some such tendency might well exist. The problem is whether this particular disadvantage of the inquisitorial system outweighs the disadvantage of the adversary system.

If the judge simply sits and listens to the two attorneys, clearly he is less likely to be personally involved with any particular theory of the case. On the other hand, the greater importance of the lawyers means that the relative excellence of those hired by the two parties is of much greater importance. If the judge decides on the basic order form of the witnesses and asks 90 percent of the questions, the man who happens to have the poorer lawyer is obviously at less of a disadvantage than if the lawyers decide the order of the witnesses and ask almost all of the questions. Since a case in which the two lawyers are of exactly equal ability must be very rare, it would seem that the inaccuracy introduced by this factor alone would more than offset the possible inaccuracy resulting from giving the judge the dominant role.

A further advantage of the inquisitorial system is a reduction of the importance of courtroom strategy. As anyone who has had much contact with lawyers knows, strategy and tactics are very important to them and lawsuits come to be thought of as contests between the lawyers. Given this attitude and the complex maneuvering that accompanies it, the smaller the role played by the lawyers, the more likely it is that the outcome will be in accord with the facts. The inquisitorial system does not, however, eliminate courtroom strategy, but it greatly reduces its importance.

If we turn from the Anglo-Saxon court system and inquire as to what system is used for other types of investigation in England and America, we find that the adversary system is almost never adopted. In the United States, if we wish to find out the facts about something, practically regardless of what it is, we do not appoint a judge and then have two attorneys present cases to him. We appoint an individual or a board to investigate, and we expect that the appointed individual will conduct the investigation himself. This is so even if the appointee is a judge. The Pearl Harbor investigation by a justice of the Supreme Court was completely inquisitorial in nature. The recent inquiries instituted in England into certain security problems were conducted by a judge, but his procedure was not "adversary." Even the advocates of the adversary system do not use it when they wish to find out something for themselves. Altogether, it does not seem likely that the adversary system would long survive competition if individuals were permitted to choose their own procedural rules.

We must now turn to another peculiarity of Anglo-Saxon law, one to which we are so accustomed that most of us do not realize how odd it is. In most courts in the world there are few, if any, restrictions on what evidence can be presented. The judge, it is assumed, is capable of weighing the evidence and gives unimportant evidence little or no weight even if it does get into the record. Although there are some exceptions to this rule, which are mainly of an administrative nature, basically the law of evidence is of little or no importance outside the area of the common law. In Anglo-Saxon areas, however, an elaborate "law of evidence" prohibits the courts from even hearing much potential evidence. This peculiar local institution to which we have become so thoroughly accustomed can be roughly divided into three general categories.

The first, although the last one to arrive on the scene, is essentially technical. An example is the rule that blood tests may be used to disprove paternity but may not be presented to prove paternity. This rule is basically a restatement of the scientific conditions surrounding the test and, as such, is completely unexceptionable. Why we should have a separate rule of this sort instead of leaving the entire matter to the experts, I do not know; but as long as the rules are in accord with science, they certainly do no harm. The rules in the second category are essentially ethical rules. The privilege against self-incrimination, for example, is normally considered part of the laws of evidence. Other examples are the rule that a wife cannot testify against her husband and that evidence obtained by improper means cannot be used by the prosecution in a criminal case.

The final category, and the most voluminous, is a vast collection of rules that prohibits the use of odd bits and pieces of evidence on the grounds that they are not very good evidence. When I took courses on Evidence in law school, the explanation given for this giant collection of rules was simply that juries were stupid. It was thought by the early judges, who set the precedents, that the juries were simple people, not used to complex reasoning and easily led astray. Certain types of evidence were particularly likely to mislead the juries and, hence, were banned. Odd though it may seem, this does appear to be the only explanation for the development of this branch of the law and it is one more argument for not using the jury system. The Anglo-Saxon law paradoxically also applies the law of evidence in those cases (Chancery, for example) in which a judge rules without the assistance of a jury.

The most widely known of these rules is that against hearsay. Suppose that A is accused of murdering B. In fact, he was playing chess with C at the time, but C has since been killed in an automobile accident. It happens, however, that the chess game was a particularly interesting one and on numerous occasions before the accident, C had talked about it to his friends, discussing the fine points of his strategy and how he had won. In these discussions, he had emphasized that the game was so interesting that neither player had moved from the table from 10:00 until 1:00; this three-hour period covers the time of the murder. Can A call these friends of C to testify as to what C had said? No, this is hearsay. In France, this testimony would be heard. In Switzerland, Denmark, and Japan it could be brought in; in the United States and England, it could not be.

Obviously, hearsay evidence is worth less than direct evidence. B's testimony that he had heard A say that Z was true is less convincing than A's testimony. Firstly, we have two potential liars involved instead of one. A may have been lying when he originally said it, or B may be lying in saying that he heard A say it. Furthermore, A was not under oath at the time he made the statement nor was he under any great pressure to be particularly careful in his statements. Most witnesses think their testimony over fairly carefully, simply because the courtroom drama convinces them of its importance. The same cannot be said of a man making a casual remark in the course of a conversation. As a last point, if all we have is B's testimony, then A cannot be cross-examined on his reasons for saying that Z was true. Altogether, hearsay is less valuable than direct testimony and the judge who weighed direct and hearsay testimony equally would be incompetent. This is not to say, however, that completely eliminating hearsay evidence is wise. The trier of the fact should have as much information as possible and hearsay is information, even if it is not as good as direct testimony. Clearly A should be asked to testify if he is available, and the hearsay should be resorted to only if he cannot testify. Clearly, also, the hearsay should not be weighed as strongly as direct testimony, but equally clearly, hearsay should not be given a weight of zero.

The argumentation against admission of hearsay, heard again and again is: "Would you like to be convicted on hearsay?" This is clearly unfair. What you object to is being convicted. The evidence used for that purpose is irrelevant except that, possibly, innocent people convicted unjustly may feel worse about it than guilty people. In any event, the hearsay rule is as hard on the defense as it is on the prosecution. "Would you like to be convicted because evidence in your favor was ruled inadmissable because it was hearsay?" Most courts accept all sorts of evidence, including hearsay, and weigh it appropriately in making their decisions. A small minority of courts, including our own, simply rule out certain types of evidence, which amounts to giving this evidence a weight of zero and can hardly improve the quality of their decisions. Surely the sensible thing to do is to present as much evidence as is available—poor evidence as well as good— and then let the judge weigh it all. This, as I have remarked, is what almost all of the world's judicial systems do.

I have discussed the hearsay rule because it is perhaps the best known of the rules of evidence. It is also typical in being based on historical precedents that have never really been thought out and in eliminating from consideration certain evidence that could be of assistance to the court. Other rules are equally silly. A witness, for example, may have taken voluminous notes at the time of the occurrence that he is asked to describe.[9] The sensible procedure, surely, would be to examine the notes and then to question the witness in order to get a cross-check and to see if there are any details that are not in the notes. Since a sizable

[9] Police officers quite regularly do this.

gap in time frequently occurs between the event and the trial, the notes would normally be more reliable than human memory.[10] Needless to say, this is not the law of evidence. The witness is required to pretend that he is relying upon his memory. He may look at his notes, but only to "refresh his memory." Obviously, this is a most inelegant procedure and equally obviously it is vastly inferior to considering both the notes and the memory.

The law of evidence is further responsible for most of the procedural quibbling that takes up so much time in American and British courts. Most of the lengthy debates as to whether a lawyer may ask a witness a particular question would be eliminated if the laws of evidence were abolished. This would not only shorten trials, but it would considerably improve their accuracy. Surely these debates tend to interrupt the train of thought of the judge and the jury and, hence, make it harder for them to appreciate the relevance of the testimony of the witnesses. When we add the fact that the laws of evidence frequently rule out the best evidence for a point, the arguments for their abolition appear overwhelming.

When I was attending law school, one member of the faculty was Max Rheinstein, a leading authority on European law (particularly German law). He was hired to testify, as an expert witness, on a point of German law. Unfortunately, he did not discover exactly what they wanted him to testify to until he got to the courthouse. He telephoned his secretary who had a good command of German. At his instruction, she looked up the relevant article in the code and read it to him over the phone. Unfortunately for Rheinstein, a court attaché happened to overhear his end of the conversation and told the opposing lawyer. The lawyer, not regarding the rules against hearsay as applying to him, objected to Rheinstein's testimony on the ground that he did not know what the code said of his own knowledge. The upshot was that Rheinstein returned to the university, personally read the article in the code, and then returned to court to testify. All of this resulted in his wasting a good deal of time, but that is not my reason for bringing up the matter. Surely the best evidence as to the German law was the German law itself. This, in fact, is

[10] But not always.

what Rheinstein depended upon. The rational first step, if one wishes to know German law, is to obtain a copy of the law (with a translation if necessary). It may be necessary to hire an expert to explain it, but the law itself is clearly the best possible evidence. The law of evidence takes a contrary view.

But this discussion of the existing Anglo-Saxon law of evidence is but a preliminary to a consideration of the problem of detecting witnesses who are lying. The entire problem of dishonest testimony and its prevention bristles with difficulties. The basic problem, of course, is that we are not very good at telling when people are lying. Even if we had some perfect method of detecting lies, there would still be many reasons why decisions might be incorrect. The human memory is fallible; most people are poor observers, and the judges, of course, make their own errors. Still, eliminating lying testimony would be a gigantic improvement. The major method of detecting lies now in use is to look intently at the witness's face in the hope that his expression will indicate that he is lying. As a method it is not very good, although there is no real evidence as to exactly how bad it is. Experiments in which a number of observers tried to guess whether various witnesses were lying or not, with statistics collected and analyzed, would appear to be both easily performed and of considerable significance. Unfortunately, I have been able to find none.

The easiest way to detect a lie is simply to have contrary evidence. The witness says that he saw the defendant commit the murder by the light of the moon, but an astronomer says that there was no moon that night. There are two problems here: one is that the astronomer may either be lying or mistaken (having made a careless mistake in his calculations) and the other problem is that the witness may be mistaken about this, but not about the rest of his testimony. What do we do when the witness says, "Oh, yes, now I remember; I saw it in the light thrown by the headlights of a passing car"? Perhaps the commonest thing for a judge or juror at this point is to simply decide that the witness is a proven liar and his testimony on other points should thus be ignored.

This is not necessarily correct. The average individual is not a good observer, a fact that has been proven by innumerable experiments, and may well be mistaken on part of his evidence simply because he observed badly. Our witness, for example, might have just looked out the window for an instant when the murder was committed and assumed the light was moonlight when it was from headlights. Last, but not least, the average man is not a quick or terribly logical thinker. A skilled cross-examination may create various apparent inconsistencies in his testimony. Nevertheless, the rule that a witness who lies in one thing will probably lie in others is surely not irrational. If we emphasize that it is "probably" and not "certainly," we are fairly safe. In fact, human testimony tends to be less reliable than "circumstantial evidence" simply because of these natural defects of the human mind. The objective material evidences are normally more to be relied upon than human memory. Unfortunately, it is rare that we find a case in which there is enough objective evidence so that we do not mainly depend on the vagaries of the human memory.

If objective evidence that contradicts the testimony of a witness normally indicates that he is lying, what about contradiction by another witness or witnesses? Clearly someone is lying, but who? [11] An obvious rule, which is unfortunately completely wrong, is simply to count the witnesses on both sides. If this rule were followed, and it must be admitted that it is followed by some juries and judges (it is actually part of patent law), then criminals could live a life of crime with complete impunity provided only that they banded together so that there would always be more of them to deny that they had committed a crime than witnesses to aver it. If you propose to make your living by robbing individuals, then you should team up with a friend so that there will always be the word of two against the word of one. Needless to say, you should only commit your robberies when there are no witnesses, but this is a sensible precaution in any event. Criminals planning to undertake crimes where there are likely to be a number of witnesses, bank robbery for example, would be well advised to organize themselves in quite large groups so that they will always outnumber the witnesses.

[11] Perhaps not. Humans are very poor observers, and differences of opinion on what appear to be the simplest matters of fact may result from honest mistakes rather than lies.

All of this is absurd, yet it is the likely result of simply counting witnesses. In fact, our courts do nothing so foolish. Rape is a particularly good crime to illustrate the fallacy of simply counting witnesses. Normally the case will take the form of the girl who testifies that she was raped and the man (or men) maintaining that she consented. Any system of merely counting the witnesses on the two sides, when combined with the "reasonable doubt" criterion, would mean that convictions for rape would be impossible. In fact, of course, the judge and juries do not depend upon this simple-minded criterion. They try to decide who is lying by carefully looking at faces, listening to voices, and observing who is most confused on cross-examination.

The denials of the accused are, in any event, not normally weighted very heavily. Perhaps the oldest test for truth is the Roman *"qui bono?"* Who gains? If two people give conflicting testimony and one would obviously have a motive for lying while the other would not, then we are likely to believe the disinterested witness. Since the defendant in a criminal trial has an obvious and strong motive for lying if he is guilty, his statement that he is not guilty is normally given little importance. The rule, however, has a much wider application. The disinterested witness is obviously more to be trusted than the one who would have a motive to lie. Even more to be trusted is the man whose testimony is against his own interest. If A testifies to certain things and this testimony will obviously hurt A, then we are likely to assume that he is an honest man who tells the truth even if it hurts him. In any event, his testimony on these matters will normally be given great weight. The problem raised by these fairly obvious rules for weighing evidence, of course, is that we may not know the real situation of the witness. He may have a good motive for lying that is not obvious. He may make a lying statement that is apparently against his interest because the truth is even more likely to injure him. Still, the basic good sense of these rules is evident.

Cross-examination is also supposed to be a test for the lying witness, although whether it is or not seems to me an open question. It may, in fact, convince the jury that a perfectly honest witness is lying. A good lawyer can usually confuse the average man who is testifying on a fairly complicated event without much difficulty. In any event, under the adversary system, cross-examination serves another important function. The lawyer who calls a witness would prefer, normally, to ask the witness only for that information that will help the lawyer's case. Witnesses frequently have information that will help both sides. The fact that the witness will later be cross-examined by the attorney for the other side means that the additional evidence will eventually appear. The original lawyer, in fact, may anticipate its production on cross-examination by bringing it out himself. Without cross-examination, this information might be completely lost. Thus, under the adversary system cross-examination is necessary, even if it does not help much in uncovering lying.

But all of these methods of detecting lying are obviously inefficient. Furthermore, all of them are merely supplementary to looking at the witness's face and guessing from that whether he is telling the truth. The weakness of this method as a way of detecting lying is patent, and the only reason we have used it is that until very recently it was the only known method. Today we have better ways of telling whether people are lying, although no one would regard them as being very good. Falling under the general (and somewhat misleading) heading of "lie-detectors," they are the subject of a great deal of emotion, but not much real thought. In the first place, these machines do not detect lies, they simply improve our observational abilities. In addition to looking carefully at the man's face, we can measure his blood pressure, watch the electrical conductivity of his skin, as well as several other phenomena that are not visible to the naked eye. Experience indicates that watching these things is a better, although still far from perfect, way of guessing whether the witness is lying than is scrutinizing his countenance. It is, of course, quite possible to combine the two methods. There is no reason why one cannot watch both the witness's face and the measurement of his blood pressure.[12]

Normally, however, these devices for displaying certain changes in the physiology of the witness are not used alone; an expert is used in conjunction with them. Furthermore, this technician does

[12] The present machines are not designed with the objective of making this easy. In this, as in many other respects, the "lie detectors" are suffering from a lack of research and development.

not confine himself to keeping the machines in repair and seeing that they are properly connected to the witness; he regards these as the least of his duties. He is an expert, in his own opinion, in telling whether the witness is or is not lying. He will normally take the witness to a specially prepared room, ask him a set of questions that he prepared while the "lie detector" makes a continuous record of various physiological variables, and then emerge with an opinion as to whether the witness is or is not telling the truth. The procedure obviously raises different issues from simply improving the methods available for judging whether the witness is telling the truth. It must be admitted that the lie-detector operators are, as a group, the best detectors of lies we have. Their opinion as to whether a man is lying or not is usually better than that of any judge who has simply looked intently at the witness's face while he testifies. Nevertheless, the lie detector operator is in a quite different class from the ordinary expert witness.

The present technique of using lie detectors takes into account only the reactions of the witness and obviously is an inferior process. The sensible procedure is to take all of the evidence, including the blood pressure of the witness, into account at the same time. This is impossible under our present method of using these devices, but there is nothing preordained about our present procedures. There is no reason why the devices that show the witnesses' blood pressure should not be arranged so that the judge and the opposing attorneys can see their dials.[13] The judge can then take the information he receives from these instruments into account in assessing the weight to give to the evidence of each witness.

Note that I have referred to the judge throughout. The procedure suggested would be impossible, at least with our present techniques, if a jury were trying the case. In my opinion, this is a further argument against juries. Present-day judges would also be unable to use the information provided by the "lie detectors"

[13] Current "lie detectors" do not register their results on dials, but there is no reason why they could not. In fact, it seems likely that methods of displaying the physiological changes of the witness in very compact and easy to understand ways would be available in these days of electronic computers.

because they do not have the necessary training. This, however, can be remedied.

Before turning to the arguments against the use of these instruments, it should be mentioned that there are some other psychological procedures that might also be helpful. To mention but a single example, reading the witness a long, carefully chosen list of words and then watching his reactions to some of them can be very informative. This procedure could only be undertaken if the inquisitorial type of procedure were used, but, again, in my opinion that is simply an argument for this type of procedure.

The objections to the use of the lie detector are seldom articulated with any degree of clarity. Basically, I think they boil down to the fact that it is new and, thus, suspect. Most of these arguments implicitly assume that the lie detector is to be used only in criminal proceedings, that only the defendant will be subjected to it, and that, somehow, it prejudices the position of innocent defendants. Since we are now talking about a civil suit to enforce a contract, these assumptions are largely irrelevant. It is generally unwise, however, to use "lie detectors" on only one witness. It may happen that there only is one witness, but normally there are more. Since a sizable possibility of error exists, we should put much less weight on indications in the blood pressure of one witness that he may be lying, than in readings from several witnesses that confirm each other.[14] Thus, if A avers that M is the case while B says $\overline{M}$, an examination of A's blood pressure that shows indications of lying is of value, but we could be much more confident if B's blood pressure showed no signs of dishonesty. If we have inaccuracy in this case, it is likely to show up as an inconsistent result—both A and B telling the truth or both lying—which would put us back in the same position as if we had not used the "lie detectors." It is possible, of course, that the errors would be arranged symmetrically so as to present a consistent but wrong picture, but the odds are against it. Furthermore, the more witnesses tested, the less likely is such a symmetric mistake.

---

[14] Actually, the readings of the physiological instruments are like judgments of expression in that they do not give simple unambiguous indications of truth or lying. For purposes of discussion, however, I have somewhat simplified the situation.

The only remaining argument against the use of the "lie detectors" is simply that they are occasionally inaccurate. Since we make use of a great amount of evidence whose accuracy may be poor in trials, it is difficult to imagine why this is an argument at all. Judging whether a man is lying by looking at his face is even less accurate than making the same judgment by looking at his blood pressure. Should we then put a screen between the witness and the judge so that the judge cannot be misled by this inaccurate information? It may be, of course, that the people who use this argument are thinking of jury trials and feel that juries, being stupid, will be unduly influenced by lie detector evidence. Thus, the dull jurors, in spite of being warned that lie detectors may lie, will assume that they are always correct and reach incorrect conclusions. Assuming that this estimate of the reactions of the jurors is correct, it seems to me an argument against the use of juries, not against the use of a recording sphygmomanometer. In any event, it is hard to believe that contracting parties would object to a provision for all witnesses being questioned under the most favorable conditions for detecting lies.

It should be noted that our present criminal procedure in fact makes use of the lie detector in a very important way, one that probably leads to much more error than the procedure I have suggested. In a great many jurisdictions it is the custom to give the defendant the option of taking a lie detector test. If the test shows him to be innocent, he is normally released without trial. If he refuses to take the test or if the test shows him to be guilty, he will be tried. Granted the inaccuracy of present-day lie detectors, these decisions by the expert must themselves sometimes be erroneous. This procedure was undoubtedly adopted in an effort to protect innocent defendants, but it must be noted that it is likely to prejudice the case of those people who have been erroneously found guilty by the lie detector operator.

It is well known to the judges and juries in most of these jurisdictions that the police and prosecuting attorney use this procedure. It is not at all infrequent for the outcome of the test to be printed in the newspapers before the trial. In any event, a regular rule such as that used in New York City to release the defendants who "pass" the lie detector test clearly should prejudice the judges and juries against those defendants who appear before them. The judges and juries know that the defendant who appears before them has either failed the lie detector test or refused to take one. It seems far more rational to permit the judge and jury to examine the results of the lie detector test along with other evidence than to use the lie detector in this way. Furthermore, it should be noted that when the lie detector is used in this way, only the defendant is tested. Those other witnesses in the case whose lying may be just as important to the outcome as the defendant's are not given the lie detector test. Thus, in many ways, this very widespread practice in our criminal law amounts to a less than optimal use of the lie detector. A conscious adoption of the lie detector as part of the regular trial proceedings could hardly help but improve matters.

Let us summarize. Using the basic assumptions outlined in Chapters 1 and 2, we have demonstrated in Chapter 4 that individuals would choose to be given freedom in the choice of courts to enforce their contracts. We have also been able to specify an "efficiency function" for courts. Chapter 5 is necessarily concerned with less clearly logical arguments. For deciding what type of court would maximize our efficiency function, we need judgments about the real world, and I have offered mine. If, however, the reader will try to think about the matter without simply relying on the customs and practices that have grown up over the years in England and the United States, I think he will find that he agrees with me. In any event, my position is that the suit to enforce the contract should be decided by a man who is specially selected and trained for that task, not a group of randomly selected, untrained men. The man selected to make the decision should take the primary role in the actual proceedings, and not be reduced to the passive role of the judge of a debate. He should be given access to any evidence that he thinks is important and not restricted by the customs developed many years ago to prevent illiterate juries from making mistakes. Lastly, he should be allowed every aid that science can give.

6

Accidents

Most laymen have a fairly clear idea of what they mean by accidents. Normally this idea itself is clear only because the layman does not understand the difficult ontological problems involved. Nevertheless, I should like to begin this chapter by accepting the layman's idea of what an accident is and only turn to the problem of defining it later. For simplicity, let us take as our example a common motor vehicle collision. In this case, the difference between the layman's definition of the term "accident" and the definitions that might be used by more sophisticated persons are of very little importance. What should the law on such accidents be? Chapter 8 discusses the issue of what type of state regulations we should impose with the idea of reducing such accidents and we will here concern ourselves solely with the issue normally dealt with in the law of torts—the payment or nonpayment of reparations to persons injured in such an accident.[1]

[1] I have been greatly helped in preparing this chapter by a book by Walter Blum and Harry Kalven, Jr., *Public Law Perspectives on a Private Law Problem* (Toronto: Little Brown and Company, 1965). Although my conclusions are not entirely theirs, it seems to me that this study greatly clarifies the basic issues and is decidedly more sophisticated than anything else in the field. In addition to this book, I was assisted by Alfred E. Conard, James M. Morgan, Robert W. Pratt, Jr., Charles L. Voltz, and Robert L. Bombaugh, *Accidents, Costs, and Payments* (Ann Arbor: University of Michigan Press, 1964). A recent and important book in this field is Guido Calabresi, *The Costs of Accidents* (New Haven, Conn.: Yale University Press, 1970).

The first aspect to note about compensation in these terms is that it makes very little difference to the final outcome what the law is. Our present law provides that, in accidents in which one party is "to blame," that party may be compelled to pay for the other party's injuries. Since we normally carry insurance to cover this liability, in practice this means that the first party's insurance company makes the payment. Let us suppose this law were drastically changed so that if a person reports to a court that he has been badly injured in an automobile accident through someone else's fault, the court will not hear him. We can be more extreme and assume that if I report to the court that I have been injured in an automobile accident caused by Smith, the court as an automatic routine requires me to pay for all damages that Smith may have suffered. The only effect of this would be to compel me to purchase a different type of insurance. There is no reason why I cannot carry an insurance policy against injuries that I suffer, regardless of their source.[2] There is also no reason why I cannot purchase insurance against the risk that someone will cause injury to me and to himself by causing an accident, and that I (the innocent party) will be compelled by a particularly wild law to pay his costs. The major effect of law in this area is to identify the person who must purchase the insurance.

Let us consider the results of a radical change in our present institutional structure. If the law of torts for cases of pure accident of the sort we are now discussing were repealed, the individual who claimed that someone injured him in an automobile accident would receive sympathy from the courts, but nothing more. This proposal will shock many people, but it is not at all obvious that it would cause anyone any particular disadvantage once the new insurance policies had been obtained. Under these circumstances, I would insure myself against accidental injury. This insurance presumably would take the form of a policy that provided me with various specific amounts of money compensation for various particular types of injury. Policies now commercially available may, in the case of total disability, provide substantial pensions for life.

[2] This must normally rule out self-inflicted injuries, although in some cases these, too, can be covered. The problem of moral risks is discussed later in the chapter.

Note that I am not suggesting that the state set up a board to make payments to those injured in automobile accidents. The reason why one should have a state board for this purpose is unclear to me. Surely our experience with the workmen's compensation boards has not been very encouraging and extending this type of apparatus to other areas would probably lead to the same results.[3] Furthermore, there seems no significant reason why people who do not want to be covered by insurance should be required to purchase it (which the state procedure would, in essence, entail) or why people who want a higher coverage should not be permitted to purchase it. If, however, it is thought for some reason (presumably ethical) that it is necessary to make certain that everybody has some minimum amount of coverage, there is no reason why a law could not be enacted requiring people to purchase it.[4] We already have laws requiring the purchase of another type of insurance as a condition for driving an automobile.

If it is thought that very poor people might not be able to afford the insurance premiums, we could presumably arrange to supplement their incomes for this purpose. It is notable that we do not legally excuse very poor people from buying liability insurance under our present system. Returning, however, to our proposal to eliminate present laws of damage to permit people to purchase insurance against injury to themselves, there are several obvious advantages. The statistics indicate that the costs of collection for people injured under present circumstances are extremely high, as much as 25 percent of the amount collected. In addition, for people who are seriously injured, the amount that they obtain under the present mechanism normally covers only a small part of their injuries. Finally, payment is normally very much delayed—occurring not at the time that the person needs

[3] Blum and Kalven, *Public Law Perspectives,* pp. 24–27.
[4] Note that our present law does not provide this guarantee of minimum coverage. I must carry insurance giving some minimum protection for people whom I injure. If, however, I am injured in an accident in which no one is to blame or in which I am to some extent at fault, there is no provision for any coverage. The current laws, of course, require me to buy insurance that will protect other people. In other words, they are an effort to eliminate an externality. The law that I am now talking about would not have this feature, but it might still be argued for on ethical grounds.

the money most, but perhaps two or three years thereafter.[5] In all these areas, a direct insurance policy would gravely reduce the economic costs.

If I have an insurance policy providing for payments to me of certain amounts for certain specified injuries, I would normally be able to obtain the money from the insurance company with little more than a letter. The threat of lawsuit, which is a necessary part of our present procedure, would be unnecessary. Occasionally an insurance company would suspect fraud and, therefore, resist payment, but this would be an exceptional rather than a routine event. In addition, the money would be immediately available as it normally is with insurance. Most insurance companies make a fetish of giving fast treatment to claims by their policy holders because they feel that this improves their sales. Thirdly, I could obtain any amount of coverage I wished, which would make it easier to match economic loss with "damages."

It must be noted that, although insurance coverage of the type I have described is a relatively new phenomenon, the Michigan study shows that payments from such direct "reparation" and from various government programs that simply help people who are injured is now becoming a significant part of total "reparation" for people injured in accidents. There seems no obvious reason why these could not be our sole dependence. The number of lawyers who would lose profitable portions of their practice is large, but this is a clear social gain. Furthermore, it would greatly reduce the present burden on our courts. Lastly, but by no means least, it would eliminate what is essentially a completely irrelevant issue. Under present circumstances, an accident, if it is a pure accident (that is, if it is nobody's fault at all), should (if we believe in the law) result in no liability for anyone. In practice, this does not often happen because judges and juries normally find that somebody has caused the accident. Still, the fact that they do make erroneous findings of facts in some cases is not an argument for requiring "fault."

Surely we should have arrangements by means of which an

[5] Connard, Morgan, Pratt, Voltz, and Bombaugh, *Accidents, Costs, and Payments.*

individual who is severely injured in a pure accident may be compensated for his injuries. At the moment, if I am involved in an accident, the court could find that the accident was a pure accident and that neither I nor the man whom I ran into was at fault. In this case, there will be no tort reparation. The court could likewise find that I was not the cause of the accident, but that the man with whom I collided was at fault. This would mean that his insurance company would be compelled to make some kind of settlement to cover my injuries. The Michigan study indicates that if my injuries were severe, this settlement would normally be comparatively modest. He himself would not in any way be compensated, even if he were severely injured. Finally under the present law, if both of us were at fault, neither of us could be compensated.

Decisions on the factual question of fault are extremely difficult to make for a wide variety of reasons, and there is no obvious reason to believe that juries are good at performing this task. But even if they were, this is an essentially irrelevant question. There is no reason why I (as a person who has not caused an accident) should find my "reparation" dependent on the question of whether the other man with whom I had my collision was or was not at fault. If the person who has not caused an accident should be compensated for his injuries, this compensation should not be dependent upon the essentially accidental fact of whether or not somebody else had done something regarded as culpable.

The dragging of culpability into tort actions seems to be an accidental consequence of the latter's historical connection with criminal law. In a sense, we are punishing a man who has committed a sort of minor crime (being a little careless in driving) by putting liability upon his insurance company. There is, of course, no reason why we should not punish people through private suits rather than governmental action, but in this area there seems no reason why we should. The seriousness of the violation of the driving codes would be a better measure of the size of the fine placed on the violator than the essentially accidental measure of how much injury happened to occur as the result of the violation.

Repealing the present law of torts for automobile accidents would cause a certain amount of transitional problems. It would take some time for people to adjust from the present circumstances in which they carry insurance against the contingency that they injure someone else through their own fault, to insurance against the contingency that they are injured in an automobile accident regardless of fault. Transitional arrangements presumably could be made, however, and I do not think they would be terribly difficult.

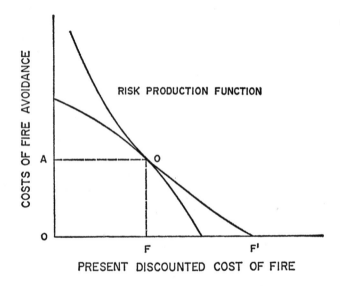

FIGURE 6–1 Fire Insurance

In order to continue this discussion, it is necessary to examine the economics of insurance. Under our present assumptions, we have no particular reason why there should be any special provisions in the law differentiating insurance contracts from other contracts. In the real world, the former are severely and often ineptly regulated by a variety of commissions, but we need not discuss this now. Later, when we turn to the law of fraud, we will see that there may be reasons for restricting the contracts an insurance company can issue, but for the moment we can set this issue aside. We can think of insurance contracts as simply being drawn by the insurance companies according to their needs. In practice, this is generally what happens, except that it normally takes some time to get any technological innovation through the regulating commissions.

For simplicity, let us consider fire insurance rather than automobile insurance.[6] On Figure 6–1, the horizontal axis shows the present discounted value of potential fires in the future to a structure that I own. On the vertical axis I have plotted the expenditures that I might make in reducing the probability of fire—installing a sprinkler system, for example. The "risk production function" shows the present discounted value of fire with each possible investment of resources in methods of reducing the likelihood (or damage) of fire.

Assuming that fire insurance is not available, I would choose the combination of risk and expenditures on avoidance of risk in which the production function of risk is tangent to my highest indifference curve.[7] Given the production function for risk that I have drawn on this diagram, this leads me to point A-F. At this point, I would be expending AO resources on things such as sprinkler systems while taking a risk of my building being burned down, which is equivalent to FO. Equation (6.1) shows this situation.

$$(6.1) \qquad AO + FO \cdot R = C$$

I have AO in protection costs, and FO is the discounted present value of a fire. If I attach to this second factor "R" as cost of risk, then the situation is as shown. It is generally assumed in discussions of insurance that individuals are risk avoiders and, therefore, that the situation is capable of improvement by transferring this risk to someone else. This transfer is not as easy as

[6] A very similar analysis of health insurance is found in Mark V. Pauly, "Efficiency in Public Provision of Medical Care." Ph.D. dissertation, University of Virginia, 1967.

[7] Note that the indifference curves are concave to the origin.

you might think. Equation (6.2) shows the insurance company's cost.

$$(6.2) \qquad\qquad\qquad FO = C_i$$

For the insurance company, of course, the number of insurance policies is so large that risk aversion is of little consequence. At first glance, then, the cost to the insurance company appears to be less than the cost to me and a bargain should be possible.

However, this is an oversimplification. In the first place, if I purchase the insurance, I would be rational to discontinue my risk avoidance activities. I will not bother to keep the sprinkler system in good working order. Most people who have used equations such as Equation (6.2) seem to have implicitly assumed that AO would remain unchanged, but this assumes that the individual does not respond to a change in the circumstances facing him. A more rational assumption would be that the individual stops trying to protect against fire. Samuel Colt refused to purchase fire insurance on his factory. He argued that it was his duty as a Christian master of property to protect it and that his attention to this matter would be reduced if he had insurance. Note that this applies only if the fire insurance is genuinely complete. Most fire insurance policies, for reasons discussed later, do not actually cover all of the cost of the fire.

For the man who has complete insurance coverage, the present discounted value of a fire occurring in the future is zero. Therefore, he would normally be unwilling to invest any of his resources to prevent it. Granted this, the cost to the insurance company of selling the insurance to the owner of the factory is not FO but rather F'O, the present discounted value of the likelihood of a fire in the event that the owner takes no precautions to prevent it. Risk aversion by and of itself is a necessary but not a sufficient condition for insurance. It is by no means obvious that Inequality (6.3) will be true, and that is the necessary condition for insurance.

$$(6.3) \qquad\qquad AO + FO \cdot R \geqslant F'O$$

In the very early days of insurance, the insurance companies may have been ignorant of these matters, but they are now very well informed about them. As a consequence, they try to design their insurance contracts in such a way that the person who purchases the insurance still has some incentive for taking precautions against fires. One method of accomplishing this goal as shown on Figure 6–2 is to vary the size of the premium according to the precautions taken.

The insurance company has a number of different rate classes

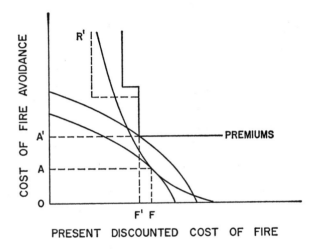

FIGURE 6–2 Fire Insurance with Varying Premiums

depending upon whether there is a sprinkler system or whether there is a fire station nearby. Note that it is not possible for the insurance company to perfectly fit this premium incentive system to the risk production function. Firstly, the insurance company cannot afford to put unlimited resources into supervising the companies insured; it does not have continuing day-to-day direct contact with the problem. This, insofar as I can tell, is what Samuel Colt had in mind when he argued that insurance increased the risk of fire.

Another and more sophisticated reason why the insurance

companies cannot make their premiums perfectly fit the risk production function is that the insurance company requires actuarial computations in order to produce its premium rates. These actuarial computations require rather large samples in each of the rate classes. Thus, of necessity, the premiums will vary in a discontinuous manner in order to bring a large enough number of "risks" into each class. Without this, the actuary would be unable to compute the proper rate.[8]

The potential purchaser of insurance, then, faces the risk production function of his particular plant and a premium schedule such as the one shown. Let us assume that without insurance, he would adjust to point AF with AO + FO · R as his cost. An insurance company appears, however, with the rate schedule shown, and he adjusts to point A'F'. Note that, on the figure, he is actually on a lower indifference curve than he was before because Figure 6–2 does not show his risk aversion. If we had a three-dimensional diagram that also showed risk aversion, he would be on a higher indifference surface. Nevertheless, with respect to just the two variables shown on Figure 6–2, he is in a somewhat worse state of adjustment than he was before. He is purchasing risk reduction by making an inferior adjustment in these two variables.

It happens in this particular diagram that he is spending more resources on fire prevention than he would have if he had been left without insurance. This is mere coincidence and no general principle is involved. Note one point, however; the purchaser of insurance will almost always find himself most satisfied if he adjusts the amount of insurance and the physical protection of his plant in such a way that he is at one of the lower left corners of the stair function of the premium structure. This means that the insurance company must keep the entire premium rate system outside the risk production function. If a mistake in calculating is made and part of the premium structure follows the shape shown by the dotted line in the upper part of Figure 6–2, then many of the insured would choose to be at the inner corner of

---

[8] In theory, it would be possible for the actuary to produce not a series of specific rates but a continuing premium rate. It is not inconceivable that in the future this particular problem will be solved.

the dotted line. The premiums would not pay for the losses and the insurance company would be driven into bankruptcy.

In the real world, the step-function of the premiums actually will not be neatly adjusted to hit the risk production function at every level as I have drawn it. It will, in fact, be somewhat to the right. We need not worry much about this. The basic question remains: is the risk reduction from the purchase of insurance greater than the reduction in the efficiency of the adjustment of resources in other ways? Once again, the simple existence of risk aversion does not by and of itself explain insurance. The risk

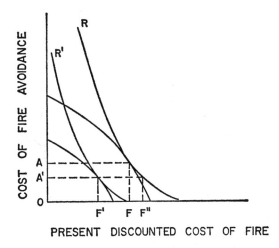

FIGURE 6–3 Fire Insurance with a Minimum

aversion must be large enough to cover losses that insurance causes by leading people to change their behavior.

Another method by which an insurance company can to some extent control the behavior of its clients and, hence, offer them lower premiums is shown in Figure 6–3.

If the insurance does not cover the entire loss, then the insured will still be motivated to engage in fire avoidance activities. In Figure 6–3, line R shows the risk production function, and I assume that the insurance covers half the losses in the event of a fire. Thus, insured faces line R′ as the risk production function for himself. This leads him to move from point AF to point A′F′ and to continue to use his resources in fire avoidance. Note that the premium is the present value of the loss faced by the insurance company F″O. Although the insured faces a discounted cost of fire of F′O, his reduction in resources spent on fire avoidance moves the "social" risk to F″. He should insure if the following occurs.

$$(6.4) \qquad AO + FO \cdot R > A'O + F'O \cdot R' + F'F''$$

Once again we cannot say from the simple fact of risk aversion whether he should purchase insurance.

One particular technique is to require the insured to pay the initial portion of the loss. This also has the effect of causing the insured to take some precautions against the loss. Naturally, all three of these techniques for controlling the behavior of the insured can be combined and all three of them will permit lower premiums, although they reduce the advantage of the insurance to some extent.

There is, however, a rather important result of declining returns on risk avoidance—that is a higher payoff in risk avoidance from the first dollar of investment in insurance than from the later dollars. Thus, as more and more of the risk is covered by insurance, each additional reduction in risk has a heavier premium cost. This heavier cost in the first instance falls on the insurance company, but through increased premiums it eventually is transferred to the insured. Thus, one would anticipate an effective declining marginal return on reduction of risk not because individuals are less averse to a small risk than to a large one, although this may well be true, but rather because the reduction of risk to smaller and smaller amounts leads to greater and greater costs in the risk avoidance measures. The result is that most people find it undesirable to purchase enough insurance to eliminate all risk.

A special case in which the existence of insurance changes the behavior of the insured is one in which the insurance payment is more than the actual cost of the fire, as shown in Figure 6–4. The insured facing a given risk production function without insurance settles on point AF. He is, however, given an opportunity by a foolish insurance company to insure his factory for considerably more than it is worth. As a result, the effect of a fire on him is not a cost but a gain, which on our present axes means that its present discounted value would be to the left of the vertical axis at F'. Under these circumstances, far from investing resources to reduce the likelihood of fire, the insured is well advised to invest resources in increasing it. The simplest method of doing this, of course, is to start a fire yourself and thus insurance companies worry a good deal about this possibility.

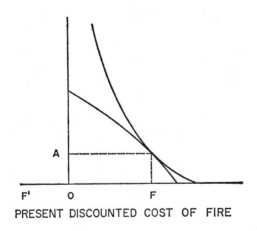

PRESENT DISCOUNTED COST OF FIRE

Figure 6–4 Incentives for Arson

The easiest protection against this situation is simply to make certain that the insurance is never large enough so that the insured will actually gain from a fire. Insurance companies, in fact, make great efforts in this direction, but they are not always successful. They also engage in a great deal of talk about what they call the "moral risk." As one could deduce from the use of the word "moral," this discussion is largely an ethical denunciation of people who act in a manner to increase their risk. The insurance companies seldom seem to realize that any adjustment to the existence of insurance, such as we have been discussing, is essentially the same kind of thing. It should, however, still be regarded as a "moral risk" if by "moral risk" we mean that people will behave differently with insurance than without it. Surely people will act differently and they would be irrational if they did not. The problem facing the insurance company is to so design its policy that such behavior on the part of its customers does not unreasonably increase its premium rate.

The insurance men also place another problem under the rubric "moral risk." Let us suppose that I purchase insurance against my medical expenses in the event that I become ill and the insurance company (misguidedly) has agreed to pay all of my medical expenses. The probability that I will become ill is actuarily computable.[9] However, the amount of medical attention I have after becoming ill is not in any way limited. I am sure that if I so desired, I could have a $10,000 expenditure out of the treatment for a common cold. One of the best-known treatments for a cold is to spend some time on the Jamaican beaches. My decision as to how much to spend on treatments if I am ill is affected very sharply by how much it will cost me to spend that amount. If any and all treatments are free for me, then I may be expected to spend a good deal more than if I faced a real cost.

As a consequence of this rather obvious fact, all schemes of medical insurance contain some kind of limitation on the freedom of the patient. The particular type of insurance that I carry, "major medical," pays only 80 percent of my expenses and has a deductible first segment. This clearly will put some restraint on my desire to spend money on medical treatment. More commonly, Blue Cross simply provides flat medical fees for various specified diseases. In places such as England where large-scale public health is provided, treatment is administratively rationed and there are long lines of people waiting for treatment."[10] In those

[9] Apparently the probability that I will become ill is very strongly positively connected with the likelihood that I will be injured by becoming ill. Arrangements under which people who are not working because they are ill are paid their full salary normally lead to considerably more illness than would occur without these arrangements.

[10] See James M. Buchanan, *The Inconsistencies of the National Health Service*, Occasional Paper No. 7 (London: Institute of Economic Affairs, 1965).

parts of the United States where contract medicine is available, we normally find that the suppliers who combine an insurance policy with the actual provision of medical service have rather stringent standards as to exactly what shall be done in specified cases.[11] This is, in fact, a highly efficient way of operating medical insurance.

It should be noted that this problem is as important for government-sponsored insurance schemes as it is for private insurance. Recently it has been suggested that the government reimburse people who are victims of crimes. This would be a deliberate move into a situation of this sort. The present insurance company sells an insurance policy against (let us say) burglary, but obtains a statement of the value of the property at the time it sells the policy. It is free to send out an appraiser to examine this property and calculates the premium based on that value. If the value of the property stolen is to be reported to a governmental agency after it has been stolen, one can fairly predict that very high evaluations will be normal. Requiring persons wishing this type of protection to make statements about the value of their property before the occurrence of the robbery would help, but not a great deal. As long as overestimates of the value of their property costs them nothing, they would be motivated to make them. An insurance system under which the individual is charged a premium based on the value he puts on the property seems to be the optimal arrangement.[12]

There is another reason why insurance companies charge different premiums to different people. A male driver under the age of twenty-five pays markedly more for automobile insurance than one over twenty-five. Clearly this rate structure does not lead to the investment of resources in efforts to change one's age. The insurance company is simply classifying people into rate categories according to the probability of their being involved in an accident without making any effort to affect their behavior. This should be distinguished from the efforts to control the behavior of the insured.

[11] It is not possible in most places because of the opposition of the American Medical Association.

[12] Those who feel that such activity should be governmental rather than private can, of course, argue for a governmental agency that sells people this kind of insurance.

If we regard risk as something that does not exist for society as a whole, then we can demonstrate from our previous discussion that insurance is an undesirable institution. I, myself, do not believe that one should deal with it in this manner, but the argument is worth developing since it does have some applications in certain areas. Let us then assume that we are simply trying to maximize a measured value of the national income and that we do not regard risk avoidance as part of that measured value because insured risks, looked at from the standpoint of a nation, are minimal. Based upon these assumptions, insurance is a basically inefficient institution. It always moves people to a location on the risk-production frontier that they would not otherwise choose and, hence, leads to a lower amount of "utility." In this sense we can obtain higher efficiency if we abolish insurance.

The argument, however, is based on the assumption that individual preferences should be maximized when they are obtained from one type of service and not from another. Thus, I, myself, may obtain utility from reducing the risk I face and, in fact, most people do. The fact that obtaining this utility reduces the amount of utility I get from other activities is no doubt unfortunate, but we usually have to pay for things in this world. If we sum utility over the entire society, assuming that this operation is somehow possible, we would find that the society with insurance would have a higher total than one without. We should, then, permit insurance in spite of the fact that it causes somewhat poorer adjustment of resources in other areas. Assuming that we are modern welfare economists and do not believe in an interpersonal comparison of utilities, the same conclusion follows.

This digression into the economics of insurance has been necessary as a background to a discussion of the second possible effect of our present accident laws. The first possible reason for a law dealing with accidents is to provide compensation for the person who is injured. If we confine ourselves to this objective, it seems clear that the simplest mechanism is to abolish the law of torts and to depend on each individual to insure himself. The second reason for a law of accidental injury, however, is the existence of externalities.

Suppose that I am a manufacturer of dynamite. I can reduce

the cost of operating my dynamite factory by building it on a small area of ground instead of on a very large acreage. Then, in the event of an explosion, my neighbors will bear part of the cost. We need not go through a welfare economics discussion of the externalities involved in this case, since it is perfectly clear to everyone that part of the costs from potential accidents are actually borne by other people. The situation can be shown once again by our Figure 6–3. The dynamite manufacturer faces the risk production function shown as R' because some of the damage an explosion causes will fall on other people. The true risk production function is R, and we can predict, under these circumstances, that the neighbors of the dynamite manufacturer would be willing to pay him a sizable amount of money to stop him from operating in their neighborhood. In the event that they were unable to organize for such a payment, the value of their property would fall.

Under these circumstances, private bargains may well develop to eliminate the externalities. The standard justification for governmental actions is that the transaction costs are so great that it is not possible to eliminate the externality by private negotiations alone. A law requiring the dynamite manufacturer to pay for the damage to his neighbors in the event of an explosion would lead to an adjustment of resources equivalent to that which would arise from free contract if the transaction costs were zero. The government thus acts to improve the market by supplementing it. It may be the cheapest way of obtaining an economically sensible end.

It would also be possible for the government to place a tax on the manufacturer of dynamite in an inhabited area and not in an uninhabited area. Needless to say, the government normally does not make perfect computations and the adjustment of the world is seldom optimal. Nevertheless, the costs of governmental activity in such an area frequently would be less than the cost of private activities. We are here comparing two imperfect instrumentalities, and there is no *a priori* reason for feeling that one is better than the other. We need in each case a careful analysis of the factual situation.

Consider an airline; under present circumstances, when an aircraft crashes the airline suffers the loss of the plane and, in addition, is compelled to make some relatively minor payments to the passengers. The bulk of the protection for the passengers (*i.e.,* the protection of their heirs), however, is the result of the insurance that the passengers themselves carry. Most of the passengers have regular life insurance policies, and a great many of them will have taken out special trip insurance just before the flight.[13] This means, once again, that we are in a situation shown on Figure 6–3. The airline faces a loss in the event of a crash shown by R′, and the total loss is shown by R. The airline would thus be motivated to invest less than the optimum amount of resources in crash avoidance.[14]

Under these circumstances, it should be possible for the airline itself to sell insurance to its passengers, thus moving its own risk production function up to R and producing a somewhat higher investment of resources in crash avoidance. This should be a mutually profitable operation with the airline being able to sell the insurance at a lower price than the insurance companies who are not in a position to improve the crash ratio by an investment of resources in safety. Note that if the airline is to bear the full cost of the crash and face the true social risk production function, it should also reimburse the insurance companies for the payments that they make in the event of a crash. This could be done very simply by selling to the insurance companies an actuarily computed policy covering this particular contingency.

It may well be that the airline companies already are investing very large amounts of their resources in crash avoidance because of the bad publicity they receive from such crashes. I think that

[13] There are, of course, a number of people who do not carry insurance at all. Being a bachelor, with no relatives dependent upon me, I carry no insurance except for a small policy that I receive as a fringe benefit from my university. Other people carry differing amounts of insurance, depending upon their comparison of the likely effects of their death on their relatives and the amount of premium. It should be noted, however, that in a sense life insurance is not a full reparation for the injury inflicted by death—the insured himself is not compensated.

[14] Note that this carries with it an implicit assumption that the airline is solely responsible for avoiding crashes. Probably this is not true. The Federal Aeronautics Administration apparently causes a fair number of crashes. I say apparently because the Federal Aeronautics Administration also investigates crashes and is reluctant to find itself guilty.

this would have been true twenty years ago, but I am by no means certain that it is true now. Air travel has become fairly well accepted and the occasional crashes that do occur are not normally blamed on the particular airline involved.

The argument thus far has assumed that the airline company carries the risk itself and does not purchase insurance from anyone else. For very large airlines this would, of course, be the rational thing to do. They could anticipate a certain number of crashes and would need insurance only against "clusters" of accidents. Naturally not all airlines and perhaps not any of them are in this enviable position. Here we return to our discussions of forcing risks upon people in order to improve efficiency. It is arguable, although I think that the argument is not very persuasive, that airlines should be prohibited from purchasing insurance.[15] Note that the owners of the airline stock could reduce their risk to any degree they wished by suitable diversification of their portfolios. Nevertheless, it seems to me that this possible restriction on airlines' insurance would not be good policy.

Why do the airlines not sell insurance? One rather obvious explanation is the elaborate, detailed, tradition bound, unimaginative, and highly decentralized regulation to which the insurance industry is now subjected. If the United Airlines decided to offer this type of insurance to its passengers and to the insurance companies who have policies on its customers, it would immediately find itself in a tremendously complicated legal controversy both with the insurance companies and with the rate-setting commission, to say nothing of the Civil Aeronautics Board. It may be that this regulatory structure, in and of itself, is the reason why this type of insurance scheme has not developed.

Surely the technical problems of the sale of insurance are not insurmountable. The airlines could announce their rates and have the amount of the insurance purchased written on the tickets, the cost being collected when the ticket was sold. (The

[15] Airlines should be prohibited from purchasing insurance *except* disaster insurance to cover the contingency that crash claims exceeded their current assets. A deductible insurance policy with the deductible amount equivalent to the full current value of their assets would, under this argument, be optimal.

travel agency at which I buy airline tickets also sells trip insurance.) This would add another item of cost reduction in that it would not be necessary to buy insurance for a full day against all causes of death, but simply a policy for death or injury caused by a crash while you are on the plane.[16]

It is also possible, however, that the basic reason why this type of insurance has not yet been developed is not the noxious effect of inept regulation, but that transaction costs would be high. Any airline company, when it first offered this type of insurance, would find its own behavior only marginally affected and, therefore, probably could not offer markedly lower premiums than do the present insurance companies.[17] If, however, the transaction costs would be high in this case, we might again turn to governmental activity as a method of reducing them. The government could legally provide an "agreement" between the parties that is not greatly different from what they themselves would reach if they were not impeded by high transaction costs.[18]

In the particular case of airline trip insurance, the arguments for private agreement being impossible because of high transaction costs are rather weaker than those arguments would be in many other areas. Consider, for example, a restaurant. The efficient way of passing the costs of the possible injury onto the restaurant-keeper, which he may inflict upon his customer through accidental poisoning, would be an insurance policy sold with each meal. Clearly, this is a case where the transaction costs would be vastly greater than the actual improvement in efficiency derived from such insurance. Here some type of governmentally imposed institutional arrangement could greatly reduce the transaction

[16] It is by no means obvious that it is rational for people to purchase these short-term coverages for special risk situations. The subject was very well discussed in Robert H. Strotz and Robert Eisner, "Flight Insurance and a Theory of Choice," *Journal of Political Economy* 69 (August 1961): 355–368. It might will be that individuals should not purchase this type of insurance and should depend upon their insurance companies for general coverage. If so, the insurance companies could buy reinsurance from the airlines.

[17] The possibility of offering insurance just for the time on the aircraft might, of course, permit much lower premiums and, therefore, make it possible to get this type of insurance started.

[18] Note that none of the numerous nationalized airlines in the world offers this type of insurance.

costs and, therefore, improve efficiency. There are, of course, more extreme cases. In many situations a person's activity may injure others who have had no previous connection with him at all. A careless construction company, for example, may cause injury to casual passers-by. It would be substantially impossible for the construction company and these accidental victims to get together on an insurance contract. Here again governmental action could improve the efficiency of the economy.

The simplest set of institutions that would lead to reasonable efficiency under these circumstances is simply to place liability on the creator of the risk—the airline, the restaurant owner, or the construction company—for the injuries that it creates. By putting the risk on the person who is in a position to invest his resources to reduce it, we will normally improve the efficiency with which the particular risk-avoiding and producing activities are carried out. Since all of us are both risk producers and victims of risks produced by other people, the net effect of this should be beneficial for each and every one of us.[19] This line of reasoning can be carried farther into an area outside the law of torts. It is possible that I will pick up tuberculosis from eating tubercular meat. It would be impossible for me to collect damages because I could probably not prove where I had caught the disease. Normally, it takes several months for the disease to manifest itself and, in this case, the damage mechanism we have been describing would not work.[20] Under these circumstances, I would be presumably willing to pay the restaurant-keeper to provide meat free from tuberculosis. Here again, however, the transaction costs would be extremely high for individual agreements. Social institutions can once again provide for some kind of inspection system, thus reducing the transaction costs.

We do, of course, have such meat inspection in the United States, and other types of inspection are quite widespread in our economy. I do not wish to argue that every single case meets the standards presented in this chapter. Nevertheless, it is at least

[19] This, of course, is only *ex ante*. *Ex post* the individual might find himself happier if this institutional structure did not exist.
[20] Roger W. Weiss, "The Case for Federal Meat Inspection Examined," *Journal of Law and Economics* 7 (October 1964): 107–120.

possible that many of them do. It should be noted that a good deal of this sort of inspection is actually carried on privately rather than by the government. The optimally efficient arrangement in any given case is a matter for empirical investigation and I have nothing to say about it here.

Let me recapitulate. Accidents raise two problems. The first is to compensate the victim of the accident and the second is to attempt to adjust compensation for individual injuries so that the costs of these injuries fall on those responsible for them, thus improving the general efficiency of the economy. It will be noted that thus far my argument could be taken as simply justifying the existing institutions. I have argued that, in the case of automobile accidents, we would be best off not to use our present liability system, but to depend upon private insurance, a radical change from the status quo. However, the criticism of our present method of assessing damages in automobile accidents is so widespread that it is practically orthodox.[21] My position on other types of accidental injury is not only generally speaking in accord with the law as it exists, but also generally speaking is in accord with fashionable points of view.

The reader, however, may still wonder why I distinguish between automobile injuries, which make up 99 percent of all accidental injuries in the United States, and the other types of injuries, and give them different types of treatment. The basic reason is that, in the case of the automobile, the individual has very strong motives to drive carefully because he does not want to be injured himself. It is true that carelessness on the part of the individual driver creates an externality and endangers other drivers. Our experience, however, would seem to indicate that putting this externality on the driver does not materially affect his driving behavior. This may be simply because our methods of determining responsibility are so inaccurate that the individual is not motivated to avoid liability. It also may be because of the fact that the individual customarily carries insurance and the insurance companies cannot make perfect adjustments in their rate classes. More likely than any of these reasons, however, is

21 For a summary see Blum and Kalven, *Public Law Perspectives*.

the fact that, for most drivers, the great disadvantage in automobile accidents is the danger of agonizing pain and/or death
to himself. The prospect of being forced to pay damages to some
other person is a relatively small factor. Thus, his behavior is
not much affected by whether or not his insurance company must
pay for the damages to others.

The other types of accidental injury are mostly injuries in
which the danger is relatively one-sided. A, through carelessness,
is not likely to injure himself but someone else, namely B. In
this case, forcing liability on A should have a significant effect
on his behavior and, hence, in these cases it is rational to do so.
Thus, the standard welfare arguments connected with externalities would imply liability in both cases. However, it would appear
that the externality in the case of the automobile accident situation is of much less importance. Furthermore, for various reasons,
courts face a more difficult problem in the automobile accident
case and, hence, probably reach less efficient conclusions.

If, thus far, I have been rationalizing the status quo (including
the intellectual status quo of criticism of the present automobile
liability provisions), I would now like to offer some suggestions
for reforms aimed at reducing legal costs that would, of course,
not cover automobile injury cases. It is possible to make considerable cuts in legal costs in this area without having any
significant reduction in efficiency. In fact, we would obtain a
somewhat better adjustment of our damage and liability institutions to the real world at the same time we made these cuts.

In the ordinary case in which A sues B for damages, alleging
that B has injured him in some way, there are two issues: (1)
Was B in fact responsible for A's injury? (2) Granting B's responsibility, how much compensation should A receive for that
injury? If we are dealing with the type of injury that people may
suffer as a result of some type of business activity, we can
eliminate the first problem from most lawsuits if we simply make
proprietors of business activities fully and strictly liable for any
accidental injuries that anyone suffers while on their property.
The issue of fact normally becomes a very simple one—where
was the man when he was injured? There would be a further
rule for such people as the dynamite manufacturer in which one

simply proves that the explosion had caused the injury to some person and not inquire as to the reason for the explosion. It will be noted that, in this case, the owner of the property would be given the appropriate motives for adjusting his resource use on the property in such a way as to minimize the total social cost— that is, the sum of the present discounted value of the risk and the resources used to avoid risk. It would also be true, of course, that the owner would find himself paying damages for a number of injuries that he could not have prevented. These additional damages would be actuarily computable and, therefore, he could insure against them. As a result, there would be a small transfer of income from the owner of the property to accident victims by way of an insurance company.

It will be noted that this suggestion is very close to the present law in many areas and, in workmen's compensation cases, it is the law. In general, it is only necessary to prove that a given worker was employed by a specified individual and was injured in the course of that employment in order for him to obtain workmen's compensation. It is unfortunately true that the workmen's compensation boards have developed a web of complex and tedious laws that has made collection much less easy than it otherwise could be; but, as we shall see, there is a way around this problem. It is unfortunate that judges and lawyers trained in the Anglo-Saxon tradition tend to elaborate things far beyond the efficient point.

There is, however, one significant element of inefficiency in the proposal I have just made. It may well happen that if Smith goes on Jones' property, Smith should be investing resources to avoid injury to himself. If Jones is totally liable, Smith may underinvest resources in this objective. I may say that I doubt that this factor is of much importance because Smith presumably is worried about being injured even if he does feel that he will be compensated for it. Still, it should have some effect. My argument here is simply that the reduction in the court costs, which comes from foreclosing the issue of fault, will more than compensate for this small inefficiency in the allocation of resources in risk avoidance.

The second problem that faces the court if a person has been injured is the monetary reparation for the injury. If we are in agreement that A must pay B damages for an injury, the value of that injury is likely to be something about which A and B disagree. A will normally think that only a small payment should be made and B will claim that a gigantic payment is necessary. One way of dealing with this problem, as is done in many of the law codes of the world, is simply to establish a table of payments for each type of injury as part of the basic law. This, however, ignores the fact that the same injury may be of much greater importance to one person than to another. Our law does neither of these things; although, in the case of workmen's compensation, fixed payments for particular types of injuries are quite common.

Note, however, that the disagreement between A and B as to the value of this "injury" could be completely eliminated if A purchased an insurance policy covering this particular type of injury before the accident occurred. If we are considering, let us say, the loss of a leg, after the leg has been lost, the person who must pay for the loss and the person who receives the payment have radically opposed interests. If, on the other hand, the person who is to pay for it is an insurance company and we are considering the purchase of insurance on the leg some time before the accident occurs, there is no difference of interest between the two parties.

The insurance company, in fact, would like to have its client insure the leg for as much as they can talk him into (subject of course to the problem of moral risk). The client, under these circumstances, can himself decide how much insurance he would like to carry, that is, how much value he is willing to put on his leg. Thus, we very seldom see lawsuits between people who have insurance policies providing for a given payment, if an injury occurs to them, and their insurance companies in which the amount of payment is in debate. If we were willing to accept in all injury claims the value of the insurance carried by the injured person as the value of the tort claim against the person upon whom the responsibility of the injury has been placed, we would eliminate this very difficult legal question from most tort cases. The problem that we face at the moment with this suggested legal reform is that most people do not carry insurance that provides specific payments for various injuries. Very likely the situation will change over a period of time, but it might be wise to undertake institutional changes that would accelerate this change.

The present situation puts considerable unnecessary costs on this type of insurance. Let us suppose that I have an insurance policy that pays me $10,000 if I lose a leg, and I lose a leg under circumstances that Smith would normally have to compensate me. Will that $10,000 be taken into account by a jury computing the damages which Smith will have to pay me? There is no clear and definite answer to this question in the United States today, but it does seem fairly certain that *ex ante* my probable collection in a tort action is lower if I have an insurance policy that has already reimbursed me than if I do not. Thus, when I buy an insurance policy, I make certain that I will receive the $10,000 if my leg is lost even if no one is at fault; but, at the same time, I reduce my probable collections in a tort action if I lose my leg under appropriate tort conditions. Suppose that I have a 1 in 1,000 chance of losing my leg and if I do, the chances are 1 in 2 that I would be able to collect tort damages of $10,000. If I have a $10,000 insurance policy against this contingency, then I still have a 1 in 2 chance of collecting tort damages, but I will probably receive only $5,000. The value to me of the insurance policy is $7.50, but its cost will be $10.00.[22] Risk aversion may lead me to buy this policy, but clearly I would buy more if the price were $7.50.

This overcharge would not be of any significance if the insurance company were capable of suing in my name to recover the amount of money it had paid me. Most insurance companies put a clause subrogating it for me in any damage action involving their policies. It would appear, however, that the insurance companies anticipate unsympathetic treatment from the courts and, therefore, do not normally attempt to recover from the person who caused the accident the damages they have paid out to the victim. If they did regularly succeed in recovering damages in these cases, they could charge markedly lower premiums and, hence, this type of insurance would become more widespread.

---

[22] In this, as in my other computations, I exclude sales and administrative costs.

The first institutional change that would seem desirable would be to make it fairly simple for insurance companies to collect in these cases. Thus, it should be possible for insurance companies to sue the person who causes injury or death to one of their clients and to collect damages that are equivalent to the payment they themselves have made. The further step of providing that recovery would be measured by the amount of insurance would (if given sufficient publicity) probably lead to substantially universal coverage.[23] It should be noted that, in a way, the proposals I have been making would lead to a slight overestimation of the value of injuries. If the individual would always collect from other people if he is injured on their property, then he would be charged somewhat less than the right amount for his own insurance. Thus, presumably he would, to some extent, underevaluate the injuries to him. It does not seem to me, however, that this would be a major disadvantage.

With these institutional changes, we would have the following situation. Firstly, most people would carry insurance against injuries regardless of the cause. In the event of an accident, they would collect damages from their own insurance company. Since insurance companies that wish to remain in business have strong motives to make certain that claim adjustment is relatively quick and involves relatively little red tape, this would normally be a speedy and fairly simple process. Occasionally litigation would occur between an insurance company and one of its clients, but litigation would be much rarer than current tort litigation to obtain reparation for injuries.

Secondly, if an individual were injured in an accident not involving an automobile, the insurance company that had paid him damages for his injuries would normally seek reparation from the person who, under our rather simple law code, would be liable for that injury. Normally no law suit would be necessary because of the simplicity of the liability system we have

[23] For those people who feel that certain parts of the population cannot be trusted to manage their own affairs, a compulsory rule requiring them to carry a certain amount of insurance would seem sensible. This, however, is an ethical problem and we cannot discuss it on our present set of assumptions.

proposed. Once again, an occasional suit would occur. In many cases, the transaction would involve only the two insurance companies. The system would do a reasonably good job of adjusting the amount of resources invested in accident avoidance. It would not, it is true, provide for a perfect arrangement of resources, but it seems likely that the saving in court proceedings would more than compensate for the imperfection in the allocation of resources.

We must now, however, turn to a problem that was discussed at the beginning of this chapter only to be set aside; what is an accident? In ordinary speech, we assume that we know the difference between an accidental injury and a deliberate injury; but, as we have seen, individual choice of behavior is involved in accidents. Suppose I am the owner of an industrial installation. The type of investment that I undertake in avoiding accidents will have a considerable effect on the number of accidents that occur. To say that it is an accident if my investments are over a certain amount, and not an accident if they are under a certain amount is drawing an essentially arbitrary line. There seems no reason, then, why we should choose any particular degree of precaution or nonprecaution as the boundary.

We can, however, distinguish a special set of cases in which individuals quite definitely decide to cause injuries. If I deliberately decide to beat someone up, this would be an example. It should be noted, however, that in some cases in which our courts now assume that people deliberately cause injury, they actually do not. These are generally cases in which the individual has gone into a business (such as bank robbery) in which there is a very high potential for causing injury. Clearly, the individuals holding up a bank who, in the process, kill someone are in really somewhat the same situation as a man who is building a bridge and, in the process, kills someone. We have tended over the years to consider these two things differently. In particular, since we want to prevent people from holding up banks, and want to help people to build bridges, we have tended to make the responsibility for injuries different. But in both cases, increased investment in risk avoidance could reduce the likelihood of people being killed.

However, if it is a little difficult to draw this distinction, there is no reason why we need it in discussing the question of reparation for injury. There is no reason why an individual who is injured by someone else should have his right to reparation in any way affected by the intent of the person who committed the injury. Thus, my wish to beat someone up is a clear case of an externality, and compelling me to pay in full the cost of that beating is a good way of getting optimal allocation of resources in society.[24] In our present law, some types of crimes do not normally lead to civil suits. Clearly this is a mistake. If a man is murdered, his family and his insurance company should have causes of action against the murderer. The fact that we are not going to rest content with giving them this cause of action has nothing to do with the question of whether they should or should not have it. Clearly they have been injured by the act, clearly this injury is an externality, and clearly we should impose the cost of that externality on the person whose activities caused the injury. This will improve the allocation of resources in society, although in this particular case we seldom think of the problem as being one of improved allocation.

This chapter concludes with a brief discussion of two points. The first of these is what type of court would we choose to deal with cases in this field. We should first begin by noting that in most cases it will not be possible for the parties to enter into an agreement in advance. This is because in most accidents the parties are strangers before the accident. After the accident has occurred, it is unlikely that we could obtain agreement among the parties as to the choice of court. Presumably one of them would like to have the decision indefinitely deferred and, if forced to go to court, would like to have the court as inefficient as possible. His opponent, on the other hand, would want quick justice and a high degree of efficiency. Requiring an agreement on the court would give great advantages to the party at fault.

This, then, is a clear case for social contrivance, and we have such a contrivance in our society known as the regular court

[24] As we shall see later, such private suits are not (in and of themselves) completely suitable in the area of crime. They must be supplemented by further action not undertaken by the victim of the crime. This does not mean, of course, that such private suits should be prohibited, but simply that we should not rely entirely upon them.

system. If the government provides a set of courts that is available for dealing with the case, and that all parties are compelled to accept unless they reach agreement on another court, then this problem will not arise. It is true that we will not obtain quite as accurate an adjustment of the court to the needs of the parties as if we could somehow permit them to reach agreement, but it is better than the available alternatives. In general, the individual should anticipate that the establishment of such a court would improve the future discounted value of his income stream. It should be noted that the considerations for the choice of an optimal court developed in the last chapter would, in general, also apply here. In particular, there is no reason why the parties should not reach agreement to move their case from the court provided by the government to some other court.

In general, we would anticipate that this would rarely happen, but the possibility of its happening should be left open. There is one particular case in which it might very well happen; that is, a controversy between two insurance companies over who is responsible for a particular injury. In this case, ironically, the insurance companies might consider the court provided by the government to be too good for their needs. An insurance company annually facing 10,000 cases of litigation of this sort would be interested in the general pattern of the outcome, not in the decision in any given case. Therefore, some cheap judicial process with a high random error would be quite attractive to the insurance company, provided that it could be sure the error was not biased. One would anticipate that the insurance companies would enter into arrangements among themselves under which this type of case was dealt with in some inexpensive and relatively inaccurate way. There is no reason why we should have any objection to this process that would surely reduce the costs of insurance.

The final question with which this chapter must deal is what the considerations we have been discussing have to do with our basic assumptions about human behavior. In general, if this system is established, it will increase the efficiency with which resources are allocated in society with respect to risk avoidance—in other words, it will internalize certain externalities and it will lead to individuals having their personal risks reduced. The present discounted value of the future income stream of individuals increases in utility terms, and thus the line of reasoning can be justified on the assumptions of Chapter 2.

7

Status

This chapter, our final discussion of the civil law, deals with a set of miscellaneous matters, all of them having to do with personal status. Sir Henry Maine, writing during the nineteenth century, argued that the law had seen a gradual movement from a status system to a system of contract. He obviously regarded this movement as progress. He saw the situation in his day as the beginning of a retrogression. When I studied law in the 1930s, the retrogression had clearly accelerated. Furthermore, my teachers (or at least some of them) seemed to regard this as a desirable change. Since that date, movements toward a basically status system of law have continued, although it must be said that status is still a minor part of our law. Special groups do have, however, all sorts of special privileges (and, in some cases, special responsibilities) as a result of their status in society. As a college professor, perhaps I should begin by discussing the specialized status of college professors. Firstly is something called educational freedom, which as far as I can see, simply means that a college professor should not be fired unless he has committed a common crime.

Since I have dealt with this problem in *The Organization of Inquiry,* I will not discuss it in detail now.[1] The point to be noted, however, is that this special set of privileges for people who hold

---

[1] Gordon Tullock, *The Organization of Inquiry* (Durham, N. C.: Duke University Press, 1966), pp. 210–219.

one particular status is representative of a vastly larger group of similar privileges. In fact, the special privileges granted college professors in virtue of their status are relatively modest compared to those granted to people such as barbers, beauticians, undertakers, and doctors. We professors have substantially no monopoly on status, and it is not likely that the income of college professors is markedly higher than it would be if "educational freedom" did not exist. It may even be less. The income of the other groups I have mentioned is, however, higher because of their legally established special status.

One of the significant developments of recent years has been the widespread development of specialized guild legislation. Under this legislation some special activity (beauty culture, hair cutting, or medicine) is declared to require special governmental control. All persons engaged in it at the time the new law is enacted are then declared eligible to continue with the activity, but new entrants are to be carefully selected in order to protect the public. The criteria for selection are turned over to a board, which is, needless to say, composed of present members of the profession. This board then uses its monopoly power to raise the economic returns in this particular field.[2]

Looking at this development from the standpoint of this book, it is clear that any individual who is a member of a group having a good political possibility of getting the state to give that group a legally protected monopoly should favor the obtaining of the monopoly. This will clearly improve his personal ability to make choices in the future by increasing the income he can spend. By the same token, however, he should be opposed to all attempts by people in other walks of life to obtain the same type of protected monopoly. It might be wise for him to enter into some kind of bargain under which his particular activity and a small number of other activities are protected. But, in general, granted the large number of guilds that have been set up by special legislation, it is probable that most people are, on balance, actually injured by the sum total of all legally granted monopolies even though they may gain from one such monopoly.

[2] See Milton Friedman, *Capitalism and Freedom* (Chicago: University of Chicago Press, 1962), pp. 137–160.

Here we have a case in which each individual group can gain from obtaining governmental aid, but where if all obtain such aid, all would be worse off. It is similar in this respect to a tariff. Like the tariff, the gains cannot be generalized. It is not possible for everyone to gain if everyone sets up a local monopoly. The individual should attempt to protect his own monopoly or establish one if he does not have it, and to destroy the others. If there are a very large number of such monopolies, it is probable that the individual (if given the choice between having all of them or having none) would be well advised to choose to have no monopoly. This, however, is only a probability, and in each case it will be necessary to make detailed calculations. Personally, perhaps as a bias, I am strongly opposed to this development of status and guild in our modern society. I agree with Sir Henry Maine that the movement from status to contract was a movement toward progress. The present movement in the opposite direction is reactionary.

As a general rule we can say that most people are better off if, in most matters, they choose what they want themselves. It is very dubious that my knowledge of what will please you is better than yours (although it may well be that in some cases this could be so). It has never actually been proven that some individuals are not well equipped to choose for other people. It may well be that you would be better off if I ran your life through a set of detailed regulations. Personally, I doubt this, but I must admit that I cannot disprove the proposition. Those scholars who feel that individual preferences are not the ultimate data, and that they themselves can tell other people how to be better off, have never been disproved. Perhaps the strongest argument against this type of attitude is simply to ask the person, who is posing the view that individual preference orderings are not the ultimate data, whether he is willing to let you run his life.[3]

Although we normally permit people to make their own choices, all societies have a certain number of individuals among them who are not given this privilege. The most obvious examples, of course, are children. The insane, and certain other cases (for

[3] I regret to say that in at least one case in which I tried this the man replied, "Yes."

example, people who are temporarily incapacitated for some reason or other) are also in this category. Obviously what we require is a way of distinguishing between people who are capable of looking after their own affairs and those who are not. The problem is particularly difficult because it is highly likely that we do not have two separate categories of the population, one composed of competents and the other composed of incompetents, rather we have a spectrum. Furthermore, probably the "incompetents" are perfectly capable of carrying on much of their daily life without supervision.

When we find people whom we decide are incompetent, our usual procedure is to try to get some person to manage their affairs. Normally, however, we do not completely trust these other persons, and some procedure is established to insure that they do not abuse their position. Again, the most obvious cases are children. In our society the child is under the control of his parents. In general, this works very well, but we do not leave the parent's discretion completely uncontrolled. There are various laws restricting what parents can do, and provisions are available for removing children from the control of the parents when warranted. Our methods of dealing with insane adults are similar but, in this case, we are more likely to give the guardian closer supervision.

Thus far, I have been describing in general terms what we now do and have said very little about what we should do. Strictly speaking, it is impossible to apply the line of reasoning used in this book to our dealings with children because the decision makers are not now children and are not likely to be children in the future. If you are reading this book, you are presumably already in full control of your own affairs and will never again be a child. Any provisions for dealing with children will not directly affect you. You would be interested only insofar as a particular child, or perhaps children in general, have attracted your emotional concern. With respect to the insane, we all have some finite probability of becoming insane and, therefore, presumably should to some extent be interested in the treatment of the insane, but I find that very few people are very much concerned with this probability.

It would appear that basically we can do little about this subject, using the reasoning upon which this book is founded. It may be, however, that intermediate stages between our present competents and incompetents could be developed. Thomas S. Szasz has argued that a great many of the insane require no confinement or special treatment.[4] He may very well be right. It seems probable that a good many of the insane would require some kind of special guardianship with respect to certain things, but could be left free to handle other aspects of their lives by themselves.

Here, unfortunately, we are dependent upon what amounts to a purely technical, medical decision in areas in which medical knowledge at the moment is very slight. It should, perhaps, be noted that as one of the results of Russian economic planning the facilities for the care of lunatics were gravely neglected. In view of the resulting shortage of facilities, the Russians introduced a special degree of lunacy for people who were insane but not dangerous. Such people were not incarcerated. Valarie Tarshish, the anti-Communist author, in fact was actually given an exit permit although he was officially classified in this category. The United States is wealthy enough to maintain large and luxurious insane asylums (even if we do not do so) but it still might be wise for us to take a lead from the Russian experience in this matter. Perhaps an intermediate category, or even several intermediate categories, would not be impractical or particularly difficult. The "Halfway House" is a step in this direction.

In practice, our methods of raising children amount to giving the child more and more responsibility as he grows older. Our criminal law, in practice, acts this way, although in theory it does not. In theory there are certain young people who cannot commit a crime because the law considers them too young, certain young people who if they commit a crime are juvenile delinquents, and other young people who are considered adults when they commit a crime. In practice, however, the courts take into account the

[4] He has made this argument so many times that citation may seem superfluous. For a particularly concise statement of his views see his, "Address at the International and Comparative Conference on Mental Illness and the State," Northwestern University School of Law.

age of the younger person involved in the commission of a crime in a gradual way, with heavier sentences usually being imposed on the older juvenile offenders. This would appear to be a sensible proceeding. The basic problem, however (when does a person become a responsible adult), is one on which we can offer no enlightenment. It may well be that it would be sensible to give some kind of examination and consider all people who did not pass it, regardless of their calendar age, as juveniles.

Another problem that raises very severe difficulties is marriage. Indeed, all problems of "family law" are difficult, and our analysis does not permit us to say much here. It may be possible to consider marriage as simply a contract and permit people to make what agreements they wish, but it must be admitted that few, if any, experiments in this direction have been made. It may be that this absence of experimentation reflects simple conservatism, but it may also be that there are good reasons why marital relations should be regulated.

So far in this chapter we have dealt mainly with areas in which there is very little we can say. We can conclude by dealing with several problems where definite conclusions can be reached. The first of these is "corporation law." If a number of people wish to jointly undertake an enterprise, their decision in this regard raises two issues. The first of these issues is simply whether they shall be permitted to engage in legal actions of various sorts (signing contracts, being sued, suing other persons) as a group, or shall be compelled always to take this action in the name of all of them individually. As far as I know, no one objects to permitting any group of people to act as a group.

Lawyers say that the corporation is a legal person. The question of whether a corporation should be considered as a person or not has even been the subject of considerable metaphysical debate. If we look at it simply as a question of whether the group of people who own United States Steel may appoint someone to undertake legal action or sign contracts, in their name, or whether they must always sign their own names individually to all agreements, I presume no one would really raise any questions as to which would be more convenient. Saying that the corporation is a legal person is a rather unwieldly way of expressing this. Whether

United States Steel has constitutional protection as a person is of really very little significance. Clearly its stockholders are persons and they have a right to constitutional protection. The only result of denying similar constitutional protection to United States Steel would be to make it necessary for the stockholders to undertake individual legal actions.

The second problem raised by corporation law is the limitation of liability. Here, again, there is no real issue. There is no reason why I, entering into a contract with someone else, cannot put into the contract a provision limiting my liability in the event that I default. Such contractual clauses are not common, but they are clearly legal. For example, if I borrow the money to build a house on a mortgage, normally the mortgage will provide that if I am in default, not only can the bank or insurance company seize the house, but they can also sue me for the difference between its value and the face value of the mortgage. There is nothing, however, to prevent us from agreeing that in the event that I default on the mortgage, the bank's ability to collect is limited to the building itself.

In practice in present-day situations most limited liability contracts are entered into through a corporation rather than individually. This, however, simply reflects present practice and does not raise any fundamental issues. If a group of people desires to get together to engage in the manufacture of steel, there is no reason why they should not put into their contracts with each of their suppliers a statement saying that collection on these contracts will be limited to the assets now involved in the manufacture of steel. Instead of this, they form a corporation.[5]

Clearly, this is merely a matter of convenience. I regret to say that the simplicity of the actual subject matter of this paragraph has escaped most legal scholars, and there is a great deal of discussion of the importance of the corporation as a way of limiting liability. As a matter of history, the limitation of liability did come in very largely with the corporation; but, if we are concerned not with how our present institution developed but whether they are desirable institutions, the concept of limited liability is only coincidentally related to the corporation. One can

[5] My discussion of the corporation has benefited greatly from the work of Henry Manne.

readily imagine corporations without limited liability, and one can equally readily imagine limited liability without corporations. Furthermore, under our present law it is perfectly possible to enter into contracts in which liability is limited; it is also perfectly possible to organize corporations with unlimited liability.[6]

Our final area is the "status" of a dead man. Our present law provides that when a man dies (if he has any significant amount of property) a person known as executor is appointed to act as the "personal representative of the deceased," in fact the man who is dead in a legal sense continues to exist until the estate is settled. This procedure, which is the mainstay of many legal practices and an entire set of courts, has normally been regarded as onerous by the common man.[7] A large number of techniques have been developed that make it possible to avoid probate. The most important of these are trusts and joint checking accounts.

In this case it would seem that the common man is right, and the law is a "fool and an ass." The historical reasons for the development of our present law of inheritance are reasonably clear, but it is by no means obvious that we should retain it. Essentially there are two different theories of "testamentary disposition." Under the first theory, I may make a particular form of gift of any property I own to other people. This gift is conditional upon my death—i.e., I retain complete use of my property until I die. If this theory is adopted (and it is the one I favor), we obtain for the individual owner of property the maximum control over that property.

The second theory of testamentary disposition is based not on the desire to give the present owner of property full control over the property (including the right to make a gift of it at the time of his death), but on a feeling that society has an interest in the disposition of the property.[8] Occasionally egalitarian ideas get

[6] We might have to use some other word in the title.

[7] At the time of this writing, one of the best sellers was, *How to Avoid Probate*, by Norman F. Dacey.

[8] There are perhaps arguments for seeing to it that certain people, *i.e.*, widows, who might otherwise become objects of public charity, are taken care of in the disposition of an estate. This, however, simply may be a recognition of a wife's contribution in accumulating this estate. In many parts of the United States the wife already owns half of her husband's property even while he is alive.

involved in the law of testimentary disposition, but clearly this is a mistake. Requiring a wealthy father to divide his money equally among his children, for example, does indeed increase the equality with which the different children are treated, but its effect on the total wealth distribution in society is substantially nil. Equitable ideas as to the "duties" that individuals owe to different relatives may also be involved in some laws in this area. Such equitable ideas cannot be deduced from our basic assumptions and, hence, are foreign to this book.

In practice in most of the United States the statement that the person who owns property may leave it to substantially anyone he wishes is fairly well descriptive of our law.[9] The only serious limitations are taxes on the estate. There are no reasons why taxes on this particular subject raise any special issues. In fact, as we shall see, one tax on inheritance is better than any other tax.

Granted that people are in general permitted to leave their money any way they wish, the law concerning inheritance falls into two categories. One, a tremendously complex and to a large extent unnecessary probate procedure; two, provisions for disposition if the deceased has left no will. Turning first to the latter situation, Jeremy Bentham suggested that a person who had left no will had indicated that he had no very strong preferences about what happened to his money and, therefore, the state should use it for governmental expenditures. This is, as any economist can see immediately, an ideal tax. There is no perceptible excess burden since the only thing that anyone needs to do in order to avoid it is to prepare a will.

Presumably, if this institution were adopted very few people would die intestate. In those cases where people died intestate, the existence of this particular form of taxation would not affect their behavior before their death since they could avoid the taxation if they wished and, hence, the only people who would "suffer" would be the occasional individual who failed to obtain a gift. Although it seems to me this idea of Bentham's is simple, elegant, and obviously sensible, it shocks most people. They talk about people whose wills are lost, who had inadvertently destroyed their will, and so on. It is clear that a person who wishes

[9] With some exceptions for a widow.

to avoid this tax on his estate would not only have to draw up a will, but would have to see to it that it was kept safe. There does not, however, seem to be any great difficulty in this. I think the real motive behind the objection is simple conservatism. What Bentham proposed, and what I am now endorsing, is indeed a radical change; and most people do not like radical changes.

There is, however, an argument of sorts for having a general law of intestacy. It might be argued that a great many people would rather not bother with drawing up a will and a standard provision in the law would permit some people to avoid this task. Thus, for example, if the law provides that if a man dies intestate half of his estate goes in life tenancy to his wife and the remainder of his estate is immediately (and the half in his wife's possession on her death) divided equally among the children, it might save trouble in that most people (who on the whole were planning on leaving their estate in that form anyway) would not have to bother with drawing up a will. There is something in this argument, but not a great deal. It is unlikely that very many of the people who refrain from drawing up wills have even bothered to find out what the provisions for intestacy are, and, hence, there is no strong reason to believe that these legal provisions would in fact carry out their desires.

In any event, it seems likely that the actual provisions for the disposition of an estate in the event of intestacy did not originate from the kind of reasoning I have outlined in the last paragraph. Originally the state felt that it had a very strong interest in the disposition of estates. This interest was expressed by requiring them to be left in certain ways. As time went by and more liberal ideas developed, individuals were permitted to avoid the rules if they wished. The rules remain, however, as a sort of residuum for those cases in which the individual has not made any specific disposition. They are, thus, interesting relics from the past rather than rationally conceived results of social engineering.

The basic problems in the field of testimentary disposition, however, are not the rules for intestacy but the probate procedure that so complicates and delays present-day transfer of property upon death. As I have mentioned, there is a recent best seller advising people how to avoid these provisions. While I was writing this section, *Readers Digest* featured an article on joint tenancy as a method of avoiding probate.[10] The same end can be attained more certainly with the aid of expensive attorneys. The wealthy are interested in minimizing their inheritance tax as well as simplifying the procedure of transmission and, hence, the devices that they use are frequently extremely complex and of very little general value. For the purposes of the rest of this chapter, we will ignore these legal devices, as well as changes in the inheritance tax.[11] Probate procedure, like the laws of intestacy, is actually a heritage from earlier times. Unlike the laws providing for intestacy, it is not of minor importance; the total costs are very great. Further, there seems absolutely no reason for these costs.

Let us consider a radically different system; assume that when a man dies, if a document called a will is found, it is regarded as simply a deed of gift. Currently, gifts by living people normally raise no particular problem. We do not have any special set of courts for them. It is, of course, true that on occasions ordinary deeds of gift will lead to lawsuits, but they are tried in the ordinary courts; there does not seem to be any reason why special courts exist for them. In fact, lawsuits concerning inheritance are relatively uncommon, and there seems to be no reason why a special court system should be set up to deal only with all inheritance matters so that the small minority of the inheritances that do lead to lawsuits may be determined by that court.

Given our present customs, the institution I have just described would raise a serious difficulty having to do with the debts of the deceased person. If the person died owing money to some people but having property that was left by deed of gift to other people, at first glance it would appear that the debtors would lose. If we observe the real world, we note that this is (generally speaking) not true with respect to gifts; gifts to prevent the repayment of debt are normally held invalid. However, there is no reason why we would need to worry about the problem. If the law were changed in the manner that I have been suggesting, then one can assume that people lending money or entering business deals with

[10] October, 1967, p. 163.
[11] There is no great difficulty in collecting inheritance taxes without probate procedure and, in fact, inheritance taxes are frequently collected on property that did not go through probate.

others would simply put special provisions into their contracts. Most loans, after all, are made on security; in these cases very few problems arise. For unsecured loans, a provision in the contract providing that if the person who borrowed the money dies the loan immediately becomes a lien on his property, would be very simple and would involve no special problems.

The new procedure might cause some difficulty when it was first inaugurated. In fact, it would probably be desirable to provide a delay between the period in which the new procedure was enacted and its coming into effect, so that people could make appropriate changes in their contracts. Nevertheless, the change would appear to eliminate much waste. The lawyers would be injured by the change and, of course, the personnel of specialized probate courts; but everyone else would gain and the gain would be large enough to compensate the losers. No doubt, the lawyers will be able to invent technical objections to it and will have the strongest possible motives to do so; but there seems to be no reason why we should pay attention to this type of sophism. From the standpoint of those who are thinking of leaving money to others and (although there is no need to pay much attention to this group) those who expect to eventually receive bequests, a reduction in the costs of transmission of property at death would be advantageous. Even if we consider economic efficiency in the old-fashioned Adam Smith sense, there is improvement. The long period in which wealth is tied up through probate would be abolished, and this would improve the efficiency with which property is used.

In this particular case, the suggestion that I have made superficially appears quite radical (although it is hard to find anything very serious in the way of an argument against it). In practice, however, the suggestion is not all that extreme. The common man is more and more turning to nonprobate methods of transmitting property to his heirs. The methods now available for this purpose (specialized trusts, joint accounts, joint tenancy of all sorts) have significant disadvantages attached to them. Permitting a similarly probate-free disposition of property by will would simplify matters, and it is very hard to see who would be hurt by the change other than the members of the probate bar.

PART III

CRIMINAL LAW

8

Motor Vehicle Offenses and Tax Evasion[1]

We now begin our discussion of the criminal law, a branch of the law that many people feel is clearly the most important. We begin with a discussion of motor vehicle offenses and later turn to a discussion of tax evasion. This may seem to be an eccentric way of beginning a consideration of the criminal law, but it seems a good idea to introduce the subject with a discussion of those branches with which the reader is personally familiar. Everyone who reads this book probably has committed a motor vehicle offense, and some may have even been arrested at one time or another for violating the motor vehicle code.

The average man feels not the slightest discomfort if he observes a policeman while walking down the street. If on the other hand we are driving, all of us feel a start of apprehension when we see a police car. Few professional criminals have had as much

[1] This chapter, in a slightly modified form, was printed in the *Social Science Quarterly* 50 (June 1969): 59–71, under the title, "An Economic Approach to Crime." The orthodox point of view was presented in a comment on my article by Walter Firey, "Limits to Economy in Crime and Punishment," *Social Science Quarterly* 50 (June 1969): 72–78.

experience with their particular type of crime as the average man has had with motor vehicle violations. The average man also has a great deal of experience with the results of motor vehicle violations. All of us have seen such violations by other people; all of us have had our lives endangered at some time or other by these violations, and almost all of us have seen the really appalling injuries that a serious automobile accident can cause. Thus we are not only experienced in violating this law; we have a clear idea in our own minds of the consequences of such violation.

After completing our discussion of motor vehicle violations, we turn to tax evasion, where the average man's knowledge and experience are, on the whole, less than that of violations of the traffic code. Still most us have at least contemplated padding our expenses on the income tax return, and we find very little difficulty in understanding why other people do it regularly. In addition, we are all fairly well aware of the consequences of large-scale tax evasion. We all know that the basic taxation rates would have to be higher or our total expenditures would have to be lower if tax evasion were permitted.

Another advantage in beginning our discussion of the criminal law with motor vehicle offenses and tax evasion is the fact that the customary element in such laws is extremely small. Most of our laws on crime evolved from antiquity and hence contain all sorts of quaint nooks and crannies. The motor vehicle law is almost entirely a creation of the twentieth century and is periodically revised extensively. The income tax code similarly is largely a recent development and is continuously being changed both by legislative enactment and by various administrative bodies. Thus we do not have to deal with the weight of immemorial tradition when we turn to these problems.

The most common and simplest of all violations of the law is illegal parking. This is a new problem. In the days of yore, there were not enough idle vehicles to raise any great difficulty. When, however, common men began to buy automobiles, the number of vehicles was such that simply permitting people to park where they wished along the side of the street led to very serious congestion. The number of spaces was limited, and rationing on a first come, first served basis seems to have been felt to be unsatisfactory.[2] Exactly why it was thought to be unsatisfactory is not at all clear. In any event, the proper governmental bodies decided that there should be a "fairer" distribution of parking space, and it was decided that individuals should vacate spaces at some specified time, frequently one hour, after they occupied them. Again, there is some difficulty in understanding why this remedy was chosen. The governments could have provided adequate free parking space, as the operators of shopping centers do, opened parking lots on a fee basis, or simply let the problem solve itself by private provision of fee parking space.

Nevertheless, the "remedy" chosen was to have people occupy parking spaces only for limited periods of time. The question then arose as to how to ensure compliance. The method chosen was to attach a penalty for noncompliance. The police were instructed to "ticket" cars that parked beyond the time limit, and the owners of the ticketed cars were then fined a small sum, say $10, by a court. Thus, the individual could choose between removing his car within the prescribed period or leaving it and running some chance of being forced to pay $10. Obviously, the size of the fine and the likelihood that any given car owner would be caught would largely determine how much overparking was done. The individual would, in effect, be confronted with a "price list" for overparking and would normally do so only if the inconvenience of moving his car were greater than the properly discounted cost of the fine.[3]

Not all overparking is the result of a deliberate decision; a good deal of it comes from absentmindedness, and part is the result of factors not very thoroughly under the control of the car owner. Nevertheless, we do not generally feel that the fine should be remitted. The absence of a criminal intent, or indeed, of any intent at all, is not regarded as an excuse. When I was working in the Department of State in Washington, I served under a man who incurred several parking tickets a week. All of these viola-

[2] We are now discussing the early development of parking regulations. The relatively recent invention of the parking meter has changed the situation drastically and will be discussed later.

[3] I am indebted to Alexander Kafka for the "price list" analogy. He insists, following his own professor, that the entire criminal code is simply a price list for various acts.

tions occurred without any conscious intent on his part. He would get involved in some project and forget that he was supposed to move his car. The city of Washington was levying what amounted to a tax on him for being absentminded. The Washington police force was not particularly annoyed with my superior; apparently, they thought that the revenue derived paid for the inconvenience of issuing tickets and occasionally towing his car away. Suppose, however, they had wanted to make him stop violating the parking laws. It seems highly probable that an increase in the fines would have been sufficient. Absentmindedness about $10 does not necessarily imply absentmindedness about $100 or even $1,000. With higher fines, he would have felt more pressure to remember to avoid parking on the public streets as much as possible, and to arrange with his secretary to remind him. Thus the fact that he was not engaging in any calculations at all when he committed these "crimes" does not indicate that he would not respond to higher penalties by ceasing to commit them.

Thus far, we have simply assumed that the objective is to enforce a particular law against parking. The question of whether this law is sensible, or how much effort should be put into enforcing it has not been discussed. In metered parking areas the government in essence is renting out space for parking to people who want to use it. It may not be using a market clearing price because it may have some objectives other than simply providing the service at a profit, but this does not seriously alter the problem. The government should maximize the net benefit obtained from the operation. For simplicity, let us assume that it is charging market clearing prices. It would then attempt to maximize total revenue including the revenue from fines and the revenue from the coins inserted in the parking meters minus the cost of the enforcement system. We need not here produce an equation or attempt to solve the problem, but clearly it is a perfectly ordinary problem in operations research, and there is no reason to anticipate any great difficulty in solving it.

But parking is a very minor problem; in fact it was chosen for discussion simply because it is so easy. In essence, there is very little here except a calculation of exactly the same sort that is undertaken every day by businessmen. For a slightly more complicated problem, let us consider another traffic offense—speeding. The number of deaths from automobile accidents, the extent of personal injuries, and the material damage are generally all functions of the speed at which cars travel.[4] By enforcing a legal maximum speed, we can reduce all of these. On the other hand, a legal maximum speed will surely inconvenience at least some people, and may inconvenience a great many.

The material costs of lowering maximum speed are easily approximated by computing the additional time spent in traveling and multiplying this by the hourly earning power of an average member of the population. This is, of course, only an approximation, leaving out such factors as the pleasure some people get out of driving at high speeds, and the diversion of economic activity that would result from the slowing down of traffic. Nevertheless, we could use this approximation and the costs of deaths, injuries, and material damage from automobile accidents to work out the optimal speed limit that would be simply the limit that minimized total costs.[5] The computation would be made in "social" terms because the data would be collected for the entire population. Individuals, however, could regard these figures as approximations for their personal optima.

To the best of my knowledge, no one has ever performed these calculations. Presumably the reason for this omission is an unwillingness to openly put a value on deaths and injuries. When I point out to people that the death toll from highway accidents could be reduced by simply lowering the speed limit (and improving enforcement), they normally show great reluctance to give any consideration to the subject. They sometimes try to convince themselves that the reduction would not have the predicted effect, but more commonly they simply quickly shift to another

[4] Recently this relationship has been somewhat obscured by the publication of Ralph Nader's *Unsafe at any Speed*. This is a misunderstanding. It is undoubtedly true that cars can be designed to reduce accidents. Recent discoveries on methods of reducing skidding by improved highway surfaces probably indicate that there is more potential in highway improvement than in car redesign. Nevertheless, for a given car and highway, speed kills.

[5] For those who object to approximation, more elaborate research, taking into account much more of the costs of slowing down traffic could be undertaken.

subject. For reasons of convenience, they oppose a substantial lowering of the speed limit, but they do not like to consciously balance convenience against deaths. Nevertheless, this is the real reasoning behind the speed limits. We count the costs of being forced to drive slowly and the costs of accidents, and choose the speed limit that gives us the best outcome. Since we are unwilling to do this consciously, we probably do a bad job of computing. If we were willing to look at the matter in the open, consciously placing a value on human life, we could no doubt get better results.

As an example of this reluctance to think about the valuation we are willing to place upon deaths and injury, a colleague of mine undertook a study of the methods used by the Virginia Highway Commission in deciding upon road improvement. He found that they were under legislative orders to consider speed, beauty, and safety. The beauty was taken care of by simply earmarking a fixed part of the appropriations for roadside parks. For speed they engaged in elaborate research on highway use and had statistical techniques for predicting the net savings in time that could be derived from various possible improvements. It was the possibility of improving these techniques that had led them to invite my colleague to make his study. For safety, on the other hand, they had no system at all.

It was clear that they did take safety into account in designing roads and spent quite a bit of money on reducing the likelihood of accidents. They did not, however, have any formula or rule for deciding either how much should be spent on safety or in what specific projects it should be invested. Clearly the money spent on safety could not be spent on increasing speed of travel or beauty.[6] They must have had some tradeoff. This rule, however, remained buried in their subconscious even though they used fairly elaborate and advanced techniques for other problems. This is particularly remarkable when it is remembered that, given any exchange value, the computations of the amount to be spent on safety would be fairly easy. If, for example, it is decided that

[6] In some cases the same improvement may increase both speed and safety, a cloverleaf, for example. In general, however, although speed, safety, and beauty may sometimes be joint products, more of one will reduce the supply of the others.

we will count one fatal automobile accident as "worth" $500,000 in inconvenience to drivers (measured in increased travel time), then with statistics on accidents and the volume of traffic, it would be possible to work out how much should be spent on safety and where.

Since the Highway Commission did not spend all of its money on safety, some such "price" for accidents must have existed, but the rather sophisticated engineers were unwilling to admit, probably even to themselves, that this was so. Perhaps more surprising, my colleagues fully approved of their attitude. Basically a "scientific" type, with a great interest in statistical decision theory, he felt that here was one place where careful reasoning was undesirable. He did not want to consider the ratio between deaths and convenience himself, did not want the people who designed the highways on which he drove to consciously consider it, and did not want to discuss the subject with me.

But even if we do not like to critically examine the process, clearly the decision as to the speed limit is made by balancing the inconveniences of a low limit against the deaths and injuries to be expected from a high one. The fact that we are not willing to engage in conscious thought on the problem is doubly unfortunate, because it is difficult enough so that it is unlikely that we can reach optimal decisions by any but the most careful and scientific procedures. The problem is stochastic on both sides since driving at a given speed does not certainly cause an accident; it only creates the probability of an accident. Similarly, our convenience is not always best served by exceeding the speed limit, so we have only a stochastic probability of being inconvenienced. There will also be some problems of gathering data that we do not now have (mainly because we have not thought clearly about the problem) and making reasonable estimates of certain parameters. In order to solve the problem, a table of probabilities rather like this is needed.[7]

[7] Note that I am ignoring all consequences of accidents except deaths, and that I am assuming that the speed limit is the only variable. These are, of course, simplifying assumptions introduced in order to make my table simple and the explanation easy. If any attempt were made to explicitly utilize the methods I suggest, much more complex methods would be needed.

TABLE 8-1

SPEED LIMIT	DEATHS PER 100,000,000 CAR MILES	COSTS OF DELAY PER 100,000,000 CAR MILES
10 MPH	1	$50,000,000,000.00
20 MPH	2	35,000,000,000.00
30 MPH	4	22,500,000,000.00
40 MPH	8	15,500,000,000.00
50 MPH	16	5,000,000,000.00
60 MPH	32	2,000,000,000.00
70 MPH	64	500,000,000.00

Obviously with this table, and one more thing, a conversion factor for deaths and delay, we could calculate the speed limit that would optimize the "cost" of using the road. Equally obviously, no direct calculation of this sort is now being undertaken. Our speed limits are, however, set by weighing accident prevention against inconvenience. The only difference between our present methods and the ones I have outlined is that we are so frightened of admitting that we use a conversion ratio in which lives are counted as worth only some finite amount that we refuse to make the computations at a conscious level, and hence deny ourselves the use of modern statistical methods.

Having set a speed limit, we now turn to its enforcement. If, for example, the limit is fifty MPH; it does not then follow that people who drive over that speed will automatically be involved in accidents, nor does it follow that driving at fifty-one MPH is very much more likely to lead to an accident than at fifty MPH. The use of a simple limit law is dictated by the problems of enforcement. If we had some way of charging people for the use of the streets with the amount per mile varying with the speed, this would permit a better adjustment than a simple speed limit.[8] In practice the police and courts do something rather like this by charging much higher fines for people who greatly exceed the speed limit. Let us, however, confine ourselves to the simple case

[8] Needless to say, the cost of driving fifty MPH in a built up area would be higher than in the open countryside.

of a single speed limit. Our method of enforcing this law is in some ways most peculiar. In the first place, if a citizen sees someone violating this law and reports it, the police will normally refuse to do anything about it. With an exception that we turn to in a moment, you cannot be penalized for speeding unless a policeman sees you do it. Think what burglars would give for a similar police practice in their field of endeavor.

A second peculiarity is that the penalty assessed is unconnected with the attitude of mind of the person who violated the speed limit.[9] Driving at seventy miles per hour may get you a fine of $100 or a ten-year sentence depending upon the occurrence of events over which you have no control. Suppose, for example, two drivers: each takes a curve at seventy MPH. The first finds a police car on the other side, gets a ticket, and pays a fine. The second encounters a tractor driving down his side of the road and a column of cars on the other side. In the resulting crash, the tractor driver is killed, and the result may be a ten-year sentence for manslaughter.[10] We can assume both men exceeded the speed limit for the same motives, but the second had bad luck. Normally, we like to have penalties depend upon what the defendant did, and not on circumstances beyond his control.

The peculiarity of this procedure is emphasized when it is remembered that the man sent up for ten years for killing someone in an accident almost certainly had no intent to do so. He was driving at a high speed in order to get somewhere in a hurry, an act that normally leads to a moderate fine when detected. The heavy sentence comes not from the "wickedness" of his act but

[9] For certain special cases, a partial and imperfect exception to this may be made. The man who speeds to get his wife to the hospital before the birth of their child is perhaps the one that gets the most newspaper attention. The general view, however, was well stated by the British Court of Criminal Appeal: "If a driver in fact adopts a manner of driving which the jury thinks was dangerous to other road users . . . then on the issue of guilt it matters not whether he was deliberately reckless, careless, momentarily inattentive or even doing his incompetent best." Regina v. Evans (1963) 1 Q.B. 412, p. 418.

[10] Note that the rule that a traffic offense is prosecuted only if seen by a police officer is not followed in the event of a serious accident. A third driver may be imagined who took the curve at the same speed and met neither the police nor the tractor. He would, of course, go free even if his offense were reported to the police.

from the fact that he drew an unlucky number in a lottery. The situation is even clearer in those cases in which the accident arises not from a conscious violation of the law but from incompetence or emotional stress (losing one's head). In ordinary driving we frequently encounter situations whereby a small error in judgment causes deaths. A man who has no intent to drive carelessly may simply be a bad judge of distance and try to pass a truck when there is insufficient room. An excitable person may "freeze" when an emergency arises with a resulting accident. Both of these cases might well lead to long prison terms in spite of the complete lack of "criminal intent" on the part of the defendant. Our laws, in essence, provide that lack of skill or mental stability may, under certain circumstances, be serious crimes.

As game theory teaches, a mixed strategy may pay off better than a pure strategy. It may be, therefore, that the combination of three different treatments is better than a simpler rule providing a single and fairly heavy penalty for speeding, regardless of whether you hit anyone or happen to encounter a policeman while engaged in the criminal act. Although we must admit this possibility, it seems more likely that a single penalty based on the intent of the individual would work better in preventing speeding. The probable reason for the rather peculiar set of rules I have outlined is simply the incompetence of the court system. If someone who disliked me alleged that he had seen me speeding, and I denied it, the court would have to decide who was lying without much to go on except the expressions on our faces. Since "dishonesty can lie honesty out of continence any day of the week if there is anything to be gained by it," this is clearly an uncertain guide. Under our present court system, permitting individuals to initiate prosecutions for speeding would almost certainly mean that innumerable spite cases would be brought before the courts, and that the courts would make many mistakes in dealing with them.

The use of two sets of penalties for speeding, depending upon factors not under the defendant's control, similarly, is probably the result of judicial inefficiency. The more rational course of a heavy fine or a brief imprisonment for every speeding conviction would very likely not be enforced by judges who do not really think speeding is very serious unless it kills somebody. That this is the restriction cannot strictly be proved, but at least some evidence can be provided for it. In Virginia, as in many states, multiple convictions for traffic offenses can result in the suspension of driving licenses. The state has encountered real difficulty in getting its judges to carry out this provision. Under the conditions of modern life, the deprivation of a driver's license is a real hardship, and judges apparently do not like to impose it for, say a speeding offense, simply because the offender has already been twice convicted. Similarly, the courts are unlikely to inflict a very heavy penalty on the man who drives after his license is suspended if he avoids killing.[11] With more efficient courts, we might be able to make our laws more rational.

It is probable that judicial inefficiency accounts for another peculiarity of the motor traffic code; that it is almost impossible for an individual to defend himself against the accusation of a violation of that code. Normally the police officer's testimony in court is accepted regardless of other evidence. Furthermore, in general, the penalty exacted for a minor violation of the code is small if the defendant does not defend himself, but high if he does. Parking offenses, for example, may commonly be settled for $1 or $2 on a guilty plea, but cost $10 to $20 if you choose to plead not guilty. This amounts to paying the defendant to plead guilty. Most of the people who get tickets are indeed guilty, but those who are not guilty normally plead guilty anyway because of this system of enforcement. A similar procedure is used in connection with other crimes, and since it is of more importance in these other areas, we will defer its discussion.

Obviously, we could apply the same line of reasoning to deal

---

[11] Possibly, given the difficulties of enforcement, a restriction of the license rather than a removal might be wise. Restricting the license of a multiple offender to a limited area, including his home, a couple of shopping centers, and his place of employment, together with a low speed limit, say thirty MPH, might appeal to judges who would be unwilling to remove the license totally. Judges might also be more inclined to give heavy sentences to people who violated such restrictions than to people who continue to drive to work in spite of the lack of a license.

with other parts of the traffic code. The problem is essentially a technological one. By the use of evidence obtained from statistical and other sources, we could compute a complete traffic code that would optimize some objective function. In practice we do not do this because of our reluctance to specify an exchange value for life. Nevertheless, we get much the same result, albeit with less accuracy and precision.

Turning now to the income tax law as a sample of tax laws in general, we must begin by noting that our first assumption does not seem to fit here.[12] Apparently, almost anyone can get special treatment under the income tax law. The laws and regulations are a solid mass of special rules for special groups of people. In apparently innumerable cases some particular wealthy man or large corporation has succeeded in obtaining special tax treatment. Under these circumstances, I can hardly recommend that people favor a tax code that does not have special privileges for themselves. Nevertheless, we can consider how a tax code, once it is set up, should be enforced.

Unfortunately, here again, our first general assumption may not apply. A great many people (special classes that readily come to mind are doctors, waitresses, and farmers) have special facilities for evading the income tax because they are often paid in cash. It is widely believed that these individuals make very good use of their special opportunities. Whether this is true or not, I am certainly not in a position to advise them to refrain from taking advantage of their situation. Furthermore, it is quite widely believed that certain groups (the farmers in particular) have been able to make use of their political power to see to it that the Internal Revenue Service does not devote as many resources to detecting evasion by them as by other groups. Once again, I cannot, on the basis of my present assumptions, recommend that the individual refrain from taking advantage of these opportunities. The tax code contains within it both a set of special privileges for individuals and instructions for evasion that apply only to certain classes. The true tax law is a residual after we have

[12] See J. Randolph Norsworthy, "A Theory of Taxpayer Behaviour: Evasion of the Personal Income Tax" (Ph.D. dissertation, University of Virginia, 1966) for a more exhaustive discussion.

knocked all these holes into what was, in 1912, a rather simple piece of legislation.

There are further difficulties. The individual presumably is interested in the taxes being collected from other people because he wants the government services that will be purchased by them. He would prefer to be left free of tax himself, but this is unfortunately not possible. He, therefore, trades the tax on his own income for the benefits that he obtains from the purchase of government services by the entire community. It is by no means clear that the present amount of governmental services is optimal for everyone. If I believed that the level of governmental services being purchased today was too high (*i.e.,* that lower tax rates and lower levels of service were desirable) I would presumably feel relatively happy about systematic evasion of a tax law on the part of everyone. On the other hand, if I felt that the present level of governmental services was too low and the taxes should be higher, I might conceivably feel that "overenforcement" is desirable.

Even if I were happy with the present level of governmental expenditures, it is by no means obvious that I should favor efficient enforcement of the revenue code. I might favor a revenue code that set rates relatively high combined with an enforcement procedure that permitted a great deal of evasion to lower rates and better enforcement procedures. Surely I would prefer the former if I would be particularly able to evade payment at the higher rates. But even if I assume that everyone will have about the same ability to evade payment (which is, in essence, our first general assumption), I might still prefer the higher rates and higher level of evasion. Nevertheless, it seems to me that most people would prefer the lowest possible level of tax for a given net return. I have been unable to prove that this is optimal, but it does seem to be reasonable that this would be the appropriate social goal.[13] In any event, that is the assumption upon which our further calculations are built. It would be relatively easy to adjust these calculations to any other assumption on this particular matter.

[13] I sincerely hope that some of my readers may be able to repair this admission.

TABLE OF SYMBOLS 8-2

C_p	=	Private cost of enforcement (includes cost of incorrect tax penalties)
C_R	=	Cost of Revenue Protection Service
I	=	Income
I'	=	Some part of income
L_C	=	Likelihood of compliance
L_d	=	Likelihood of detection of evasion
N	=	Social return on tax (excess burden not subtracted)
P	=	Penal rate for detected noncompliers
R	=	Tax rate
T_r	=	Tax Revenue (net of direct enforcement costs)

Under these circumstances and on these assumptions the return in taxation to the government for various levels of enforcement can be seen by Equation (8.1):

$$(8.1) \quad T_r = L_C \cdot R \cdot I + (1 - L_C) \cdot I' \cdot L_d \cdot P - C_R$$

Once again we have a fairly difficult-looking equation that is actually quite simple. The first term is the likelihood that individuals will fully comply with the tax laws multiplied by the tax rate and income. Note that this is deliberately somewhat ambiguous. It could be taken as any individual's tax payments or the payments for the economy as a whole, depending upon which definition we choose for income. We add to this the probability that an individual will attempt to evade payment of taxes on all or part of his income, times the probability of detection, times the penalty he will be compelled to pay on a detected evasion. This gives us the total return that the community will receive. There is, of course, the cost of maintaining the inspection and revenue collection system that is subtracted from this output in the final term C_R.

In Equation (8.2) we see the conditions for an individual's decision as to whether or not he should attempt to evade the tax payment on a particular portion of his income.

$$(8.2) \quad L_d \cdot P \cdot I' < R \cdot I'$$

It indicates that if the likelihood of detection times the penalty he must pay on being detected is less than the standard rate, he would be wise to attempt evasion. It will be noted that both in this inequality and in the previous equation there is an implicit assumption that the individual will be able to pay a fine if he is found to have evaded the tax and that this fine will settle the matter. This is not a bad approximation of the situation in tax law. In other parts of the law, this is normally not true and hence there is a very great difference between tax law and the law of burglary. The reason that the individual is normally able to pay a fine is simply that, in general, in order to get into income tax difficulties you have to be well off. No one plans to have zero assets in order to avoid the necessity of paying income tax fines.

Nevertheless, although this is a very good approximation, it is not entirely accurate. The income tax authorities do sometimes attempt to put people in prison for tax evasion. In general, the Internal Revenue Service has a dual system. If you make a "tax saving" that is relatively easy for them to detect, they will normally "adjust" your return and charge you a relatively modest fine. If, on the other hand, you do something that is quite difficult to detect (normally a directly dishonest rather than a somewhat misleading statement), they assess a much heavier penalty. No doubt this is a sensible way of minimizing enforcement costs.

There is another peculiarity of the income tax policing process. The policeman himself (*i.e.,* the internal revenue man) normally simply assesses a deficiency on the face of the form. This is usually the only legal proceeding. In minor cases the individual normally pays although he may complain. It is highly probable that in this matter, as in other small-claims litigation, there is a great deal of inaccuracy. Since these are small matters, the use of a relatively inaccurate procedure is optimal. For major matters, however, very elaborate legal proceedings may be undertaken. These proceed at first through the administrative channels of the Department of Internal Revenue, and, only if all administrative methods are exhausted, turn to the regular courts.

Returning, however, to our basic equations, it will be noted that the likelihood of quiet compliance (*i.e.,* the likelihood of the

income tax payer making no effort to evade) is a function of the
likelihood of detection of evasion as shown in Equation (8.3).

(8.3) $L_0 = +fL_d$

The likelihood of detection of evasion in turn is a function of
two things as shown in Equation (8.4).

(8.4) $L_d = +f(C_R) + f'(C_p)$

The first of these, of course, is simply the amount of resources
that we put into the revenue service. The second, however, is the
quantity of resources that we force the tax payer to put into keeping records and filling returns and doing other things that make
it easier to enforce the tax. Thus Equation (8.1) is socially in-
complete. Equation (8.5) shows the net social benefit or loss
from the tax including the factor C_p.

(8.5) $N = L_0 \cdot R \cdot I + (1-L_0) \cdot I \cdot L_d \cdot P - C_R - C_p$

It will be noted that these computations ignore the problems of
excess burden.

C_p is an interesting and very comprehensive term. It not only
includes the trouble of filling out the income tax forms but also
the necessity of keeping our accounts in a form such that the Internal Revenue Service may survey them. It includes the possibility that we will be audited even if we have not violated the
law. It does not include any penalty that we might incur if we
have violated the law because that is included under P. It also
includes a number of other things that are somewhat less obvious.
For example, it includes the inconvenience we may occasionally
suffer when the Internal Revenue Service is investigating a potential violation of the internal revenue code by someone other
than ourselves. We might for some reason have some evidence
that the Internal Revenue Service wants and be compelled to
furnish it. It also includes the possibility that the Internal Revenue
Service will wrongly suspect us and will assess an incorrect fine
upon us. Lastly, of course, it includes legal expenses involved in

all of those mentioned. Thus it is by no means a small figure. When we turn to other types of crime, we will find it necessary to divide the equivalent of this figure up into a large number of components, and this will make our analysis much more complex.

Still, under our present circumstances, the problem is relatively easy. We could simply maximize N. An examination of this equation indicates some mildly paradoxical consequences. We could, for example, be in favor of increasing enforcement even though we know it is likely to raise our own payments. It will be noted that nowhere in the equation is the assumption that we will obey the law while others will not. If we really believe that the government's money is being spent for something worthwhile, we then make a gain of some nature from increasing N. It is true that the N in our equation very crudely represents this gain since it takes a total figure rather than a marginal figure, but we need not worry about it. Once again, when we turn to other crimes we will produce more elaborate and more complex equations.

It should be noted that we might feel it desirable to include a risk aversion factor. If the penalty for evasion of the tax is quite large, say twenty-five times the tax that is evaded, and if we feel that there is a fair probability of the Internal Revenue Service's going wrong in assessing such penalties, then our term C_p would be large.

These are refinements, however. Basically, we could calculate an optimum tax enforcement policy from a set of equations such as those given. If the reader considers his own reactions, he will realize that his attitude toward the income tax authorities is based upon something like this reasoning. He does, of course, hope that the income tax authorities will give him special treatment and does his best to obtain it. Insofar as this special treatment has already been taken into account, his behavior would be appropriately described by Equation (8.2). His behavior with respect to general social policy in this period would then be described more or less by a desire to maximize N in Equation (8.5). There may be people who have strong moral feelings about their own payments under the income tax, but I have never run into them.

In this chapter we have discussed two areas of the law with which the reader is likely to have fairly heavy personal experience.

We have demonstrated in both cases that very simple computational tools permit defining an "optimum law." Application of these computational tools would, it is true, require the development of certain empirical information we do not now have, but they are nevertheless suitable guides to further work. In addition, our computational tools in this respect are simply formalizations of the thought processes now used by most people in dealing with these matters. When we turn to other crimes, we will find that somewhat more complex tools are necessary. Nevertheless, the basic line of reasoning will be very similar to that which we have employed in this chapter.

9

Jurisprudence: Some Myths Dispelled

Most Americans feel that the commission of a crime is likely to be followed by imprisonment, that people who are in prison are there as the result of a trial, and that in the United States people are not kept in prison by administrative decisions. These beliefs are mythological. Most crimes are not simply the preliminary to punishment for the criminals, most people who are in prison have not had anything that we would recognize as a trial, and administrative decisions keep people in prison and (in effect) extend their sentence. There are, in fact, a good many people in prison who have actually been put there by an administrative decision. Having said so much, however, I would add that I am by no means convinced that it is undesirable that these myths are false. Chapter 9 is devoted to dissipating a set of myths, but should not be regarded as necessarily critical of our present judicial system. It is not obvious that we would be better off if our judiciary functioned in closer accord with popular mythology.

In order to see how unlikely it will be for crime to be followed by punishment, we need look no further than that high point of establishment opinion, namely, *The Challenge of Crime in a Free Society, A Report by the President's Commission on Law En-*

forcement and the Administration of Justice.[1] As part of this study, the commission undertook some statistical investigations of crime. Although this statistical information is not ideal, it is the best we have.

The first thing to note is that many crimes never even get reported to the police. It is not known how large a percentage of crimes are unreported or at least unrecorded, but the commission hired the National Opinion Research Center to investigate this problem by asking individuals whether they had been victims of crimes. This research design is not ideal, but it should produce reasonably good data. It is a commentary on the state of our law enforcement statistics that such a research project should be needed. According to the results in this survey (which is reproduced herewith as Table 9–1), only about one-half of all serious

TABLE 9-1
Comparison of Survey and UCR Rates
(*Per 100,000 population*)

INDEX CRIMES	NORC SURVEY 1956–1966	UCR RATE FOR INDIVIDUALS 1965	UCR RATE FOR INDIVIDUALS AND ORGANIZATIONS 1965
Willful homicide	3.0	5.1	5.1
Forcible rape	42.5	11.6	11.6
Robbery	94.0	61.4	61.4
Aggravated assault	218.3	106.6	106.6
Burglary	949.1	299.6	605.3
Larceny ($50 and over)	606.5	267.4	393.3
Motor Vehicle theft	206.2	226.0	251.0
Total violence	357.8	184.7	184.7
Total property	1,761.8	793.0	1,249.6

SOURCE: *Uniform Crime Reports for the U. S.*, issued by J. Edgar Hoover, Director, FBI, 1965, pp. 21 and 51. The UCR national totals do not distinguish crimes committed against individuals or households from those committed against businesses or other organizations. The UCR rate for individuals is the published national rate adjusted to eliminate burglaries, larcenies, and vehicle thefts not committed against individuals or households. No adjustment was made for robbery.

[1] *The Challenge of Crime in a Free Society, A Report by the President's Commission on Law Enforcement and the Administration of Justice* (Washington, D.C.: U.S. Government Printing Office, 1967). A large number of task force reports are also available from the Printing Office.

crimes are contained in police statistics (the uniform crime reports); presumably this means that only about one-half of such crimes are even reported to the police. Probably the ones that are not reported are less important on the whole than those that are reported, but it is still clear that a great many serious crimes are not reported.

The flow chart reproduced from the President's Commission Report (Fig. 9–1) shows the outcome of crimes that have been reported to the police. Approximately two and three-quarter million significant crimes were reported in 1965, the base year, which means that at least $5\frac{1}{2}$ million crimes were actually committed, the remainder not being reported. The number of arrests resulting from this $5\frac{1}{2}$ million crimes was 727,000 or about one arrest for every seven crimes. Of the arrested, approximately one-third were juveniles who were removed from the remainder of the flow chart. The number of people under detention after conviction of a crime among adults is 362,000 and among juveniles only 62,000, as shown by Table 9–2. The percentage of juveniles who are actually imprisoned is lower than that of adults. Nevertheless, let us assume the juveniles committed one-third of the crimes and that two-thirds of the crimes committed were committed by adults. With this conservative assumption the imprisonment figures at the right end of the chart are the result of the commission of approximately $3\frac{1}{2}$ million crimes.[2] It will be noted that only 63,000 people were sent directly to prison as a result of these crimes, which works out to about one person sent to prison for every sixty crimes committed. Of course, another 35,000 persons were sent to jail (which means a short sentence), and there was another group of people who received "'unsupervised sentence, fine, etc.," some of whom were fined. The fact remains, however, that the danger of imprisonment if you commit a crime in the United States is quite low.

The statement that crime does not pay is frequently made. Surely the statistics shown offer no supporting evidence for this

[2] The people who were actually sent to prison in 1965 no doubt frequently had committed their crimes in 1964 or even earlier. In the absence of any evidence that there has been a sharp change in the flow through the process; however, the use of the imprisonment and the number of crimes as being directly related will cause no great error.

TABLE 9-2

*Daily Average Number of Inmates in
American Correctional Institutions in 1965*

Institutions primarily for adults:	
Federal prisons	20,377
State prisons	201,220
Local jails and workhouses	141,303
Total	362,900
Institutions primarily for juveniles:	
Public training schools	43,636 [a]
Local juvenile institutions	6,024
Detention homes	13,113
Total	62,772
Grand total	425,673

SOURCES: National Survey of Corrections and U. S. Department
of Justice, Bureau of Prisons, "Statistical Tables, Fiscal Year
1965," pp. 2 and 172.
[a] Includes 1,247 Juvenile and Youthful offenders in Federal Bureau of Prisons institutions.

maxim. Indeed, in the United States, the people who are involved
in what is known as "organized crime" apparently make a very
good thing out of it. The President's Commission Special *Report*
on organized crime makes this clear.[3] Even if we do not concern
ourselves with "the Mafia" and confine ourselves instead to crimes
such as burglary, assault, and robbery, it may well be that the
present discounted value of these crimes is positive. We cannot
be sure that this is true without further data, and it is indicative
of the general level of criminological research that the President's
Crime Commission did not look into the matter.[4]

It is certainly possible that crime is an attractive profession in
the United States for the person who is not much concerned by
moral scruples and who is willing to take rather large risks. This
is particularly likely since the criminals who are captured have a
low average intelligence. The usual explanation for this phenomenon is that criminals are stupid. Actually, the evidence simply in-

[3] *Task Force Report: Organized Crime* (Washington, D.C.: U.S. Government Printing Office, 1967) especially pp. 2–4.
[4] I am engaged in an effort to produce the necessary data.

dicates that criminals who are captured are stupid; they may not be a random sample of the total population of criminals. It is quite possible that an intelligent man entering into this profession could expect a much lower rate of capture and hence would have a much higher payoff on his career than the stupid people who make up the bulk of the population in our penitentiaries. This is, however, only a possibility. The characteristics of criminals who are not caught are unknown, and the characteristics of the criminals who are seldom caught are hard to deduce from our present data. Although we cannot prove it, it would seem probable that one of the major causes of the high crime rate in the United States is the fairly low detection rate that a careful criminal would face. If stealing $1,000 gives you a fifty-fifty chance of going to jail for two years, you are less likely to take up the profession of burglary than if a similar crime gives you a one-in-a-hundred chance of going to jail for two months.

Furthermore, the figures collected by the President's Commission in a sense overstate the likelihood of conviction for the professional criminal. In the first place, surely some of the people who have been convicted are innocent; subtracting these would give a lower probability of being convicted for a person who commits a crime. Secondly, "crimes of passion" make up about 10 percent of the total number of crimes committed in the United States. The conviction rate for such crimes is markedly higher than for crimes calculated for material gain for the simple reason that a crime of passion is normally not committed with any care. Some rather rough manipulation of the uniform crime report data indicates that the conviction rate for crimes of passion must be at least three times as high as that for crimes of calculation.[5] We must, of course, keep in mind that many of the criminals are convicted of more than one crime at a time. Thus a burglar who is caught committing a burglary may be tried for three or four

[5] These data are compiled from the 1962 issue of the *Uniform Crime Reports,* Table 11, p. 87. I reasoned that murder, rape, and aggravated assault would all contain a considerable number of crimes of passion, and the other types of crimes would not. Needless to say, this is far from a definitive calculation, but poor figures are sometimes better than none at all.

burglaries, possibly because some of the loot from the other burglaries was found in his home.

Let us now proceed along the flow chart provided by the President's Commission from the arrest to the trial period (Fig. 9–1). In the first place, it will be noted that the number of cases in which "no complaint is filed or the charge is reduced" is considerably greater than the number in which there is a formal accusation and detention for trial.

Furthermore, there is a small group of persons whose case is dismissed after they have been formally indicted. The decisions here are purely administrative and, considering the number of people involved, perhaps more important than those of the trials themselves. However, few readers will object to the police and the District Attorney having the right to refuse to proceed to trial, when they feel that this is desirable.

When we reach the disposition level, three possibilities are shown: bench trial, jury trial, and guilty plea. It will be noted that "guilty plea" is listed in contrast to "trial." This is correct; there is no trial in these cases. Let us, however, begin by discussing the two forms of trial. About two out of three of the accused who choose to go to trial select a trial by a judge, rather than a trial by jury. This is in spite of the slightly higher likelihood of conviction in the bench trial. The number of accused persons acquitted by judges is about 20 percent of those who choose the bench trial, and the number acquitted in jury trials is about 25 percent. The accused is permitted to choose between a judge trial or a jury trial, and presumably chooses the one that he thinks has the best present discounted value for him.[6]

Approximately 39 percent of the people convicted of serious crimes in the United States are sent to prison, about 22 percent are sent to jail, about 35 percent are given probation, and the remaining 6 percent receive unsupervised sentences. The people who take the risk of a trial and are convicted have a higher probability of going to prison than those who plead guilty. The basic reason for pleading guilty is the promise of a reduced punishment.

[6] See Kalven and Zeisel, *The American Jury,* especially pp. 17–22, for a discussion of the factors that may lead the defendant to choose a judge or a jury.

Criminal Justice System Model Figure 5
with Estimates of Flow of Offenders
and Direct Operating Costs
for Index Crimes in the United States
in 1965.

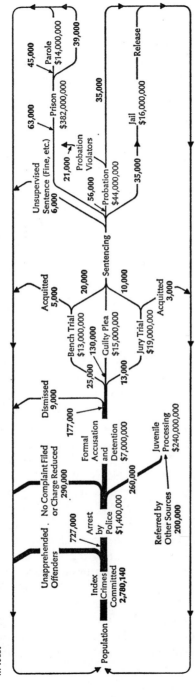

FIGURE 9-1

Number in boldface indicates estimated flow of persons arrested for index crimes.
Numbers in regular type indicate estimated costs incurred at processing stages.

SOURCE: The Challenge of Crime in a Free Society: A Report by the President's
Commission on Law Enforcement and Administration of Justice (Washington:
U.S. Government Printing Office, 1967), pp 262-263.

Thus if you plead guilty you have considerably less than a 39 percent chance of going to prison. In fact, as we shall see in our later discussion of the confession process, the accused normally knows exactly what sentence he will get at the time he makes his plea. Thus if committing crimes in the United States is not a particularly dangerous activity, even confessing to them is not tremendously risky.

The reason for giving a lighter sentence to someone who has confessed than to someone who has been found guilty as a result of a trial is not obvious. The custom, however, is part of the judicial practice in practically every legal system. There seem to be two main reasons for this practice. The first is to spare the state the expense of the trial. Actually, however, the costs of the trial are not very great when compared to the cost that both the state and society undergo when a man is imprisoned, so this would normally not call for a very large reduction in return for a confession. The second, and more important reason for giving a man who confesses a lower sentence is simply to reward confessions. Assume you are accused of a crime. If you go through the trial there is at least some chance that you will be acquitted. It is true that you will have to undergo the cost of the trial, and in the case of a wealthy man, this may be a large cost, but it probably would pay you to do so unless the evidence is extraordinarily strong. Trials sometimes have the most unlikely outcomes. If you confess, you are certain to be punished. If you do not confess, you have a finite chance of getting off. If the punishment will be the same whether you confess or not, confession would be irrational.

Let us turn to the way in which confessions are normally obtained. For this purpose, let us re-examine the figure showing the amount of evidence and degree of likelihood of guilt that we used in the chapter on contracts. There the likelihood that the plaintiff should prevail was shown on the vertical axis; in this case the vertical axis shows the likelihood that the accused is guilty. Again, the amount of evidence is shown on the horizontal axis. In criminal cases, we deliberately introduce an element of bias. The reasons for this bias and a discussion of its probable rationality are deferred to another chapter. For the time being, let us accept the fact that bias does exist. Thus the decision line has been drawn on the diagram not to minimize total errors, but to reduce the number of errors that involve convictions of people who should not be convicted. It is not possible, short of refusing to convict anyone, to completely eliminate convictions of innocent people, but we can make the erroneous findings of innocence more common than

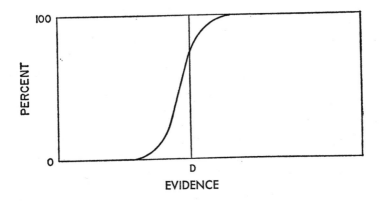

FIGURE 9–2 Evidence and Outcome in a Criminal Proceeding

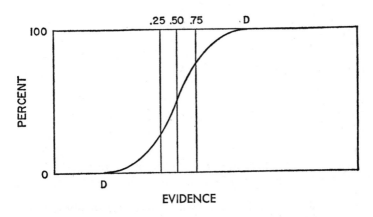

FIGURE 9–3 Negotiated Pleas in Criminal Proceedings

the erroneous conviction of an innocent person. The line D, which shows the amount of evidence necessary for conviction has been drawn in Figure 9–2 to introduce this type of bias.

Figure 9–2 looks at the matter from a standpoint of whoever is to make the ultimate decision, the judge or the jury. Figure 9–3 shows the same problem from a standpoint of an attorney considering the situation before a trial. He is unable to perfectly forecast the behavior of the judge or jury and from his standpoint, therefore, their behavior is not shown by a vertical line, but by another S curve such as D in Figure 9–3. Note that D on Figure 9–2 and D on Figure 9–3 are really the same thing, from different points of view. In both cases, they represent the behavior of the judge and/or the jury.

The skilled attorney confronting this line makes estimates of the likelihood of conviction of his client in terms of the evidence. I have drawn in three such likelihoods as three vertical lines, one showing a three-quarter probability of conviction, one showing an even probability of conviction, and one showing a one-quarter probability of conviction. If the probable sentence after trial and conviction is ten years, and the defense attorney feels that his client has a three-quarter chance of conviction, the defense attorney would be willing to make a deal with the prosecuting attorney for a confession in return for a reduction in the length of sentence that exceeds one-quarter.[7]

The district attorney may be delighted to make such an arrangement. The district attorney does not have sufficient staff to make it possible for him to try all cases. This, of course, is known to the defense attorney. Again, the district attorney normally wants to have a high conviction rate on those cases that he does try. Frank Hogan of New York, for example, is very displeased if any case is brought to trial without a conviction.[8] As a predictable consequence, his assistants would be willing to make deals with defense attorneys in which very substantial reductions in sentences are exchanged for confessions. Most cases in New York are handled by confession. The federal courts are another

[7] In practice the decision as to what sentence properly discounts a risk of three-quarters or one-half is a little difficult because the sentence will occur in the future. Therefore, it is necessary to use a rather complex discounting formula to reach an accurate present value. I have not done so here mainly for simplicity, but it is likely that my desire for simplicity in this case parallels that of the attorneys making the decision.

[8] Martin Mayer, "Hogan's Office is a Kind of Ministry of Justice," *New York Times Magazine*, 23 July 1967, p. 7.

area in which a high percentage of cases are handled by confession; as a matter of fact, 90 percent. In courts in which a very high percentage of the cases are handled by confession, one can feel fairly confident that the prosecutor is offering quite favorable terms to the defense attorneys.

TABLE OF SYMBOLS 9–3

C_c	=	Court costs
C_l	=	Cost of Lying
D_c	=	Disgrace resulting from confession
D_t	=	Disgrace resulting from conviction at trial
E	=	Evidence
L_c	=	Likelihood of conviction
P_c	=	Punishment resulting from confession
P_t	=	Punishment resulting from conviction at trial
P_u	=	Publicity case has received (if high, prosecutor may have to proceed despite high Q_d)
Q_d	=	Quality of defense
Q_j	=	Quality of trial system
R	=	Risk aversion factor
R'	=	Prosecutor's aversion to low conviction ratio

Let us once again turn to high school algebra in order to put the matter more precisely. The conditions for confession are shown by inequalities 1 and 2, respectively, for the guilty individual and the innocent individual. Once again, these equations are somewhat formidably appearing but are actually very simple.

$$(9.1) \qquad R \cdot L_c(P_t + D_t) + C_c + C_l > P_c + D_c$$
$$(9.2) \qquad R \cdot L_c(P_t + D_t) + C_c > P_c + D_c + C_l$$

In each case the costs of standing trial are on the left side of the inequality and the costs of confession on the right. The inequalities are, with the exception of one factor, identical. Basically, the punishment that is likely to result from conviction at a trial added to the disgrace that results from conviction at trial is multiplied by the likelihood of such conviction and risk factor. To this is added the court costs. On the right side we find the punishment that would result from a confession and the disgrace that would result from a confession. Another item that may or may not be of any significance is the cost of lying, which simply represents the fact that some people at least dislike lying and, therefore, will take this dislike into account. For the guilty person, the cost of lying is on the left side of the inequality because he lies by saying that he is not guilty; for the innocent person it is on the right because he lies by pleading guilty.

The cost of lying might seem a way of sneaking ethics in through the back door in this equation. My impression is that it would be a rather small factor for most defendants in a serious criminal case. In any event, I should like to defer further discussion of this factor until later. It is, of course, clear that the difference between P_t and P_c is the control variable available to the prosecutor. He has no control over the individual person's risk preference and very little control over L_c, so if he wishes to induce confessions he must offer a punishment after confession that is sufficiently less than the punishment if there were a trial and conviction to counter balance $L_c \cdot R$. If he makes such an offer, then the defendant should accept.

The conditions for the prosecutor are shown in Equation (9.3). Note the risk premium.

Prosecutor

(9.3)
$$R' \cdot L_c P_t - C_c > P_c$$
$$L_c = f(E, Q_d, Q_j)$$
$$R' = -f(P_u)$$

This risk premium is rather unusual in form, in fact it might better be called "loss aversion." The prosecutor, of course, has many cases and is not unduly concerned with any one of them. He is, however, interested in maintaining a fairly high level of convictions. As we have noted, the prosecutors, in fact, obtain convictions in three-quarters or more of the cases they try. What the prosecutor has, therefore, strictly speaking, is not a risk aversion factor but a desire to have a certain percentage of convictions. This means that he is unlikely to go to trial unless L_c is at least .75. The defendants know this and take it into account. Thus the R' that shows risk aversion actually varies with different values of L_c. Otherwise the equation is fairly simple. It points out that if the likelihood of conviction times punishment minus the court costs is less than the punishment to be given if confession is obtained, then the prosecutor would be willing to accept the confession. The principal difference between this equation and that of the defendant is the switch of the court costs from one side to the other, together with the disgrace factor in the defendant's calculus.

This desire on the part of the prosecuting attorney to have a good record of convictions plays an interesting role. On the whole it means that, unless the evidence against the defendant is quite good, he will not be prosecuted. In the mythology there is a great deal of talk about the court procedure itself being biased in the direction of the defendant. There seems to be little if any empirical evidence that our procedure is in fact so biased. There are a few parts of the rules of evidence and a few parts of our procedural rules that might give the defendant an advantage. In general, however, our procedural rules and the laws of evidence are about as much of a handicap to the defendant as they are to the prosecutor. It may be that the verbal formula of "reasonable doubt" is in itself a protection for the accused. It would be interesting to have empirical evidence on this point.

Whatever one can say about the bias of the trial procedure, toward or against the defendant, it is clear that the prosecutor's desire to have a good percentage of the cases he tries end in convictions leads to some protection of those defendants against whom the evidence is weak. Assuming that the courts have no bias at all and do not give the defendant the benefit of the doubt, the prosecutor as we have noted only undertakes those cases in which he feels he has at least a three out of four chance of conviction so that many people against whom the evidence is relatively weak would not even be tried. Note that if this attitude on the part of the prosecutor is combined with a similar bias on the part of the court, it might make a very great amount of evidence necessary for conviction. It should also be noted, however, that if the courts happen to be biased against the accused, then this practice on the part of the prosecutor would not necessarily mean that only those against whom the evidence was overwhelming were convicted.

As we have noted, most judicial systems arrange a reward for the person who confesses; he is normally given a lighter sentence than the person who does not confess. If I feel that I have about an 80 percent likelihood of conviction if I stand trial, and there is a provision in the law that says that any person who confesses is given a sentence 75 percent of the sentence of the person who is convicted after a trial, I would be wise to confess. From the standpoint of the government, this proposal provides some saving, i.e., the saving involved in not holding a trial, and little loss. Out of a collection of trials they would end up with only a slightly smaller number of years of imprisonment imposed on the people tried than they would have had if they had gone to trial in each case. If they are trying to prevent the commission of crimes by making the present discount value of the crime negative, a high probability of a somewhat low sentence is as good as a low probability of a high sentence.

In discussing confession, I have said nothing about the guilt or innocence of the accused. There is no real reason why this should have any major bearing on the matter. A person who feels that the evidence is such that he has a certain probability of conviction will, if he is rational, confess if he is given a suitable reduction in sentence. If he is a typical middle-class American, it may be that the disgrace of confessing to a crime is so great that the reduction would have to be extremely large in order to overcome it. In talking to various middle-class people, I have found that they say that no one who is innocent would confess to a crime, regardless of what he was paid for doing so. I suspect this reflects naïveté. In any event, most people who are accused of crimes are very decidedly lower-class people, who frequently have already been found guilty of committing another crime. In general there is no reason to believe that they have an extreme aversion to confessing to a crime they did not commit.

In this connection, I found it rather interesting that most of my friends were unwilling to discuss whether they would confess a crime of which they were guilty. Nevertheless, they are, in essence, alleging that human beings are so constituted that they will confess to crimes of which they are guilty and not confess crimes of which they are innocent. Although I think they exaggerate its importance, there can be no doubt that some such tendency exists.

It is surely so that most guilty persons will have at least a little less reluctance to confess than innocent persons. How large this difference is will, of course, vary greatly from person to person and according to circumstances. Basically, however, the reason for confession is that the evidence seems to indicate that you are better off if you confess than if you don't. Whether you are guilty or not is in most cases of less importance, unless the calculation of other factors is very close.

One of the interesting characteristics of the literature on negotiated pleas is the lack of an open and thorough discussion of the likelihood that innocent defendants may find it wiser to plead guilty. The only direct discussion of the matter that I have been able to find, and it is a very brief one, is provided in the Appendix A to the Task Force *Report on the Courts* of the President's Commission on Law Enforcement and Administration of Justice.[9] This contains the single sentence, "Even counsel may see the occasional practical wisdom of pleading an innocent man guilty." [10] There follows a short and inconclusive discussion. Indirectly, the same subject is dealt with in a number of places including the President's Commission's report itself, the Task Force's *Report on the Courts,* and Donald J. Newman's book, *Conviction.*[11] In all of these sources, however, instead of discussing the possibility that an innocent defendant may be led to plead guilty, the point discussed is the desirability of minor precautions.

These precautions, which are normally suggested as reforms rather than as descriptions of actual practice, are usually limited to an investigation by the judge to find out whether or not there is a *prima facie* case against the defendant. This avoids the main issue. Unless there is fairly good evidence against the defendant, he is unlikely to plead guilty. The plea bargaining process should normally eliminate people against whom there is no prima facie case. It would seem certain, however, that some innocent persons confess because it is the best alternative available to them.

There is, furthermore, no obvious reason why we should find

[9] Arnold, Anchor, "Perspectives on Plea Bargaining."
[10] *Ibid.,* p. 114.
[11] Donald J. Newman, *Conviction* (Boston: Little, Brown and Company, 1966).

TABLE 9–4
Negotiate Guilty Pleas

STATE (1964 STATISTICS UNLESS OTHERWISE INDICATED)	TOTAL CONVICTIONS	GUILTY PLEAS	
		NUMBER	PERCENT OF TOTAL
California (1965)	30,840	22,317	74.0
Connecticut	1,596	1,494	93.9
District of Columbia (year ending June 30, 1964)	1,115	817	73.3
Hawaii	393	360	91.5
Illinois	5,591	4,768	85.2
Kansas	3,025	2,727	90.2
Massachusetts (1963)	7,790	6,642	85.2
Minnesota (1965)	1,567	1,437	91.7
New York	17,249	16,464	95.5
Pennsylvania (1960)	25,632	17,108	66.8
U.S. District Courts	29,170	26,273	90.2
Average (excluding Pennsylvania) [a]			87.0

SOURCE: The President's Commission on Law Enforcement and Administration of Justice, *Task Force Report: The Courts* (Washington, D.C., U.S. Government Printing Office), p. 9.
[a] The Pennsylvania figures have been excluded from the average because they were from an earlier year, and the types of cases included did not appear fully comparable with the others.

this undesirable. People would only confess to a crime of which they are innocent if the evidence against them is strong enough so that they feel there is a reasonable probability of conviction. The sentence to be given to them in return for their confession would be appropriately discounted in terms of the evidence against them. Thus if all innocent persons chose to go to trial rather than to confess, one would anticipate that the erroneous outcomes of the trials would lead to about as many net years of imprisonment among these innocent persons as would the plea bargaining process. The distribution of prison sentences would of course be different.

There is, however, one aspect of the present plea-bargaining process that is decidedly objectionable. It is, in general, necessary to go through a little ceremony in which everyone concerned denies that negotiations have taken place and maintains that the plea of guilty is not the result of a threat or promise.[12] This hypocritical ceremony should be abolished, and the agreement between the prosecuting attorney and the defendant's counsel should be treated in exactly the same way as any other out-of-court settlement. Judicial supervision here is not more important than it is in a large automobile damage suit.

Thus far, I have been discussing the plea-bargaining process in what one might call a Utopian manner. In actual practice, it is unlikely that either the defendant or the prosecuting attorney would engage in such subtle calculations as we have described. As Herbert J. Simon is fond of pointing out, when you have a complicated problem, the usual human reaction is to resort to simple rules of thumb. We do have complex cases. The case cited by Jerome H. Skolnick in *Justice Without Trial* in which two burglars who had committed (between them) at least 500 burglaries got off with almost no sentence at all, is an extreme case, but good bargaining can lead to very great gains on the part of the defendant.[13]

Normally, however, we find a rather rough system under which precise and difficult calculations are not made.[14] Still this rather rough set of rules of thumb approximates our sophisticated calculations. Once again, I would reiterate that I am not criticizing the institutions described. I am simply pointing out that what happens is not what the common man thinks happens. The procedure merely means that different people who are convicted of the same crime receive different sentences depending upon the strength of the evidence. A person against whom the evidence is weak may receive, not a discharge, but a light sentence. If there were no negotiated confessions, he would get a trial at which he

[12] See the President's Commission's Report on Law Enforcement and Administration of Justice, *Task Force Report: The Courts* (Washington, D.C.: U.S. Government Printing Office), p. 9.

[13] Jerome H. Skolnick, *Justice Without Trial* (New York: John Wiley & Sons, Inc., 1966), p. 178. It may be argued that I have oversimplified this case, in which other factors were involved. The reader is referred to the actual text of Skolnick's book for a more complete description of the matter.

[14] This rather rough system is described in considerable detail in Donald J. Newman, *Conviction*.

would have a small chance of getting a heavy sentence and a large chance of getting no sentence at all. Since he has a voluntary choice of going to trial, presumably he prefers the confession, but there is no reason why we should object. We can, after all, simply raise the average sentence a little bit.

The principal argument against the negotiated confession would seem to be that the attorneys are not likely to be quite as well informed about the evidence at the time they engage in negotiations as the judge and jury would be after the trial. Things do come out at the trial, and time does indeed sometimes bring out new evidence. Furthermore, the two attorneys are unlikely to be completely candid with each other. Basically each will try to convince the other that he has more evidence than he really does, and each will discount his opponent's statements, whether appropriately or not. Furthermore, in some cases one attorney or the other will prefer to withhold evidence until the trial rather than mention it to his opponent. Also, the principal purpose of the negotiating process looked at from the standpoint of the attorneys is the saving of time, and therefore *ipso facto* they spend less time on negotiating than they would on the trial itself. For all of these reasons the negotiation of confessions probably introduces a certain amount of random noise into the judicial process. It is not obvious, however, that this is undesirable. It also reduces the social resources invested in trials and this may balance the random errors introduced.

Let us now consider the administrative routes to prison. We begin with the fact that both the police and the district attorney have administrative discretion as to whether or not to proceed with the case. The police must first investigate the crime and decide who they think is guilty; they are privileged to stop at any time if they think their resources could be better invested elsewhere. The district attorney furthermore can then refuse to proceed with the case.[15] Most people would agree that these two types of administrative discretion are completely acceptable. As a result of this discretion, there is, as previously pointed out, an in-

[15] In Newburgh, New York, this type of discretion has substantially abolished the law against simple assault. See James Q. Wilson, *The Varieties of Police Behavior* (Cambridge, Mass.: Harvard University Press, 1968), p. 136.

teresting modification of our traditional criminal law in most jurisdictions. It is not constitutionally possible to compel the defendant to take a lie detector test or even to ask him to take a lie detector test and then use his refusal against him on trial. A great many jurisdictions, however, routinely give the defendant a lie detector test. If he passes it, he is released in most cases. An example of this may be taken from New York City, where the district attorney's office as a regular routine permits any defendant to take a lie detector test, and if the lie detector test is in his favor normally drops prosecution.[16]

As a bit of administrative discretion, this procedure is not open to criticism (although it should be noted that it is not the best way of making use of the lie detector). Nevertheless, the fact that it is done and that all the judges and a certain number of jurymen know that it is done means that a defendant facing trial is normally believed by those people who make the ultimate decision for or against him either to have flunked a lie detector test or to have failed to take this opportunity to clear himself. Thus in practice the lie detector has been brought into our procedure although it is not mentioned in court.

It will be noticed in the chart in the President's Commission report that of the people who are convicted of crimes, 56,000 are put on probation and of these, 21,000 are eventually sent to prison for violation of their probation. The process of sending someone to prison for a violation of probation is essentially an administrative one. The probation officer usually makes the decision. He normally has to make a routine report to the judge and the defendant may find it possible to protest, but in practice the probation officer's decision is final. Thus 21,000 people a year are sent to prison by essentially administrative decisions, usually for rather minor matters. Most probation violations involve something that is not a crime—changing one's address, for example. Furthermore, it seems in some cases that the "probation violation" is in fact an accusation of another crime. Smith is found guilty of robbery and placed on probation, but two months later his probation officer sends him to prison, and the probation violation is an al-

16 Martin Mayer, "Hogan's Office."

leged second robbery—a robbery for which he is never given any formal trial. But again there is no reason to believe that this is improper; it is simply different from the myth.

In fact, the probation official and his administrative discretion are important in the actual sentencing of a man who has been convicted by a genuine trial. The President's Commission recommends that the probation report be made use of for, in essence, convicting people for a newly invented crime.[17] If their recommendation is carried out, a person who is reported by the probation officer to be a member of the administrative hierarchy of the Mafia will receive a very severe penalty. The decision as to whether he is a senior member of the Mafia will be made by the judge in chambers as a result of a confidential report by the probation officer. Clearly this is administrative justice with a vengeance.[18]

In the prison itself administrative justice has always been an ordinary part of administration. Today there is a "good-time" system, under which a prisoner who does not cause significant difficulty for the prison administration is given a reduction in his sentence. Normally this is one day off his sentence for every four days in which he behaves himself. If he never gets into trouble, he will get off with a 20 percent reduction in his sentence. If he gets into trouble, the "good time" that he had accumulated before will be lost to him and he must begin accumulating again. The decision as to whether he will receive "good time" or not is entirely an administrative matter for the prison authorities.

We see here an example of word magic. If the law provided that the guards might add 25 percent to the sentence of any prisoner who they thought was not behaving himself, there would be a terrible scandal. Giving them the power to cut 20 percent off the sentence, mathematically the same thing, however, does not seem to be a matter of much note. In actual practice, of course, the two are identical. Most sentences are given by judges who are aware of this custom, and surely if the law were changed to permit

[17] *The Challenge of Crime in a Free Society, A Report by the President's Commission*, p. 203.
[18] *The Washington Post* has recently been urging the denial of bail to some accused if the judge thinks that they are dangerous.

25 percent addition to sentences instead of 20 percent reduction, they would reduce their sentences accordingly. The only difference between the present law that permits a reduction in sentences and a law that permitted guards to increase the sentence is in the form of words used. It is a telling indication of the importance of word magic that no one, insofar as I know, has ever complained about the present system.

The use of the "good-time" system by prison administrators and the absence of any objection to it on the part of prison "reformers" also indicates that the people who are in prison can be influenced in their behavior by the traditional techniques of the carrot and the stick. This seems obvious, but unfortunately a great many of the specialists in criminology deny that criminals are deterred by punishment. Why they think that a man's decision to rob a bank is not influenced by the penalty that he will receive for doing so, but that his decision as to whether or not to join a prison riot will be, is something that I do not understand. Furthermore, in my cautious interrogation of criminologists upon the point I have never received a coherent explanation.

The carrot and stick technique is used to keep prisons orderly in another way. Most prisons have disciplinary arrangements under which prisoners who have in some way transgressed the rules, or who are at least thought to have done so by the guards, are administratively confined in much more stringent and strict conditions. In a sense, they are moved to a special prison called "solitary," which is as much more unpleasant than the regular prison as the regular prison is than outside life. Again this imposition of a very considerable punishment on prisoners by administrative orders does not seem to cause any concern among reform groups.

In any event, many prisoners at any given time are in prison because the guards have taken away their "good time" by administrative decree. Another administrative board capable of doing the same thing is the parole board. Here, again, we have a case in which word magic is important. A provision that a board could triple the sentence would surely cause great indignation. The present situation in which it can slash the sentence to one-third does not cause any indignation. Substantially, the two are identical. The judge in deciding on the sentence takes into con-

sideration the fact that the convict is only certain to serve the first
third of it, and that whether he serves the remaining two-thirds
depends upon the discretion of an administrative board.

Under present circumstances, if the judge sentences a man to
prison for six years, he feels that he should be kept in prison two
years and perhaps four years more at the discretion of a board.[19]
If there was a board that was permitted to triple sentences, the
judge would probably give a two-year sentence. The additional
sentence that a prisoner may receive by annoying the parole board
or, for that matter, simply making it administratively difficult for
them to parole him, is very large. As a general rule, such minor
matters as the ambition and work habits of members of the parole
board have considerable effect on the period of time a prisoner
spends in prison. Thus, again, we have an administrative body
determining whether or not people will be in prison. Furthermore,
once a man is paroled he can be sent back to prison again by a
purely administrative decision, normally by his parole officer.

Altogether, although there do not seem to be any statistics on
the point, it seems fairly certain that at least two-thirds, and perhaps three-quarters, of all prisoners in the United States at any
given time are in prison because a parole board, a guard, or a probation officer decided that they should be. In all cases, of course,
they have appeared at some time before a judge, mostly to register
a guilty plea. Nevertheless, the relevant decision, the decision that
keeps them in prison, is an administrative one.

A final feature of the parole process must be mentioned. Parole
boards are more likely to release people who (they feel) have
repented of their crimes. This a natural consequence of their
efforts to determine whether or not prospective parolees are likely
to commit further crimes. Quite naturally, the parole board does
not feel that people have repented of their crime unless they say
that they have. They are, in fact, very dubious of the repentance
even when it is expressed.

This puts the innocent man who has been convicted after a
trial in a difficult position. It is not absolutely certain that he will
not receive a parole if he does not confess to his crime and ex-

---

[19] I am here ignoring "good time."

press repentance, but the odds are against it. In consequence, a large percentage of prisoners who are convicted through regular trials later confess in order to obtain a parole. This makes it very difficult to measure the accuracy of our judicial process. A confession sends about 90 percent of all federal prisoners to prison. Of the 10 percent who don't confess before they go to prison, the great majority confess in order to obtain a parole. In all cases they are being paid very heavily in the form of sentence remission to confess, and, therefore, their confessions are suspect.

This is merely a statement that the present system makes life difficult for researchers, not that it is a bad system in itself. To repeat a statement that I made at the beginning of this chapter, its point has been to dispel certain myths that are widely held. This chapter is not intended to criticize our present judicial institutions. I do not know whether the institutions that I have been discussing are desirable or undesirable. The fact that they do not operate in accord with publicly held myths is no evidence one way or the other. There is no reason why we should regard ill-informed popular opinion or the views of men who about 200 years ago adopted our present judicial procedures as scientific evidence. If I do not criticize the system, however, at least the reader should realize what it is. Our discussion of the law should not be based upon myth nor should we confine ourselves to pointing out that reality does not fit the myth and from that fact arguing that reality should be changed. Perhaps it is the myth that should be changed.

10

Jurisprudence: Some General Problems

Chapter 9 was devoted to dissipating certain myths about our criminal procedure. This chapter is devoted to a discussion of certain truths that almost everyone already knows but that for some reason are not mentioned in most books on law. The first of these truths, that which we normally call the "criminal law," is only a small and arbitrarily selected segment of the total activity of the state in repressing criminal activity. Whether justice is done in some particular case may be as much or even more affected by how many detectives are assigned to that case as by what happens in court. Inadequate investigation may lead to very serious mistakes in the judicial proceedings.

Furthermore, if we look over the world in general, we observe that the very rigid Anglo-Saxon distinction between the court and the preliminary proceedings that lead to a person's being brought into court is not widely copied. In many countries the court and the police force are melded into one organizational body. This was true in the early days of the Communist regime in Russia and it is true of the present Communist regime in China, although the matter is somewhat disguised, and at the bottom level—the traffic court—it is true in the United States. As a general rule people accused of traffic offenses never have any contact with anyone except employees of the Police Department or, in a few cases, of the Revenue Department, which collects on the tickets.

In fact, if we look around the world we frequently find a melding of police and judicial activities in which the judicial power is the superior of the police power. In the Old West, the District Judge was in essence the Chief of Police. He had supervisory control over the United States Marshalls who were the principal police force of the area. Arrangements of this sort are not uncommon. It was the early system from which the modern English police force developed. In addition, the continental institution of *Juge de l'Instruction* is similar. It is a matter of definition whether this official is a policeman or part of the judiciary. The entire tradition of Mohammedan law is based upon a mixture of administrative and judicial activities in the same person. Under the old system in China the magistrate was simultaneously the chief judge in his own court, the chief of police, and the prosecuting attorney.

In the United States we normally have different personnel sitting as judges in trials and engaging in bringing the person to trial. I am not criticizing this custom, but I would point out that much that is of importance occurs at the pretrial level. Viewed from the standpoint of a criminal, the government must surmount a set of hurdles if he is to be convicted. First, the police must decide that he committed the crime and arrest him. The police fail to do this, as we have seen, in 90 percent of all crimes. Second, the district attorney must decide that he should stand trial. Third, the judge or the jury must convict him. And finally, if he decides to appeal, the conviction must be upheld on appeal. Failure of process for suppression may occur at any one of these four levels. It is just as much of a failure if the police fail to discover who committed a crime as if the Supreme Court of the United States releases a criminal. The only difference is that the police failures receive less publicity. Still it is at the police level that the largest opportunities for improvement now exist. If the police could double their detection level, this would have a much greater effect upon our total crime rate than would almost any change in the judiciary. If we assume (and I see no reason not to assume it) that the percentage of criminals convicted would not change, then the probability of a prison sentence for a criminal would almost double.

This is, however, largely a matter of administration and technique in the police area. I have very little to say about this except that I believe that there are prospects for very great progress in this area. The government has gravely underinvested in criminological research. Furthermore, it has refused for various reasons to make use of more efficient techniques in many areas. Changes in these matters would not be dramatic and might not appear to be policy decisions. Nevertheless, they could work a very great improvement in the way we treat criminals and, for that matter, the way we treat innocent persons who are suspected of crimes.

Proceeding forward from police activity, a person who has been arrested by the police is normally held pending trial or released on bail. In their present form both of these practices date back to the Middle Ages, and it seems to me that drastic reform is desirable. Let us consider first a man who, for one reason or another, cannot post bail. He is in prison sometimes for very long periods of time awaiting trial. Clearly this is hard on a man who has not been found guilty of any crime. The reason for holding him is that he might run away. As I hope to demonstrate in a moment, this is not necessarily an insoluble problem, but let us temporarily assume that there is a good reason for holding the person in prison. No doubt there would be at least some persons who would have to be held in prison awaiting trial.

The question then arises, if the federal government or the state government needs to keep the person in prison, why does it not compensate him for his time? The only argument I can see against this is simply tradition. In the late Middle Ages, a person who was in prison not only was not paid but he had to pay the jailer for his food. If he were later found innocent, he could not be released until he paid these bills. We have abandoned this barbarous practice, but we have retained the equally barbarous practic of keeping him in jail without compensation. Assume that it is necessary for the enforcement of criminal law to keep a certain number of people under detention for varying periods of time before trial. If we do not compensate them, we are placing a special tax upon them, and there seems to be no reason why such a special tax is desirable.

Paying a person who is in prison awaiting trial the fair value of his services, together with a reasonable amount for the general inconvenience of living in an uncomfortable jail, would be a considerable improvement in what Aristotle called distributive equity.[1] Furthermore, from the standpoint of most of us, the prospect of having to pay slightly higher taxes if we are not accused of the commission of a crime in return for a guarantee that if we are so accused we will be fully compensated for our time spent in a cell awaiting trial would appear a good bargain. There is, however, another advantage in requiring the police to pay people awaiting trial the opportunity cost of their imprisonment. It would lead to a very great administrative interest in methods of reducing the number of people so imprisoned, and the amount of time that they are imprisoned.[2] If we assume that the police and other administrative authorities are interested in reducing the amount of time that people spend in prison awaiting trial, these techniques are not hard to find. Bail is an old and almost barbarous technique, but there is no reason why a simple modification of the law should not permit most accused to be freed to await trial without having to post bail. If failing to appear for trial, after having been formally informed of the trial date, is made a serious crime, it is reasonably certain that very few people would fail to turn up.[3]

There are many other areas in which what are regarded as difficult constitutional problems could quite easily be settled by simply paying people for things that we now take from them by force. As an example, consider the present-day search procedure in the United States. The police may not enter upon my property in order to search it without first having obtained a warrant from

[1] If the prisoners were paid a fee that included the inconvenience of living in a jail, one could assume that jails would very rapidly be improved so that this inconvenience (and the fee) was reduced.

[2] It should be noted that *some* people are in prison more or less voluntarily. For various reasons they are deliberately delaying their trial. There is no obvious reason why people who are imprisoned under these circumstances should be compensated.

[3] Arrangements would have to be made to prevent defendants from avoiding being formally informed.

the magistrate. Exactly why this is supposed to do me very much good if my property is searched is unclear. The police, in practice, normally evade these requirements in any event.[4]

If we substituted for this a law providing that the police may at their discretion search any person's property, subject, however, to putting everything back in the same order they found it before they began the search and paying a reasonable fee for the intrusion, I would predict that the entire problem would vanish. In fact, I would predict that a number of people would attempt to get the police to search their property because it would be a convenient way of obtaining a little extra cash. Noncriminals in general are somewhat put out by having their property searched but not enough that a rather small fee would not completely assuage the hurt.

The present situation is quite to the contrary. The police search and are not required to put things back the way they were found, although frequently out of good manners they will do so, and do not make compensation for their searches. An extreme example may be found in the case of the three civil-rights workers who were murdered in Mississippi. The FBI obtained information as to where the bodies were buried by the payment of approximately $30,000 to an informer. They then went to a dam that was being built by a private person on his property and destroyed it in the process of searching for the bodies buried in it. Suppose, however, they had with their perfectly valid search warrant destroyed the dam looking for the bodies and not found them. Under our present law, they would be under no obligation to restore the dam to its previous condition. Clearly this is not a desirable state of affairs. Our law on this matter is largely held over from a previous and barbarous state in England in the late Middle Ages, a time when most governments were impecunious and harsh, and the English government was more impecunious and harsh than most. The restraints put upon the king were perhaps rational, granted the nature of the Royal Government at that time, but they are quite irrational under modern circumstances.

[4] Their methods are numerous and complicated. See Tiffany, McIntyre, and Rottenburg, *Detection of Crime* (Boston: Little, Brown and Company, 1967), pp. 99–207.

We can think of further areas, many of them in fact, in which the present system of permitting the police to do something or prohibiting them from doing it should rationally be replaced by simply requiring them to pay for doing it. In some cases this is very difficult. Suppose, for example, the police become curious about me and arrange to have me followed by a man who (whenever possible) sneaks up close to me and listens to my conversation. This is perfectly legal in the United States today. It would be very hard to arrange a system of payments for me for the inconvenience that this may or then again may not cause me, because obviously the police do not want me to know it is happening. It nevertheless might be possible, even in this case for the police to make suitable payments after the event. This same rule might be applied to such things as telephone tapping and bugging. Once again, if a rule providing for reasonable payments were made, I suspect the real problem would not be a police desire to spend large parts of their budget on unnecessary and undesirable searches, seizures, and wire tappings, but a desire on the part of the private citizens to get themselves searched, bugged, or wire tapped in order to obtain these fees.

Payment as part of police activities is what is normally meant by "scientific police methods" in English discussions. The Bow Street runners when they first brought "scientific methods" to England actually depended very largely on simple straightforward payments of money for evidence. This is still the English tradition, although it is perhaps disappearing now. In the United States, we have been very reluctant to use this system, even though as I mentioned before the FBI has purchased information at a very high price upon various occasions. Our courts have tended to feel that purchased testimony is unreliable, and there is much to be said for this point of view. It certainly is true, however, that purchased information that is confirmable is desirable information. The case of the location of the civil-rights workers' bodies is a good example. The money was paid, and the bodies were then found. If the bodies had not been found, clearly no innocent person could have been convicted.

Unfortunately, in the United States the fact that we restrict payments for evidence, or other information, has lead to the use of "stool pigeons" that in many ways is much worse. Under this system, various minor criminals are given a "license" to continue their minor criminal activities providing only that they inform police officers of the minor criminal activities of other people.[5] This system in many ways combines the worst of both worlds. The information obtained is paid for, and the method of payment protects some people engaged in the commission of minor crimes. Switching to a system of direct monetary payments would be an improvement.

It must, however, be remembered that paying witnesses is a risky business because of the possibility of false testimony. This is, of course, a possibility in any court system, but particularly so if you pay witnesses. In general, a witness who has been paid for producing his evidence should be regarded as somewhat less reliable than a witness who has not been paid, and his testimony should not be given great weight unless it can be corroborated. In most cases, of course, the witness, if he is genuinely reporting a crime, will have some information that the police do not already have and can be checked after he has told the police. Corroboration, therefore, is normally not too difficult.

Still, this type of testimony is inferior to voluntary testimony. The reason for desiring that it be added to our present system is simply that it is more evidence. Our present witnesses would not be driven away and we would obtain further witnesses. Furthermore, large payments to people who turn in their friends and colleagues make it very hard for criminal organizations to retain their internal coherence. Criminals, after all, are criminals and they are as likely to commit "immoral" acts against their confederates as anyone else when there is much to be gained. Thus, the undermining of criminal morale and the cohesion of criminal organizations will be a secondary consequence of large payments for information. Once again, however, great care must be used in dealing with such evidence. We have here another place to use the polygraph.

Once the police have made up their minds as to who they think committed the crime and feel they have enough evidence to pro-

[5] See Jerome H. Skolnick, *Justice Without Trial* (New York: John Wiley & Sons, Inc., 1966), pp. 126–132.

ceed, they then take the matter to an attorney. In England this attorney is usually a barrister who is hired by the police for the individual case. In the United States he is a permanent official of the government. It is probable that the English system leads to a somewhat more even match of the attorneys on the two sides. In cases where the police anticipate that the defense will be in the hands of an exceptionally competent attorney, they hire an exceptionally competent one themselves. On the other hand, in cases where they feel that the defense will be poorly handled, they don't waste their money on a first-rate man. In the United States, the district attorney is a relatively constant quantity, which means that a defendant who can afford first-class counsel will normally be better represented than the government, and the average defendant normally has a poorer attorney than the government. In any event, the attorney decides whether to continue with the case. There is little to be said about the decision to give the prosecutor this discretion. In the United States, we have another preliminary procedure—a Grand Jury, or in some states a special judicial proceeding. Insofar as it has any rationale at all, it makes it difficult to persecute individuals by initiating prosecutions on obviously inadequate evidence. It probably, however, has very little effect on anything. Certainly we find no need of a similar process in the civil courts.

Turning to the court itself, we should begin by noting that the function of the court is largely to find out what happened at some time in the past. In *most* cases the legal situation is fairly straightforward. Smith did or did not shoot his wife. Once we know what happened, we have little or no difficulty in determining what the legal consequences of that act are. There will, of course, be cases in which we do not find the legal situation quite that simple, but these are decidedly the exceptional ones. Furthermore, in most cases under the criminal law, where there is a real question as to the law, it makes little difference. There are cases in which there is real doubt as to which of two legal rules applies, and consequently there are cases where at the time the act was committed it was uncertain what the law was. In consequence, although a decision as to the legal consequence of the act will have to be made, in terms of deterrence, it makes relatively little difference what that decision is. Anyone who gets himself in a situation in which the law is unclear is taking a risk, a risk proportional to the lack of clarity.

The fact that courts are predominantly engaged in finding out what happened in the past is obvious to any outside observer, but would not necessarily be obvious to anyone who studied Anglo-American law in law school. In these schools, almost no attention is paid to the problems of fact finding, that is, determining what really happened, and a vast amount of attention is given to a study of the minutiae of the law. The presumed reason for this phenomenon is that the proceedings of the courts are recorded in the words of the judges themselves. The judges normally state what they think happened and then discuss at some length its legal consequences. As a result of this method of teaching law the difficult problems of guessing what happened tend to be slurred over and are largely omitted from the training of legal personnel.

Training fact-finding organizations, the courts, in the procedures of application of the law with very little attention being given to the facts and technicalities of evidence seems odd. How we got into this is a problem of history that will not be discussed here. It does seem clear, however, that steps should be taken to remedy the situation. Judges should be given training in such things as fingerprint analysis and the scientific aspects of real evidence. In addition, if it is possible to tell whether a witness is lying by any method, the judges should be given training in this field. Of course, it may be that nothing much can be done about detecting lying. It is of some interest that continental legal training does include some attention to the facts and does not deal entirely in the law as does ours. This may have something to do with the fact that continental law is a great deal simpler than ours.

Turning to the trial process, there are three general methods of selecting the people who will determine the facts. In a number of cases in Anglo-Saxon countries people are selected at random and instructed to make a unanimous decision as to the facts. In the cases in which this method is used, this decision is in theory, and to a considerable extent in practice, subject to no appeal. Appeals in the American system and to a large extent in the

English system are, in theory, only possible on the legal consequences of the finding of facts or on the legal details of the proceedings of the courts. They do not deal with the factual matters
determined by the jury.

The second basic procedure for selecting people to make decisions in court is to choose an individual. This method was the
basic procedure in Roman law, and oddly enough, is the most common method in modern British and American law. As we have
seen in criminal trials, judge trial is more common than jury trial.
Minor cases are uniformly tried by single magistrates. Juvenile
cases are also tried before one person as are all cases in equity.
In the United States, those civil cases that are "law" cases are
tried by a single judge if the parties decide to waive a jury. In
England juries have been largely unavailable in civil cases since
the beginning of the century. On the Continent, on the other hand,
a great many cases are tried by a board of judges. As a general
rule, these judges are legally trained individuals, although as we
have noticed, continental legal training involves a certain amount
of schooling in interpreting facts. In some cases, however, certain laymen have been introduced into the court.

The appointment of a single official as a judge raises relatively
few issues unless we contrast it with the board of judges. At first
glance it might appear that the continental system of having several judges at most trials is clearly superior to the old-fashioned
Roman or modern American and British procedure of having only
one. Surely the American court systems in which all appellate
courts consist of more than one person could be evidenced as supporting this view. In general, in the United States, the higher the
appellate court the larger the number of judges sitting on it. All
of this would seem to indicate that in judicial numbers there is
strength.

The arguments for the use of a board of judges instead of a
single judge are, however, by no means completely convincing.
Resources are inherently limited. If we assume that the people
who appoint judges are capable of selecting better judges over
worse judges (and without that assumption we can hardly argue
for the selection of judges at all), they should be able to obtain
a better single judge than the average of five members of a board.

It is not even that simple. Clearly we could afford to pay a single judge five times as much as we could afford to pay the average judge on a board of five. Perhaps we could pay even more because the board of five would probably spend more time on each case than would a single judge. Thus it should be possible to obtain very materially better personnel by using the single judge system rather than the board of judges. In practice we appear to feel that a single judge is suitable for the actual case but for appeals we need a board. It is hard to say anything definite about the desirability of a single judge as opposed to a board of judges, but this would seem to be an empirical problem that could be solved by suitably designed experiments. Lacking such experiments, I simply note that there are these two different techniques and proceed to discuss other matters.

A somewhat similar issue is raised by the appeal process. As we have already noted, the most important decisions made by a court (the decisions as to fact) are, at least in theory, not appealable. The reason for not permitting an appeal of factual matters is simple tradition. However, a rationalization, and not a bad one, has developed. This rationalization is that the people at the trial see the witnesses and are able to judge to some extent whether they are telling the truth or not or whether they are reliable people. This, however, points to a peculiar characteristic of our appeal process. It is not a rerunning of the trial in an effort to use better personnel and reach a better conclusion. On the contrary, it is simply an examination of the record compiled at the trial, and as this rationalization I have just given indicates, this record is far from complete. There seems to be no reason why a judge might not be just as readily mistaken in his judgment of a witness's veracity as in his judgment of other matters. Prohibiting any rectification of such errors on appeal is hard to understand.

Another argument for permitting an appeal on the law is that it is thought desirable to have a law that is uniform within a particular jurisdiction This argument will be dealt with at some length later. At this point, we will only say that uniformity should mean that equals are treated equally. Inequality can come as easily from a misapprehension of the fact as from a misapprehension of the law. Furthermore, uniformity is not an infinite good, and we should not be willing to pay an infinite price for it.

Before proceeding with the discussion of uniformity, let us first consider the appeal process in itself. As we have already noticed, in Anglo-Saxon law, a good deal of the work in any court is not subject to appeal. The findings of the jury, the chancellor, or the judge is supposed to be final on a great many matters. Other court systems have permitted no appeal at all, the most notable of which is the Mohammedan system that seems to have worked well over a long period of time depending upon summary proceedings with a total absence of appeal. When the Communists seized power in Russia, they actually set up a court system that was in many ways copied from the Mohammedan system. As a general rule, the arbitration courts that have been voluntarily established to deal with contract problems also function without appeal. It is thus by no means obvious that an appeal system is desirable.

What then are the arguments for providing appeal? The first and most naïve is that the court of the first instance may make errors and it is desirable to have someone to correct them. The problem with this argument is that the appellate court may also make errors and therefore, if the initial court has reached a correct decision, the decision by the higher court overruling it may put the law in a worse situation than it would have been had the original decision been left unappealed. In order for the higher courts with appellate authority to have an effect of reducing the number of errors in the law, there must be some reason to believe that they themselves make fewer errors than the lower court whose decision they reconsider. In general, appellate courts are somewhat more highly paid and somewhat more carefully selected than the lower courts. Furthermore, in the United States at any event, the lower court is usually one man and the upper court is usually a board that may, or then again may not, give the upper court the advantage.

Still, it is by no means obvious that the higher courts will indeed make fewer errors than the lower courts, particularly when the higher courts are denied access to certain information such as the appearance of the witnesses. We can, however, assume for the sake of argument that in a well-organized appellate court system the higher court would make fewer errors on the law than the lower court, and therefore the possibility of appeal to the higher court would lead to fewer errors. Immediately two questions are raised. Who appeals, and why not simply make the entire court system as accurate as the appeal court? Taking these questions in reverse order, if all cases are appealed, then it would require as many (or perhaps more) judges in the appellate courts as in the trial courts. Thus abolishing the findings of the trial court judges and letting the supposedly superior judges of the appellate courts sit on the original trial of the case would seem to be a good idea. This logic seems invulnerable as long as we assume that all cases may be appealed. When we realize that for one reason or another only a rather small number of cases are actually appealed, we see the possibility of improving court functioning by using the appellate system.

The first obvious reason for only a few cases being appealed is that in a great many criminal cases the defendant is represented by a public defender who seldom takes appeals. In many other cases, the financial resources of the defendant are limited and he cannot appeal. Similarly, in civil cases the amount in question may be small enough so that an appeal is not sensible. Although there are some restrictions on the right of appeal, it does seem that financial resources are really the basic reason why some cases are appealed and others are not. The lawyers, of course, also take into account the likelihood of winning, but this is something of a gamble in any case, and there certainly will be considerable delay on appeal that normally benefits whichever side has lost the first round. Thus, in a sense, the appeal process permits the more important members of the community to have two or even three goes at their cases, whereas the less influential individuals are only given one. It may well be that this is an excellent idea in terms of limiting social tension. It may also be that the cases that are appealed are the most important and, therefore, the ones in which correct decisions are most important.

There are, however, less naïve explanations for the appeal process. The first of these would be that it provides a desirable discipline on the trial judge. The knowledge that he may have his decision reversed and have his superiors make public statements that he is not quite bright surely will put pressure on him to be careful. In this respect it is unfortunate that a similar pressure is not put on him to be careful about the facts. The Swedes go further and permit disappointed litigants to sue the judge, alleging he has brought in a wrong decision. It should be noted that the judge in general will be able to guess fairly accurately which cases are to be appealed and which are not. He need pay little attention to the prospects of appeal if the defense is by a public defender. Similarly, if it is a civil suit and the amount involved is small he can safely assume that there will be no appeal. Still it would not be wise to rule this particular factor out. It may work a small improvement in the behavior of the trial courts, but it is an improvement.

The second non-naïve argument for the use of appellate courts is the maintenance of the uniformity in the law. People offering this argument will say that they do not wish the law to vary from judicial district to judicial district. This naturally brings up the whole question of the uniformity of law. Most people seem to be convinced that the law ought to be uniform, but the reasons given for this preference are not terribly convincing. It is not necessary, for example, that the law be uniform in order to be predictable. We could have a highly nonuniform law that was nevertheless extremely predictable. It could, for example, provide that your punishment in the event that you committed murder depended on the first letter in your last name. This would be nonuniform but highly predictable.

The genuine arguments for uniformity are twofold. First, it makes it easier for individuals to "know" the law if the law is the same over a large number of cases; and second, if we believe that the law represents some desirable standard, presumably the best standard is the same everywhere. Elaborating upon the first argument, I can devote less time to learning the law if it is the same in Athens as in Chicago. In those cases in which I might be concerned with the law in Athens, I could simply apply my knowledge of the law in the United States. As Bruno Leoni has pointed out, this line of argument would also indicate that it is desirable that the law be uniform over time, *i.e.,* that it not be changed or be changed very slowly. The need for people who move from one area to another to learn new law is paralleled by the need to learn new law if the law is changed. Most people, however, will not accept uniformity as having an absolute value. They are in favor of the law being fairly simple and fairly easy to understand, but they do not feel it is an infringement on their rights that Greece has a different law from their state, or for that matter that their state has a different law from the next state. Similarly, they do not object terribly to changes in the law. Still it must be admitted that the argument does have some validity. The wider the range in time and space of any given law the less resources need be invested in relearning the law.

The second argument, that the law is an ideal standard, and that that standard should be the same everywhere, is basically an ethical one. It is, of course, true that if we had some reason to believe that our law of contracts were the best of all possible laws, then we would be doing other people a favor by forcing it down their throats. But in practice most differences between law codes do not involve a clear-cut superiority on one side. There is, in fact, an excellent reason for not having uniformity if we are really interested in working toward a good legal system. Empirical investigation will be necessary to produce an ideal legal system. Clearly this will involve the use of the experimental method. For this purpose we must establish some method by which a proposed change in the law can be compared with other or older provisions of the law. The method, of course, is simple and well established in science—it is the method of controls. Thus, if Texas changes its law of burglary, and Illinois does not, and we observe the two states in action through a period of fifteen to twenty years, we should be able to obtain at least some idea of the effects of the new law. It would be even better if we arranged a formal experiment. Kalven, Zeisel, and Buchholz recommend this very highly.[6]

It will be noted that the arguments for an appeal system are not overwhelmingly strong. Our present appellate system is supported more from custom than from careful thought. The implicit assumption that the higher courts correct the errors of the lower courts and commit no errors of their own may also be involved. If we are to have appeal, however, it would appear desirable that the lower courts be unable to predict in advance what aspect of their behavior will be examined, and which case will be appealed.

[6] See Kalven, Zeisel, and Buchholz, *Delay in Court* (Boston: Little, Brown and Company, 1959), pp. 241–250.

A possible procedure would be to arrange for a random sample of cases to be automatically surveyed with great care by a superior court. This should fulfill most of the duties of the appellate system and could do so in a much more efficient manner.

This suggestion may seem extremely radical, but in practice it is not too different from the military court system. In this system all convictions by court martial are automatically reviewed in Washington. This is a very old and traditional system that has recently been supplemented by a more conventional appellate court system.

The appeal court system, particularly since the foundation of the United States and the development by our court system of the modern version of *stare decisis,* has not only served to review trials but has actually created new law. It frequently happens that some matter comes up that is not clearly and obviously covered by the law. The court is forced to make a decision, and the tradition at the moment is that, if it is a higher court, this decision is regarded as the law for all future similar cases. It is not exactly obvious why this should be the custom. It was not so in the original common law or in the Jurisconsult law of Rome, which so closely resembles the common law. In both of these systems a judicial decision, although final for a given case, was not regarded as binding on future cases until much the same case had come up several times and had been considered by several different authorities. The rigid rule of the single precedent seems to have come out of the practice of the American Supreme Court in its early years and does not seem to have been carefully thought out.

It should be noted that the filling in of the gaps in the law by court decisions does not necessarily reduce the uncertainty of the law. Each little piece of patchwork may simply move the zone of uncertainty a little bit without reducing its size. In any event, it is impossible to make the law fit all possible future cases, and we should not attempt to do so. The continental system with a fairly brief law code and the courts not absolutely bound to follow previous decisions in every case provides a simple system and does not seem to have any other great disadvantage. If we assume, as all of the arguments for judge-made law must assume, that the legislature will not keep the law up to date, then we must also accept something like the common law. There is, however, no reason why individual courts trying individual cases should be the authority that supplements the inadequate legislature. The French administrative court that produces an authoritative interpretation of the law in general terms rather than with respect to individual cases does as well. Thus, we could have the law itself and a gloss on it made by a selected group of judges. It would not be necessary to wade through thousands and thousands of judicial decisions in order to determine the rights of a party to a dispute.

We now turn to the situation that arises after the courts have reached a final decision. If the matter is a civil suit, most people would agree that the court should proceed to enforce its decision. It should seize the property of the defendant, if it is decided that the defendant owes money to the plaintiff and does not make the payment, or in some cases it may put him in prison. Admittedly, the enforcement of the decision will work considerable inconvenience on the person against whom the decision is made and some of the decisions will be wrong. Nevertheless, we must accept the fact that the courts are sometimes wrong and the unfortunate man who is wrongfully compelled to pay $50,000, perhaps losing his house and business, is indeed unfortunate and nothing can be done about it.

If, however, the defendant is found guilty on a criminal charge, we customarily turn to some other procedure to deal with him. It is true that if the defendant is to be fined, we treat him like the defendant in a civil suit who has lost, and similar procedures are undertaken to collect the money. In most cases, however, the defendant in a criminal case either is indigent and cannot pay the fine or is not given the alternative of a fine but is subject to other penalties. It is these other penalties, in particular imprisonment, to which we now turn. A reading of the literature on penology will quickly convince any student that he is dealing with one of the most confused areas in modern thought. Exactly why this should be so, I do not know; but in fact it is so.

In general, a discussion of penology is conducted as a sort of debate between two schools of thought that I shall call the "curative" and "punitive" schools. As a matter of fact, this debate is about little since one normally finds that the two parties to the debate are in general (although not detailed) agreement about many practical matters and their basic philosophical positions are not logically inconsistent. It is possible to apply both curative and punitive measures simultaneously. Normally, the people who argue for a curative type of approach to prisoners are strongly in favor of various forms of education and vocational training for prisoners, and frequently are also in favor of psychiatric treatment for them. One will also normally find, however, that they feel (even though they don't say very much about it) that more serious crimes should be followed by longer imprisonments than less serious crimes, and that discipline in the prison can best be kept by the imposition of punishments for violations.

The advocates of punishment, on the other hand, will normally talk a great deal about the need to make prison life a true punishment and are sometimes (in England) in favor of flogging. Normally, however, they also favor the prisoners, being put to work while in prison. I have never run into one who feels that those prisoners who are in need of psychiatric attention should not receive it. Thus, the difference between these two "schools of thought" is largely a matter of verbiage and emphasis.[7] Unfortunately, much of the work in penology is, as I have mentioned, a debate between these two quite consistent positions.

My position is that potential criminals should not anticipate a positive present discounted value from the acts of the crime that they are contemplating. This would mean that a criminal faces a possibility of suffering some amount of unpleasantness, which, suitably discounted, is greater than the benefit obtained from the crime. Since, however, we normally imprison people for this purpose, it seems only sensible that they be occupied at something, and there surely is no reason why they should not be oc-

---

[7] Richard Wagner, on reading the original draft of this book, pointed out that the two approaches lead to a different procedure for varying lengths of sentence. The advocates of punishment, if they were consistent, would have the period of time spent in prison a simple function of the crimes committed by the criminal. The curative people, on the other hand, would want it to be the function of "response to treatment." Logically, I cannot disagree with Wagner, but my reading of the literature indicates that the advocates of the two sides are not as logical as he.

cupied at learning a useful occupation. If there were some danger, and in practice there is not, that the learning of a useful trade in prison might be a positive incentive to commit crimes, then this could be offset by appropriately increasing the length of the prison sentence or the unpleasantness of the prison.

The present-day prisons are unpleasant places to live (some more unpleasant than others) which offer very little in the way of training or treatment to their inmates. In some institutions for juveniles, this is not necessarily true, but in general it applies to almost all prisons. Whether it is possible to convert prisons into educational or curative institutions is a question to which I have very little to contribute. The difficulties are immense. Thus far, what controlled experiments have been made have been mostly unsuccessful. It is probable that if our prisons have any desirable effect on their inmates, it is solely because they are unpleasant and people having once been in them do not wish to be sent back. It seems likely that the major educational effect is counterproductive. The individual is thrown into an environment in which his most important social contacts are with fellow prisoners. Among these fellow prisoners the major criminals seem to have a dominant role. Thus, the major real educational effect of our present-day prisons may well be the training of the individual in improved techniques of crime and equipping him with a network of connections that can later be used in a life of crime. Clearly, changing prisons from educational institutions of this sort is highly desirable. Nor do I think this is beyond the ingenuity of man.

11

Theft and Robbery[1]

Perhaps the easiest way to make a living, and certainly one of the oldest, is to take another's property. I might take your money, not for my material gain but because the thought of your starving filled me with joy. In this case, the motive would be the inflicting of injury on the person robbed, and we shall leave its discussion to Chapter 13 and concentrate in this chapter on those cases in which the motive for taking another's property is material gain.

The system of private property (or state property, in a Communist system) requires that property be kept in the hands of its owner (which may, of course, be the state). This is so obvious that it is often said that even professional thieves would favor laws against thievery. This protection could theoretically be provided by the owners, but this is an extremely inefficient system.[2] Each individual would have to devote a considerable amount of his time and energy to standing guard over his possessions. In addition, the weaker members of the population could not guard their possessions even if they tried. Note that you could not hire protection without at least some rudimentary capacity of self-defense because the people capable of being guards could help

---

[1] See Gary Becker, "Crime and Punishment: An Economic Approach," *Journal of Political Economy* 76 (March–April 1968): 167, for an essentially similar treatment of the problem.

[2] See my "The Welfare Costs of Tariffs, Monopoly, and Theft," *Western Economic Journal* 5, No. 3 (June 1967): 234.

themselves to your property without the tedium of standing guard. This line of reasoning is so obvious that it might be thought that no one could possibly doubt it, but the anarchists do.

TABLE OF SYMBOLS 11-1

C_c	=	Court cost
C_o	=	Conscience cost
C_r	=	Crime rate, likelihood individual will be victim of crime
C_t	=	Cost of being victim of crime
D_t	=	Direct profit of crime
I_c	=	Cost to individual of investigation of crimes that he did not commit
L_c	=	Likelihood of conviction
L_d	=	Likelihood of detection
L_{fc}	=	Likelihood individual will be falsely convicted for crime he did not commit
L_s	=	Likelihood individual will commit crime
P	=	Payoff (may be negative)
P_c	=	Cost of maintaining police, prisons, and courts
P_r	=	Private cost of protection against theft. Includes nonproduction
P_u	=	Punishment
R	=	Risk aversion factor

Turning once again to our high school algebra, Equation (11.1) shows the payoff obtained from the various possible institutions for dealing with theft.

$$(11.1) \qquad P = L_s[D_t(1-L_d) - L_d(C_c+L_cP_u)-C_o] \\ - P_c - I_c - L_{fc}P_u - C_rC_t - P_r$$

Once again it is an extremely complex-looking equation that has relatively little in the way of mathematical content. For any given level of enforcement of laws against theft—and this level may be zero—the individual will have a particular likelihood of committing that particular crime. This is shown by the L_s. The area within the square brackets is the payoff to be expected from such a crime. It consists of the profit to be made from the undetected crime less the likelihood of the crime's being detected together with the penalty that results from being detected. Note that, if you are detected, some type of legal costs will certainly fall upon you (assuming, of course, that we have a law against the crime) but being sent to prison is a matter of probability rather than certainty. Finally, there is a cost of conscience for the person who feels that theft is wrong.

A number of additional costs then are associated with the existence of theft and measures to combat them are shown in the factors that follow the square bracket. Note that the payoff from the institution of theft is a negative number, *i.e.,* the average individual would prefer that the institution not exist. Note also that if we do not have laws against theft, a good part of Equation (11.1) vanishes, and we get Equation (11.2), which is almost certain to be a much larger negative number than is Equation (11.1). Thus, the individual is likely to feel that laws against theft are desirable and the problem is in essence optimizing Equation (11.1) rather than making up one's mind between Equation (11.1) and Equation (11.2).

$$(11.2) \qquad P = L_s D_t + L_s C_o - P_r - C_r C_t$$

I must, however, digress about the cost of conscience in the equation. My real reason for putting it in is to simplify the presentation in the last chapter of this book, my return to ethics. A full discussion of the matter is deferred until then. We should, however, note that people do in fact have such conscience costs that affect their behavior. It should, perhaps, be noted also that the person who has the strongest conscience is most inhibited from stealing and, therefore, is disadvantaged by the institution. This is particularly true if there is no (or very weak) legal protection against the crime. A man who had a very strong aversion to committing theft would be under a disastrous disadvantage if he lived in a society described by Equation (11.2). But I must leave further discussion of the conscience problem until later. For the present I should like to have the reader consider conscience as existing but not being a major part of our main chain of reasoning at this stage. He can perhaps consider that he is dealing with Justice Holmes' "Wicked Man," who had no conscience problems at all, and for whom C_o would be zero.[3]

[3] Oliver Wendell Holmes, *The Common Law* (London: MacMillan & Company, Ltd., 1881).

In passing, we may note that a great many people apparently assume that for themselves C_o has such a high value that they would never commit a crime. This may be true, or then again it may not. For a person who feels this way, however, the principal effects of the institution of theft are costs with no gain anywhere. The individual who is never going to commit a crime himself may be the victim of a crime, may find himself unjustly imprisoned as a result of a false charge of crime, and certainly will end up paying taxes to support the police and court apparatus. He is likely to be interested in reducing these three factors and perhaps in making trade-offs among them. A very large part of the public discussion of crime is confined to these three areas. This probably reflects the opinion of most of the people involved in the discussion that, for them, the possibility of their committing a crime is zero.

Putting the problem in its most general form, however, and assuming that we do have some institutions for the repression of theft and robbery, then an individual considering whether or not to commit such a crime would make his decision on the basis of Inequality (11.3).

$$(11.3) \qquad D_t(1-L_d) > R \cdot L_d(C_c+L_cP_u) \\ + C_o - I_c - L_{fc}P_u$$

The profits of the crime, together with the probability that it will go undetected are on the left side of the inequality figure, and the costs together with a risk aversion figure are on the right. Note that costs are opportunity costs. If he does not commit a crime, there is some finite possibility that he will nevertheless be sent to prison for it and some finite possibility that he will be inconvenienced by the investigation. These factors therefore should be offset against the costs of the crime. For most of my readers, these items are small, but in some slum neighborhoods exists a significant probability of people being unjustly convicted of a crime. For people in this environment, it is likely that the cost of crime is lower than for the intellectuals reading this book.

Inequality (11.3) is roughly approximated by Equation (11.4).

(11.4) $$\frac{D_t(1-L_d)}{R} = L_d \cdot L_c \cdot P_u$$

Equation (11.4) might be said to be (roughly speaking) the social control equation. If we can increase any of the terms on the right, we can reduce the crime rate. All of these factors are under control of the government.

(11.5) $$L_c = {}_f(C_c \cdot I_c)$$

Equation (11.5) indicates that L_c, the likelihood of conviction, is a positive function of court costs and, in a much more minor way, the cost to individuals of being involved in an investigation of crimes that they did not commit. The appearance of I_c here simply indicates that in general if we increase our prevention and police activity, we are likely to inconvenience innocent bystanders. It is, of course, a very minor cost. It should be noted that in Equation (11.6) the likelihood of false conviction is a negative function of the same two factors.

(11.6) $$L_{fc} = {}_{-f}(C_c \cdot I_c)$$

Increased investments in police, courts, and the bothering of witnesses will both increase the number of criminals who are convicted and reduce the number of innocent persons who are unjustly convicted.

Equation (11.7) indicates that the likelihood of initial detection of the criminal is the result once again of police costs and the bothering of individual persons who are not directly involved in the crime.

(11.7) $$L_d = {}_f(P_c \cdot I_c)$$

It will be noted that we can lower the crime rate by increasing either L_d, L_c, or P_u. In Equation (11.8) a number of things that could be expected to deter criminals are collected on the right side.

$$(11.8) \quad C_r = -f[(L_c - L_{fc}), (C_c - I_c), L_d \cdot L_c P_w, C_0]$$

Note that the improved detection of criminals permits a reduction in punishment without increasing the crime rate. If we can raise either the rate of detection or the rate of conviction, this permits us to reduce the sentence we give to the convicted criminal while obtaining the same "deterrence."

As a general rule, people who are in favor of "tougher" police and court procedures are also in favor of longer sentences. On the other hand, the people who favor giving criminals shorter sentences are also normally great enthusiasts for various procedural techniques that make it less likely that conviction will be obtained. Although there is no direct logical contradiction in either of these positions (we might have either too heavy or too light a net $L_d \cdot L_c \cdot P_u$ in our society), it would seem more sensible to favor either a tougher court procedure with lighter sentences or more safeguards in the court procedure with heavier sentences.

Before we discuss the institutions that will give the best payoff for Equation (11.1), let us examine the range of institutional structures that might be established with respect to theft. Under the Common Law, two quite different procedures were available. Firstly, as part of the law of torts, the individual whose property had been stolen could proceed against the thief in a civil suit. If he were successful, he could either get his property back or force the thief to pay him its value as assessed by the court. This particular approach to thievery is not used much in practice. In fact, suits in conversion or for return of property normally do not involve anything that we would recognize as theft.[4] The reason, of course, is that cases of genuine theft normally lead to criminal prosecutions. Nevertheless, the law is clear, if someone steals my car, I can sue him in conversion and make him pay me for it.

Even though civil suits play almost no role in the present day, let us consider them at some length. Suppose that the standard remedy for theft were a suit for the return of the stolen property, and, for simplicity, let us assume that in such cases the police and courts never make mistakes. If you steal my car, there is no chance of the police failing to catch you or of the court deciding

[4] They sometimes involve embezzlement.

that it was your car in the first place. This procedure would make the stealing of cars useless as a business, for you obviously couldn't sell something you were going to have to return, but you could go through life using other people's cars.[5] You steal my car, and while the suit is pending you drive it. When you have to return it, you simply steal somebody else's, and so on.

The remedy for this state of affairs is simple enough: make the thief pay a fair rent for the period in which he held the property plus, probably, a few dollars for the inconvenience to which he put the true owner by taking the car without permission. This would, I think, be a most superior state of the law. It would mean that no one would ever take anyone else's property, except in emergencies. If, however, I had a very great need of a car immediately, I could simply take any that I saw subject to later payment. I would, of course, run the risk that the owner would also need the car for emergency purposes, in which case the payment for his inconvenience might be extremely high.[6] On the whole, however, this system would give a high degree of flexibility to the property system in times of emergency. It is indeed unfortunate that we cannot use it.

The problem, of course, is that we may not know who has stolen the car. Private suits would require that the thieves be identified. Today we depend upon the police to find the person who stole our property, and the thief is then prosecuted. Let us divide these two steps and assume that the police still locate the thief, but that once he is located the owner also sues. It would seem reasonable in this case that the police also sue for their expenses in hunting down the thief. Thus a citizen who took a car in an emergency could promptly inform the police and limit his liability, while the man attempting to make a career of crime would try to keep his theft a secret and pay more if he were caught. Let us retain our assumption that the courts make no mistakes, and, therefore, there is no prospect of a miscarriage of justice. If the accused took the car, the court will so rule; and if he did not, he will be given a judgment accordingly.

---

[5] If sale at an assessed value were the remedy rather than return, the assessed value would then almost certainly be high enough so that there would be no profit.

[6] Assuming, of course, that there is no other car about for him to take.

If the police caught the thief every time, then there is no obvious reason why this system would not work reasonably well. Under those circumstances, thieves might be largely paupers who could not pay damage judgments, but let us put off a discussion of this problem until later. The police, however, will not catch every thief. Consider, for example, the situation if they caught every other thief.[7] Suppose that the average car is worth $2,000, and that the police normally expend $500 in investigating each missing car. If I steal twenty cars a year, I will have to return ten of them and pay the police "finding fees" of $5,000, but I will net $15,000 for relatively little effort. Clearly, this would be an excellent career for an ambitious young man. Unfortunately, as in all businesses where the profits are supernormal, competition would be attracted. Shortly there would be so many thieves that ownership of a car would become almost an empty form. It probably would even become impossible for the thieves to sell their loot at reasonable prices.[8]

Suppose, however, that the rate of police successes is taken into account and the man whose car has been stolen is given the right to sue for twice its value in damages. The average thief would then lose $500 (police fees) for each pair of cars he steals. Clearly, this would not be profitable. The owners of cars who were not thieves would face a fifty-fifty chance of double or nothing in the event that their car were stolen. Presumably, insurance companies would be willing to sell them "insurance" under which the car owners would be compensated whenever their car was stolen, but would surrender the right to recover from the thief to the insurance company. Although this system would work out all right for the police, the insurance company, and the car owner, it would not necessarily be "fair" to the thief.[9] Different thieves

[7] No existing police force even approximates such a favorable performance.

[8] It was mentioned earlier that even thieves would favor laws against theft. Here, they would favor strengthening the law.

[9] Not necessarily to the police. Placing the cost of the police services on the thief who is caught has some rather complicated implications. The more thieves that are caught the larger the police budget, and hence the less likely you are to get away with stealing a car. A fall off in thievery, however, would lead to a decline in the takings of the police and hence to a cut in the police budget. This would then make stealing safer and

would have different degrees of skill. There would be newcomers to the business who were caught practically every time, and highly skilled craftsmen who were caught only once every twenty or so times. The first group would pay a disproportionate part of the damage suits. Our objective in setting up this system, however, is not to enforce some sort of implied contract between the thief and his victims but to protect people against having their cars stolen.

Looked at from this point of view, the system would surely reduce the number of cars stolen and would probably weed out all but the most skillful of thieves. It would, however, permit a good deal of thievery by skilled and intelligent criminals. With this change in the ability of the average thief, the effectiveness of the police might well fall. Perhaps they would only catch the thief in every fourth robbery.[10] An obvious remedy for this situation would be to raise the possible damages to four times the cost of the car. This, in turn, would surely force more criminals, the moderately skilled ones, to seek another line of endeavor. The process could be continued. Presumably, there is some ratio, say damages of $200,000 per car stolen, at which no one, no matter how skilled and lucky, would be interested in stealing cars.

Would we really want to put a damage claim for $200,000 on the man caught stealing a car, particularly since the person might be caught while stealing his first car? Most readers will probably think this is a silly problem; they may have felt that our whole discussion of damage claims as a way of preventing theft is simply foolish. In fact, we are considering issues fundamental to the theory of crime, but in a radically different context from that normally used. The "change of scene" will, I hope, improve our understanding of these issues. Another, obviously correct, objection to the question that begins this paragraph is that it is based upon other premises than those outlined in the first two chapters. Although this is true, let me at least ask the question.

lead to an increase. The problem is similar to the carnivore problem in population ecology.

[10] This is, in fact, the rate maintained by the very efficient London Police force for all crimes. (C. B. Norton, "Letter to the Editor," *London Times,* 20 August 1963, p. 9.)

Let us make just one change in the radically simplified model of the last few pages. A large number of real-life criminals are insolvent and could not pay damage claims. Furthermore, if the result of being caught stealing a car were merely a damage claim, then it would be sensible for car thieves to plan to be perpetually poor in capital goods, like merchants who continuously skirt bankruptcy. They might have a large income but they would have no property. They would live in expensive furnished apartments and drive rented Cadillacs. Although they would be able to continue in their profession, they would be driven into bankruptcy periodically by large damage judgments that they could not pay. Thus it would be impossible to compensate the owners of stolen cars out of collections in damage suits; the owners must buy insurance or take precautions against theft. The damage mechanism also had a second effect. It made the business of car stealing an unprofitable one, and hence one that did not attract many entrepreneurs. The fact that many criminals are insolvent, and all of them can become insolvent if they wish, makes it impossible to pay owners of stolen cars out of the receipts from damage suits. Can we nevertheless impose costs on the criminals so that car stealing is not a suitable way of making a living?

All known societies have answered this question "yes," and have had methods of imposing costs on the thief. These costs cannot, by the very nature of the problem take the form of monetary collections.[11] They involve, therefore, the direct infliction of costs upon the thief, whether in the form of branding, ear clipping, hanging, or imprisonment. Thus, the individual thinking of taking up theft as an occupation must weigh the profits against the likelihood that, say, for every tenth car he steals he will be caught and sentenced to five years in prison. Our discussion of the amount of damages, thus, becomes relevant. As Equation (11.3) showed, the "cost" to be imposed is a function of the efficiency of the enforcement mechanism. If anyone stealing a car could be immediately caught, the most minor punishment would be sufficient—a $5 fine, for example. If police only caught every other thief, then a punishment equivalent to a fine of about $4,000 would be necessary.

[11] Although this is frequently provided as an alternative in the event the thief can pay the fine.

Similarly, the differential skills of the thieves would mean that a level of punishment that would keep the incompetent out of the business would still leave it a good racket for the well-trained specialist. The highly skilled criminals who operate the "gangs" of our large cities apparently feel more than amply compensated for their occasional prison sentences. Although we do not have much data on which to make a judgment, they are probably right.

Again, as in the damage suit case, raising the cost of getting caught would, presumably, eventually make even the most skilled operators move out of the business. But here the question of how much of a punishment we wish to impose, raised in connection with the damage suits, becomes relevant. Most people do not believe in death sentences for automobile theft.[12]

Looking at the matter rationally, the crime rate is a function of a number of things, among which the likelihood of getting caught and the likely punishment are important. If we hold the likelihood of getting caught constant, then the crime rate will decline as the punishment goes up. A one in ten chance of getting a slap on the wrist is quite a different thing from a one in ten chance of being executed. There can be no doubt that the Communists are correct in their belief that death penalties for economic crimes will deter them. If the punishment is to serve this purpose, however, it must be known to the potential criminal, which means that you must give it publicity. It might, in fact, be sensible to exaggerate its unpleasantness. Thus, when a new prison is put up the authorities might well make statements to the press to the effect that it would be an awful place in which to be confined, instead of pointing out its "humane" features.

In law school I learned that judges and juries were reluctant to impose severe penalties, which meant that raising the punishment for a given crime automatically lowered the likelihood of the criminal's being punished at all. Thus, for example, the "four-time loser" laws, which provide life imprisonment on the fourth conviction for a felony, amount to giving three-time losers a license

---

[12] The Communists, of course, do sentence people to death who have stolen or embezzled property, or sometimes people who have merely "speculated." Since they announce such executions in the newspapers, it must be assumed that they are proud of them, and that, therefore, at least some people follow the line of reasoning we have outlined to its ultimate, rational conclusion.

to commit petty crimes. Juries, my professor said, will not send a man to prison for life on a minor charge. The odds of conviction are, in this view, a declining function of the punishment imposed. Since a one in four chance of a year in prison may be a better deterrent than a one in one hundred chance of a ten-year term, the milder punishment may work better than the more severe one. The problem would appear to be largely one of control over the courts. If the courts can be organized in such a way that they carry out the law as it is given to them, this problem would not arise. If, on the other hand, the courts followed their own ethical system instead of the law, or mixed the two together, then this fact must be taken into account when drawing up the basic law.

We have, however, tried to keep ethics out of the discussion insofar as possible. Let us, therefore, assume that the courts will carry out the law as it is given to them, and will not impose their own personal ethical system upon it. This permits us to ignore the effect of the severity of the punishment on the likelihood of conviction. We can simply select a suitable punishment in view of a given likelihood of the criminal's being caught. The situation in which the punishment also effects the likelihood of conviction is more complicated and will normally not permit as satisfactory a solution, but in the real world we may be in this suboptimal situation. For the purposes of our study, this complication will be ignored.

Is there, then, any rational reason why we should not follow the Communists' example and impose the death penalty for minor crimes? Surely this would reduce the crime rate. For the rational man, it would appear to be all gain with no loss. He would himself make rational calculations, and hence never commit a crime for which the discounted value of the punishment exceeded the probable profit. The system would give him the maximum protection from crimes committed by others, since the deterrent effect would surely reduce the crime rate even if the criminals weren't highly rational. The only offset would appear to be the possibility of erroneous conviction. Since the courts are clearly not always right, each individual will always have the possibility of being convicted of a crime that he did not commit. Such things are unpredictable, and no one can really protect himself. The raising of the penalty on a crime is, thus, a straightforward increase in the cost of an erroneous conviction. Surely this is a factor that should be taken into account, although the weight it is given will depend upon the efficiency of the courts and the police. In well-functioning systems it should, I imagine, be a very minor item in determining punishments. In situations where false convictions are fairly frequent, on the other hand, it could be a major factor.

The problem can be dealt with a little more rigorously, although it is by no means sure what actual explanation is dominant. Presumably as the punishment for a given criminal act is increased, the likelihood that anyone will commit that crime declines. Normally, however, there will be at least some occasions on which the crime would be committed in spite of high penalties because there would be some opportunities to commit the crime under circumstances when detection seemed extremely unlikely. In general, one would anticipate, however, that the number of crimes committed would decline as the severity of punishment increased. If we assume the opportunity for committing crimes with different probabilities of detection is distributed normally, however, the "payoff" in terms of reduction in number of crimes as the penalty was increased would steadily decline. Further, individuals might regard this as a declining return investment in terms of utility, as well as in terms of technology. Under the circumstances, the marginal return to the individual from an increase in the penalty rate on some crime would be a declining function.

The cost to an individual of raising the punishment rate would mainly take the form of the possibility of his being unjustly convicted under the new punishment scale. Presumably, as the punishment is increased and the total number of crimes committed is reduced, the likelihood of incorrect convictions also goes down proportionately. Thus, an increase in the penalty which reduced the total number of crimes might leave the objectively calculated present discounted cost of possible unjust conviction not much changed. If, however, people have an aversion to risk which increases as the size of the risk goes up (which seems likely), they would face an increasing marginal cost on this side of the balance sheet. Thus, the marginal benefits from increasing the weight of the sentences is subject to declining marginal returns and the cost is subject to increasing marginal weight. Under the circumstances, the optimal punishment would not be infinite and might be fairly low.

But how about the "natural sympathies" of Adam Smith? Certainly the man who gives money to orphanages on Christmas may feel that he should be equally charitable to convicted criminals. The decision that a robber should be given four years instead of five years may be taken on exactly the same set of motives as the decision to make a gift to the American Cancer Society. Since this involves preferences, we cannot in our present state of knowledge make any judgment upon it. Presumably, there is some sort of exchange between security from theft and the pleasures obtained from not making the punishment for thieves heavy, but we have no idea of the ratio. Furthermore, it seems likely that it varies greatly from individual to individual. Thus, all we can say at this point is that people are likely to be at least a little charitable to convicted criminals. If we had exact statistics on the effect of changes in the extent of punishment upon the crime rate, the individual's judgment would no doubt be more informed than it is now, but there is no reason to believe that it would be identical from man to man. Under the circumstances, we can only regard the charitable motive as, to some extent, offsetting the purely practical considerations.

Our present law distinguishes between theft and robbery, the latter being marked by force or the threat of force in removing the property, whereas the former normally involves stealthy removal. For our present purposes we can ignore this distinction. Everything we have said about theft would also apply to robbery. In addition, although robbery is normally thought to be worse than theft, particularly if there is actual violence, this is essentially a moral judgment that we need not follow. Robbery with violence, in fact, is likely to be easier for the police to handle since the victims normally have seen the robber. With the resulting higher conviction rate, a somewhat lower penalty would be sufficient to deter robbery as a profession.

This contention, that robbery should (if anything) be punished less severely than theft, will strike most readers (and certainly most police officers) as extreme. Uniformly the use of violence in a crime is penalized heavily. Similar crimes without violence are punished more lightly. It seems to me that this may be a mistake. Acts of violence that occur as by-products of an effort to obtain someone else's property can be prevented if you make the obtaining of the other person's property in and of itself an activity that has a negative present discounted value. The only murder trial that I ever attended concerned a murder in which the victim had been killed for $5. I once shocked a group of intellectuals, all of whom generally believed in much lighter punishment of criminals than I did, by suggesting that if in the jurisdiction in which it was committed, thefts of $5 were detected approximately one time out of five, a suitable penalty for committing such a crime would be $27 or $28. The discounted value of the punishment would have exceeded the potential gain.

The concentration of police resources on violent crimes and the severe sentences on criminals who commit such crimes may be taken as an attempt to change the type of crime committed. But surely this is not a very high priority social goal. In a sense, our present behavior in this field, as in so much of the law, is simply a hangover from the Middle Ages. We have not carefully thought the matter through and, therefore, do not realize that we can prevent the use of certain production methods by preventing the production.

Let us now, however, turn to the question of the court that should try cases in this area by considering courts trying any kind of criminal case, since the analysis will be identical for any other crime. In our current mythology, it is always said that the court system should be biased against conviction, *i.e.,* instead of attempting to convict when the evidence is stronger for conviction and acquit when the evidence is stronger for acquittal, the courts should only convict when the evidence is stronger than a fair preponderance. Various magical phrases such as "beyond a reasonable doubt" are used to describe this system. As was mentioned before, there seems to be a lack of convincing empirical evidence that our courts actually behave this way, but the myth says they do and we can now inquire whether they should.

In Figure 11–1, I have plotted evidence and percentage of de-

fendants found guilty in the manner to which you have by now
become accustomed. If the courts attempted to decide according
to the fair preponderance of the evidence, they would use the rule
indicated by line A. If, on the other hand, they are biased in favor
of the accused, they would follow the rule represented by line B.
Note that if they follow the rule represented by line B, there will
be few cases of erroneous findings of guilt and many cases of erroneous findings of innocence. If we return to Equation (11.1),
which shows the payoff on various types of institutions in dealing
with theft, we will note that change from line A to line B will
make two changes. The likelihood of conviction (L_c) and the likelihood of false conviction (L_{fc}) will both go down. In order to

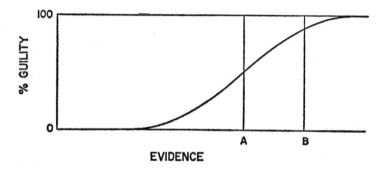

FIGURE 11–1 Bias in Criminal Proceedings

avoid an increase in the crime rate, we would have to increase
the punishment (P_u). It is by no means certain that this change
would benefit people who are erroneously accused. It is possible
that they would find that the combination of a new lower probability of being unjustly convicted with the higher penalty if convicted makes them worse off than they were before. Still, this is
only a possibility. It might well be that providing the highest payoff under Equation (11.1) (which, of course, means the smallest
negative number for P) would involve some such bias. This is essentially a technological question and one that can only be dealt
with when we have far more information about the nature of the
enforcement process.

It is, of course, quite possible that the common view in this matter that we should so bias our court proceedings so as to make what we might call type 1 errors more likely than type 2 errors, is the correct policy. We cannot say. What we can say, however, from an inspection of our equation is that improvements in procedure will be helpful. If we can increase L_c, reduce L_{fc}, and leave C_c unchanged, then we would get an unambiguous gain. Here we have a *quasi-Paretian rule*. If we have a number of factors, the interaction of which we cannot now measure, it may nevertheless be possible to make unambiguous improvement in the real world by improving one of them without worsening any other. Thus costless improvements in the accuracy of the court process or the detection process will have an unambiguously positive payoff. Furthermore, these two improvements would reduce the product of L_{fc} and P_u.

Here again, we find that improved efficiency in our apparatus for finding out what actually happened (the "police" and "courts") would have a clear and decided benefit. In general, improvements in the accuracy of our system can come in either of two ways: increasing the resources devoted to it or adopting improved procedures. The first, of course, carries with it the cost of the resources invested. The second is essentially free. We should not permit customs that descend from the Middle Ages to bind us today. Improved procedure should be considered not in terms of sacred rules but as a matter of science and technique. Problems of innocence and guilt, of imprisonment and the crime rate are too important to leave to the judgment of men who died long ago.

12

Fraud and Information Control

It may surprise the reader to hear that some intelligent and well-informed people believe that fraud should be legal. These people are normally associated with the "Austrian school" of economics, and the arguments they offer against making fraud illegal are worthy of brief consideration. Although fraud, like robbery and theft, is an effort to obtain property that is not properly yours, it does raise rather different issues. In the first place, it is normally fairly easy to avoid being defrauded. A few simple precautions—such as not buying gold stock unless it is listed on an exchange—will usually be sufficient. Secondly, it is normally impossible for the person perpetrating the fraud to conceal his identity. This means that he will not be able to continue in a career of fraud unless he changes his environment fairly frequently.

These two factors mean that fraud is never likely to be a major influence upon the economy regardless of how lightly the law treats it. The small minority of economists who argue that there should be no laws against fraud point out that fraud is almost unknown in markets where the same sellers deal with the same buyers over long periods of time. In any event, legal restrictions on fraud are, from any point of view, less important than those on theft and robbery.

In practice, the laws against fraud take these arguments into account to some extent. The normal prosecution for fraud results from an inability to repay. If the person who has perpetrated the fraud is willing and able to repay, there will usually be no prosecution. This is not true with theft and robbery. The jury system, of course, makes prosecution for fraud particularly difficult. Many successful frauds are too complicated for the jury to understand and, hence, successful prosecution against fraud defendants is difficult if not impossible. This is particularly true of that type of fraud called embezzlement. The record of prosecution of reasonably skilled embezzlers is so poor and the danger of suits for false arrests is so great if prosecution fails that few victimized firms and prosecuting attorneys are willing to take the risk. Normally, an embezzler who works out a complicated plan of embezzlement and who does not confess will find that he is simply fired when he is discovered.

Nevertheless, neither fraud nor embezzlement is likely to be a permanent career. Both require getting the confidence of someone, which is difficult to do if you are either a stranger or a man with the reputation of a defrauder. Each fraud, however, either ruins your reputation and/or requires that you move; hence, continued fraud is unlikely.

It might be argued that the more intelligent part of the population would have a net gain from making fraud legal. They would be relatively immune from fraud themselves, and the legal situation would give them the right to defraud their less intelligent fellow citizens. It seems unlikely, however, that this would really work out to the advantage of even the most clever part of the population. The legalization of fraud would surely lead to a great proliferation of protections against it. Business deals would become much harder to negotiate if each party had to be continually on his guard. Fraud normally involves misinforming people, and any increase in the quantity of misinformation in a system will always reduce its efficiency. Altogether it seems likely that the less that fraud is attempted, the higher the national income will be. It would be a small factor, but still worth some investment of resources.

The laws against fraud, although difficult to enforce if juries are depended upon, are easy to enforce if the court system is reasonably efficient. It is usually fairly obvious who is the guilty person. The man who sold you the gold stock may have suddenly left town, but at least you can recognize him. The man who works out a complicated plan of embezzlement may have covered his tracks so carefully that he is hard to pick out of the mass of other bookkeepers, but this is exceptional. Normally, once the embezzlement is discovered, it is fairly easy to tell who was responsible. The embezzler must, if he is to be successful, run a continuing fraud, and this is normally impossible. Most embezzlers get involved in embezzlement without much prior thought, perhaps as a result of a sudden need of money. By a single embezzlement, they may make enough money to retire, particularly given the difficulty of getting convictions, but they are unlikely to have the opportunity to do it twice.

In order to clarify the issue, let us once again turn to our high school algebra exercises. Equation (12.1) shows the payoff to an individual who plans fraud if there is no law against it.[1]

$$(12.1) \qquad P = BLP_n - C_o - (1-L)C_rL_r$$

TABLE OF SYMBOLS 12-1

B	=	Benefit expected to be derived by potential liar from the action being urged
C_{in}	=	Cost of information
C_o	=	Conscience, internal cost of lying
C_p	=	Costs of punishment
C_r	=	Injury to reputation through others' knowledge that an individual has lied
I_i	=	Injury suffered by victim from carrying out action urged by liar
L	=	Likelihood that lie will be believed
L_p	=	Likelihood of punishment if lie is not believed
L_r	=	Likelihood that injury to the reputation will occur if lie is not believed
P	=	Payoff
P_n	=	Persuasive effect of the lie: probability that the lie, if believed, will bring about the desired action

[1] The following discussion is based largely on the author's "The Economics of Lying," *Toward A Mathematics of Politics* (Ann Arbor: University of Michigan Press, 1967), pp. 133–143.

As usual, the equation is basically simple. The benefits to be obtained from successfully deceiving the person whom you are attempting to defraud times the likelihood that your lie will have a persuasive effect, *i.e.,* lead him to undertake the action you desire, are at the left. We subtract from this the conscience cost (which we discussed to some extent in the last chapter and will return to again in Chapter 14) and the probability that the lie will not be believed, together with the injury to the reputation of the individual that will be occasioned by the disbelief of the lie. Those persons who argue that fraud should not be illegal are, in essence, saying that the $C_r \cdot L_r$ is so large and L is so small that this equation would normally show P as a negative number.

Equation (12.2) shows the net payoff to the individual to whom the lie is addressed. The I_l in this case is the injury that he will suffer in the event that he believes the lie, and the lie has the desired persuasive effect. As a consequence, P is actually a negative quantity—an injury in all cases where it is not zero.

(12.2) $$P = I_l \cdot L \cdot P_n$$

Even if I_l is equal to B, *i.e.,* if it is a straightforward transfer of funds from one person to another—a fake sale of gold stock or something of that sort—it is clear that the benefit achieved by the potential confidence man is less than the injury suffered by the victim. In most cases, of course, there is no such simple transfer and the benefit received by the confidence man is much less than the injury to his victim.

Note, then, that if it were possible, the potential victims of fraud would be willing to pay potential confidence men to desist. A bargain could theoretically be struck between these two groups. In practice, of course, no such bargain is possible because the people who plan frauds must, of necessity, conceal that fact from their potential victims. Nevertheless, we may call this difficulty an extreme case of a transaction cost and, therefore, can say that such a payment would be a Pareto-optimal change. Here, as in many other cases, it may be possible to use the government to minimize transaction costs. In particular, a procedure under which resources are used to repress fraud may be a suitable procedure.

Before turning to this matter, however, let us consider Equation
(12.3) in which the potential victim invests resources in obtaining information in order to reduce the likelihood of fraud.

$$(12.3) \qquad P = I_l \cdot L \cdot P_n + C_{in}$$

If we compare Equation (12.3) with Equation (12.1), it is once
again clear that the net cost to the potential victim of fraud is
greater than the net benefit to the person who might gain from the
fraud. It is not true, of course, that the P in Equation (12.3) is necessarily lower (a larger negative number) than the P in Equation
(12.2). Although in Equation (12.3) the potential victim of fraud
is investing resources in obtaining information to protect himself
against fraud, this would have the effect of reducing the value of
L. If he has invested his resources rationally, the negative payoff
from Equation (12.3) would be less than the negative payoff of
Equation (12.2).

Let us now consider the situation if we have a law against
fraud, *i.e.,* some cost will be assessed on a person who is detected in committing or attempting to commit a fraud. Equation
(12.4) shows the payoff for attempted fraud under these conditions.

$$(12.4) \qquad P = B \cdot P_n \cdot L - C_o - (1-L)(C_p L_p + C_r L_r)$$

Note that I have collapsed the likelihood of detection and likelihood of conviction terms of the equations in earlier chapters to
simple costs of punishment and likelihood of punishment. This is
merely for simplicity and does not change the argument. It is, of
course, clear that the payoff under Equation (12.4) is lower than
the payoff under Equation (12.1). Marginal individuals who are
contemplating fraud under conditions given in Equation (12.1)
would be dissuaded under the conditions given in Equation
(12.4).

However, the cost of establishing the punishment system would
be greater than the benefits to be obtained thereby. Looked at in
terms of present discounted value, I would contemplate the possible benefits that I might obtain from being successful in committing

fraud under Equation (12.1) less the possible injuries I might suffer from being the victim of fraud under the Equation (12.3), and weigh that against the situation that would occur if we were in the situation described by Equations (12.3) and (12.4). For the potential victims of fraud or for a professional confidence man (when he is not trying to defraud someone else), the principal difference between the two situations is the different value of C_{in}, which could be lower if there were laws against fraud, and of L, which would consequently also be lower. The first question would be whether the present discounted value to me of reducing these two factors in Equation (12.3) is greater than the injury I will suffer from the reduction in the payoff from any potential frauds I might undertake in Equation (12.4). It is reasonably certain that this calculation would favor the enacting of laws against fraud.

The sole problem remaining is whether there are major costs of enforcement in connection with the law against fraud. The only sizable cost that I can see is the real possibility of judicial error and consequent conviction of innocent persons. In many cases, the only witnesses to the act of fraud are the two parties involved. Since the successful confidence man is necessarily a plausible fellow, it is possible that he will be able to convince the jury that he is telling the truth and that the victim is not. If this is so, it will be possible for people to get out of contracts and place their partners in contract in prison by simply lying in court. It is probably the danger of this type of miscarriage of justice that led to the rules restricting oral testimony that would tend to alter a written contract. If we were confident of the court's ability to detect lies, we could relax these rules.

Nevertheless, the problem of prosecution for fraud does not seem to be overwhelmingly difficult. There is, in fact, one area in which the prosecution of fraud would seem to be remarkably easy. One way of committing fraud is to sell something to the public through false advertising. In this particular case, the proof that false claims have been made is ridiculously easy. The only problems in court would be whether the claims in fact were false and whether the businessman might not have, perhaps, believed them himself. The latter possible defense in this case could be eliminated if we had a rule that people engaging in large-scale adver-

tising campaigns are required to assure themselves to some reasonable degree as to the accuracy of their statements.

It is an interesting fact that we have not, in general, turned to
the standard law of fraud to deal with this problem. It is not
obvious why this should be so. It is true that the development
of nationwide advertising was rather quick and an adjustment of
the court system to this new type of crime may have been difficult.
Nevertheless, it would seem that the easy way of dealing with
this particular type of fraud would be to appoint special bunco
squads and special divisions in the prosecuting attorney's office
rather than to set up federal governmental agencies such as the
Federal Trade Commission. This is particularly so since most of
these federal administrative agencies do not have the full powers
that are given to district attorneys and the courts. The penalty
they can impose upon people who commit fraud is considerably
lighter than the penalty imposed by regular courts.

Regular court procedures were not, however, the methods
chosen and we now have a number of special governmental bu-
reaus engaged in dealing with dishonest advertising, which is not
treated as simple fraud. Note that, in general, it is not possible
for private persons to sue for damages in such cases. If you were
to sell me a piece of land under conditions that the court would
consider fraudulent and you had sufficient funds, I could sue you
and get the money back. But in general if you defraud me by
engaging in a nationwide advertising campaign, and the amount
of money that I personally lose through my believing your advertising is small, our court system provides no remedy.

Theoretically, there are two types of private suits that would
be possible in this event. First, one would anticipate that the competitors of the company engaging in the fraudulent advertising
would be able to sue for the damages that they suffered from the
resulting loss of customers. Unfortunately, as the result of a
rather peculiar legal decision made in the latter part of the nineteenth century, this type of suit is impossible. The courts refused
to permit this kind of suit on the grounds that it would be hard
to determine what the damages were. It is, of course, difficult to
determine the proper amount of damages, but it does not seem
that this would deter the courts. They are willing to decide the

monetary damage of having a girl's nose bent slightly. It does not seem that it would be any harder to calculate damages against a man who had made false claims and, hence, injured his competitors. This would be particularly true since the major effect of permitting such suits would be to make it more unlikely that people would make false claims. Thus, the potential purchasers would be benefited even if the amount of damages were improperly computed.

This particular remedy has the fairly obvious advantage that a company's competitors are more likely to be both in a position to detect its false advertising claims and better motivated to take action against such claims than any other group in society. Thus, using these competitors as policemen would seem to be a rational policy. In the antitrust area, of course, we do use this technique. We permit private persons or companies who are injured by monopolies to sue for triple damages. It would be sensible to permit similar suits by competitors who were injured by false claims in advertising.

A second method of enforcing rules against false advertising would be to encourage the customers to sue in the form of a class suit. This is a rather unusual form of litigation. Essentially, a lawyer who is looking for business finds a large number of people who have each been injured slightly. He then collects three or more of these people, and they institute a class suit in the name of all of the others so injured. If the suit is successful, the defendant in the suit is compelled to make restitution to the large collection of people who have been injured, and the judge awards a standard percentage fee for the lawyer. Obviously, it is a very lucrative practice for lawyers; only our obsolete rules restricting entrepreneural activity on the part of lawyers make it rare. Here, again, we have a method that could make false advertising claims extremely expensive.

Turning from direct fraud, there are also other areas in which control of information may be desirable. First, let us consider statements that, although not directly dishonest, are likely to deceive. We can include in this category things such as packaging, which makes the contents appear larger than they are, and other methods that deceive the unwary but not the careful purchaser.

By turning back to our equations, it is again obvious that the purchasers or potential purchasers would be willing to pay the potential sellers to desist from this kind of activity because it will permit a reduced investment by the potential purchasers in obtaining information. Once again, it is not possible to have a direct agreement between the two parties in these matters because of the transaction costs, but governmental activity may reduce the transaction problems and, therefore, be desirable from everybody's standpoint. In this case, the traditional law of fraud is not (strictly speaking) applicable. The objective is to make it easier to purchase safely.

If legal restrictions on this type of activity are sensible under our welfare criteria, the question of organization is much more difficult. Specific laws requiring accuracy in the packaging or the labeling of commodities are difficult to draft. If the enacting of specific legislation is difficult in this field, the use of administrative agencies has also not been very successful. Apparently the type of information that seems useful to a governmental regulatory board is not the type that seems useful to actual purchasers. The Securities and Exchange Commission, for example, has required all new issues of securities to be accompanied by a thick disclosure booklet that meets its approval, but purchasers of securities seldom read these booklets.[2] It is perhaps significant that there is a debate currently going on in the economics profession as to whether the Securities and Exchange Commission has had any desirable effect at all.[3] The only effect that all parties to the debate are agreed on is that the cost of preparing these booklets is high enough so that it is no longer possible for small companies to go into the public issue market.

It may be, however, that these difficulties in making the actual sale nondeceptive simply indicate the ineptitude on the part of the specific regulators and are not a permanent characteristic of regulatory commissions. Surely we can hope so. This is an area in which experimentation and research might have a high payoff. The

[2] The booklet is required by law to carry a false statement that it has not been approved by the Securities and Exchange Commission.

[3] For a summary see Henry G. Manne, ed., *Economic Policy and the Regulation of Corporate Securities* (Washington, D.C.: American Enterprise Institute, 1969).

elimination of deceptive information from the total information stream would be a net improvement in efficiency. Requiring parties who have differential access to some type of information to provide it to people with whom they are dealing with also, in most cases, be a net improvement. The only problems are practical questions of organization. These practical problems may be insoluble, and certainly the agencies now engaged in enforcing this type of regulation have made very little progress in solving them. But experiments aimed at their solution would be a rational investment of resources.

It should be noted that a great deal of supervision and enforcement of standards in the commercial area is undertaken not by the government but by private organizations. A particularly conspicuous example is the Howard Johnson Company, which enters into contracts with local restaurant owners under which they are required to provide a highly standardized set of services to their customers. The improved information flow that results from this has been vastly profitable to both Howard Johnson and most of the local owners. There are a great many other areas in which private persons commercially provide standardized and/or improved information.

Another special problem concerns contracts. If we consider the contract of insurance, for example, the average man never reads it and has small understanding of its contents. This has led a number of states to establish organizations that provide a standard contract (or to be more exact, a wide range of standard contracts) that the insurance companies are compelled to use. In practice, this reform has not worked out very well, partly because the insurance companies have been able to influence the agencies in various undesirable ways and partly because the agencies themselves tend to be incompetent and resistant to new ideas. Nevertheless, in theory, one can argue for the provision of standardized contracts. Normally, one would want to permit the parties to make another contract if the standard contract did not meet their requirements, but the provision of standardized arrangements might be a way of simplifying the information flow.

There are other areas in which the establishment of standards would simplify the information problem for the buyers and sellers of a commodity. The grade labeling of meat would be an example, and surely does no harm as long as the people who benefit by it pay for it, and as long as it is possible for meat that is not grade labeled to be sold. The basic problem with grade labeling or setting standards is that most commodities can vary in a very large number of different ways. The establishment of standards involves a setting off of reductions in one attribute against improvements in another. It may well be that, for some people, the particular trade-off used by the governmental regulatory commission is not ideal. Thus, they would prefer a somewhat different set of qualities, and we should leave them free to obtain this different set in the market.

In addition to commercial problems there are a number of other areas in which false or very careless statements are made—and their elimination would be desirable. The most obvious single area is also the area that is best known by the average man to be extremely dishonest. This is politics. Under present circumstances, except for very slight restrictions under the law of libel, false statements by politicians are completely and totally uncontrolled by law. It is only if the C_r portion of our equation seems to be particularly high for a given politician that he need worry about dishonesty. It is, I suppose, obvious that our previous reasoning would lead to the conclusion that making false statements in the course of a political campaign (or, for that matter, on the floor of Congress) should be severely punished. Unfortunately, here again we run into extremely difficult practical considerations.

The practical problem is not that it is difficult to detect this type of fraud but that the person who is successful is put in a position to protect himself against any governmental action.[4] Here again, however, it would seem that research and experimentation are called for. Perhaps some arrangement under which a reasonably impartial judiciary is supplemented by a prosecuting apparatus in the hands of the opposition might work. I would hesitate to make any specific recommendations, but it certainly is important and we should invest considerable resources in this area of research.

[4] Treason never prospers. What's the reason? When treason prospers, none dare call it treason. Sir John Harington, *The most elegant and wittie epigrams of Sir John Harington* (Princeton: Princeton Univ. Press, 1916).

Turning to another area, a false statement by Smith about Jones that injures Jones is grounds for a suit for libel or slander. The arguments normally given for this depend upon what are essentially property rights on the part of Jones in his own reputation. This, of course, assumes that it is desirable that Jones have property rights in his reputation and, as far as I know, no one has demonstrated this. It is, however, true that on the whole the average person would be better off if the number of false statements that he encounters in his daily life were reduced. This would mean that the information that he receives is somewhat more reliable and he is required to invest less in checking statements that come to his attention. Permitting suits in libel and slander presumably has some effect in reducing the number of false statements with which the individual is bombarded.

It should be noted that our method of dealing with libel and slander is not the only possible one. The Brazilians, for example, do not permit libel suits against newspapers. They require, however, newspapers to permit a person who has been criticized to answer in the paper. There are some signs that a somewhat similar provision is being introduced into our radio and television law. Whether this is better or worse than libel actions is not clear.

Lastly, it seems reasonable that the reduction of the total amount of noise in the form of false statements that we obtain from the media would be desirable. It would permit us to have a given level of information with a reduced investment in checking. Thus, if a popular journal runs an article on, say, a small island off the coast of Australia that is romanticized to a considerable extent and reflects what they think their readers would like to think about the island rather than what actually exists, no one is obviously injured. Actions for fraud, libel, or slander would not lie. Yet the net effect of this article is that, in a real sense, society is somewhat less well informed than it was before. It now, or at least some members of it, believes things that are untrue whereas before it had a zero information level. Furthermore, anyone who wanted to find out about this particular island might find this particular article; this surely would make his information-gathering activities somewhat more difficult and somewhat more hazardous in outcome than they otherwise would be.

Restrictions on this type of false information raise even more severe practical problems than the restrictions we have discussed thus far. It is unlikely that any private individual would be motivated to take action. Surely there is no one who could sue.[5] Furthermore, the danger in governmental restriction is extremely high. Once again, however, it seems that we should at least do some research.

In a sense, the first part of this chapter was devoted to laboring the obvious. We proved that fraud is a bad thing. Some of the later conclusions that are drawn from the same line of reasoning, however, will be regarded by many readers as not only nonobvious but absurd. I can only suggest that the line of reasoning that I have followed and that leads to these surprising results does not seem to have any serious defects. The proposals are largely proposals for experimental investment of resources. It does seem to me that we should look into the possibility of exercising more control over the dissemination of misinformation. The problem of instituting such controls without at the same time preventing dissemination of information that is for one reason or another objectionable to the government is extremely difficult. It may be insoluble, but I see no reason for accepting the status quo until we have thought much more about it.

[5] Possibly the competing news media might be permitted to sue in this case. They would have at least some motive to bring such suits and might serve as policemen.

13

Crimes Against the Person

The usual distinction between crimes against property and crimes against the person is simple and straightforward, and involves the nature of the crime. A more basic distinction would be between crimes that are intended to improve the material well-being of the criminal and crimes that are merely motivated by a desire to injure someone else and, thus, give the criminal utility. Crimes against the person falling in the first class can be dealt with by the reasoning given in Chapter 11. In discussing crimes motivated by a desire to injure, we should note that there are some crimes against property of a similar nature. It sometimes happens, particularly in family disputes, that a person will engage in, for example, arson, not because he anticipates any particular direct gain from it but because he wishes to injure the person whose property is burned down. This is a crime against property, but it is very similar to the crimes against the person to be discussed in this chapter.

Crimes that are not motivated by desire for material gain are actually much less common than materially motivated crimes. The commonest single example is injuring somebody in a fight—such as a barroom brawl. In such cases, the desire to inflict bodily injury is usually transitory. Less commonly, there are cases of the planned infliction of injury as a result of hatred or dislike of the person injured. This is sometimes the motive for murder. In other cases the crime of murder is committed primarily to get rid of the person murdered, but not to make a direct material gain or to satisfy hatred. Thus, for example, a man who would like to get rid of his wife may murder her without necessarily feeling any violent aversion to her personally. She is in his way, but is not a hated object.

Last, but by no means least, we have crimes in which violence is worked upon the victim for reasons of direct pleasure in the act by the perpetrator. The commonest example of this, of course, is rape. There seem, however, to be a number of other rather similar crimes, in particular some types of sex crimes in which children are the victims, and there have been cases in which sadists have obtained pleasure by torturing their victims. Usually, again, the victims are children, and usually some type of sexual assault is included. The last group of crimes is the result of severe mental derangement, and I shall not discuss them further.

In order to consider the simplest possible case of a crime committed for the purpose of inflicting injury, let us begin with a most rare crime—carefully calculated assault. Consider a person who has a desire to injure another person and is contemplating doing so. For present purposes, we need not inquire as to why he wishes to injure his victim. It may be that he is a sadist who likes to inflict pain; he may have a violent feeling of hatred toward the person who is to be injured; or the injury he is contemplating may be murder and he may simply wish to get the person to be injured out of his way for one reason or another. In all of these cases, the criminal will gain satisfaction from his criminal act and the victim will, we can safely assume, have his utility reduced.

If we wish to avoid interpersonal comparison of utilities, we could only say this and then inquire as to whether the victim would be willing to pay enough to the person planning the crime to stop him. This is the standard Paretian way of avoiding interpersonal comparison and, with this type of crime, it is not particularly helpful. It would be possible, for example, to make a living by threatening violence and then collecting the payment made to avoid it. The contrary procedure—requiring the person contemplating violence to purchase from his victim the right to commit the violence—would have the disadvantage that in many cases it would eliminate the motive for the violence. If I am trying to injure a person and must actually make him slightly better off by giving him full compensation for any injury, obviously I cannot accomplish my goal.

We are, thus, in an area in which the standard welfare tools do not work very well. Most of us would simply engage in interpersonal comparison in this case, but without some kind of interpersonal comparison of utilities, we cannot say that laws prohibiting people from using force and violence against other persons solely for the purpose of working injury are undesirable. It will be recalled that we included among our assumptions the proposition that individuals did not get more pleasure out of inflicting pain on others than the pain they would receive from the same amount of injury upon themselves. With this assumption and risk aversion, it is easy to demonstrate that people would be opposed to making assault and battery and other crimes of violence legal. It should be noted in this connection that, although there would presumably be some strong, vigorous people who, in their youth, could anticipate inflicting far more injury on other people than they themselves would receive, all of us are going to become older. The youth of twenty who injured a number of other people might find that the latter part of his life was extremely uncomfortable. Thus, we can argue, on the base of this special assumption, that laws against force and violence are desirable.

It is possible that there are some people in society for which this assumption is not true, *i.e.,* they obtain more pleasure from the inflicting of violence than the pain that they would suffer from receiving similar violence. If there are such persons, we could arrange a special "violence" club for them in which they would be able to inflict violence on each other. Granted the assumption, this would be a desirable institution from their standpoint and there is no reason why anyone else should object to it. Historically, it is clear that there have been many cases in which people have gained positive pleasure from fighting. In fact, it is possible to argue that young males in general get a positive payoff out of fighting and certainly many drunks act as if they do.

Whether this is something we should prohibit in terms of *our* judgment of their behavior is, of course, different from the question of whether it is Pareto-optimal. If both parties to a fight, duel, or brawl obtain pleasure from it, there is no welfare reason why outsiders should interfere.[1] In any event, the rules prohibiting the use of violence on a person whose own personal preference function is not such that he gains more out of the chance of inflicting violence than he loses from having violence inflicted on him is clearly justifiable, as long as we leave people who have other preference functions free to commit violence upon each other.

Having decided that crimes against a person (outside the violence club) should be controlled by law, we are still left with a most difficult problem: what amount of punishment fits a crime of this sort? For theft the problem is easy. We can simply make the punishment heavy enough so that the present discounted value of the punishment is greater than the present discounted value of the loot, and the computation can be done in material terms because the object of the crime is material. In our present case, the object of the crime is to receive an immaterial satisfaction from the act itself. Computing the cost that will make it unlikely that people will undertake it is, therefore, much more difficult. I regret that I can offer nothing very impressive in the way of such computation. In fact, as we shall shortly see, the problem in real life is even more difficult. Nevertheless, we have here a case in which empirical tools would work. We could experiment with raising and lowering the penalty for this type of crime and find out the effect on the number of such crimes.

It would, of course, be desirable to make clear to the potential criminals the size of the penalty they are risking and the likelihood that they will be caught. In the case of the carefully calculated crimes we are now discussing, the probability of punishment is high. Once again, it may be that our present methods greatly overemphasize the amount of deterrence that is necessary for this type of crime. Unfortunately, this type of crime is closely

---

[1] If the state has an institution that automatically provides payments to people who are crippled (and fighting of one sort or another is likely to lead to such crippling), then perhaps a suitable tax on the fighting to pay the full cost of this possible payment would be rational.

connected to the next type we are to discuss and may be practically indistinguishable from it. If so, it may be that the fairly light penalty that would be necessary to prevent carefully calculated crimes of violence will have to be replaced by the heavier punishment necessary for the next type of crime.

Most crimes of violence are not carefully calculated. They are either by-products of other crimes intended to improve the well-being of the criminal or a result of something such as a barroom brawl. The former case has already been discussed, but the latter case has not been touched upon. Up to this point we have been talking about what must be a very tiny category of crimes against the person—those crimes that are carefully thought out and are intended solely to injure someone.

All of the crimes discussed thus far are, if we except only some of the automobile offenses, crimes of calculation. This does not mean that the individual who commits the crime has done a lot of careful thought but that they are the type of crime that we can well imagine a person deciding to commit even after careful consideration. They could involve calculation even though in some cases they may not. Many of the crimes against a person, however, are not of this sort. They result from losses of temper. Sometimes they involve a desire to fight, particularly on the part of someone who is drunk. In a few cases, they involve a sudden strong emotional drive that the criminal does not or cannot resist.

At first glance, it might seem that this type of crime cannot be prevented by providing a penalty for committing it. Since the crime itself is not the result of much in the way of rational thought, we might assume that rational criteria would not stop people from committing such crimes. If, however, we think a little bit about our ordinary day-to-day behavior, we will realize that the degree to which we give in to our emotions is affected by the consequences. While preparing this chapter, I happened to be in England and came across an article in the *Daily Mail* in which the President of the Football League remarked that English football had recently been disgraced by a number of acts of violence on the field. He proposed to deal with this problem by imposing very stiff penalties on the players who lost their tempers.[2]

---

[2] Len Shipman, *Daily Mail*, 25 August 1967, p. 14. "Suspension of up to three months or half a season will have to be introduced for persistent

One might think that such control would be impossible, but a little thought about the way people actually behave will indicate that it is not. Furthermore, no one wrote to the Editor and said that the President was imbecilic in thinking that he could stop people from losing their temper by making it painful. In most walks of life we depend upon such controls. Parents will teach their children not to lose their temper by punishing them. The police are unkind to people who lose their temper on being arrested, and this also has an effect.

In this field, there seems to be a certain amount of double-thinking in much popular discussion. Perhaps this can be illustrated best by a page from *Time* magazine. The issue of 3 September 1967 began with a long discussion of Negro rioting and remedies that could be used to prevent it. It was the theme of the discussion that police force would not stop the riots. The following article, however, dealt with Mace, which inflicts a great deal of pain and suffering on a rioter without much further damage to him. This article began by saying that Mace can do a great deal to prevent rioting. Clearly, the editors of *Time* did not realize that they were using two different criteria in their two successive articles. Regardless of the truth or falsity of the first approach to rioting, the second certainly will work. This does not, of course, indicate that it should be our sole dependence.

Most of the acts of violence that are not committed in the course of a crime aimed at improving the material well-being of a criminal are the result of a loss of temper or something of this sort. The category of calculated crimes of violence that we discussed at the beginning of this chapter is probably very small, and it is a difficult administrative problem to separate the two types. It may well be necessary to treat all crimes against the person as if they were the result of a loss of temper.

offenders. Now is the time to act, particularly in the cases where players lose their tempers. I don't mind so much the cases where a player is sent off for tackling from behind, for instance."

"What has to be stamped out immediately is the incidence of players going berserk for a split second. I mean players who retaliate violently after they have been fouled and start kicking and lashing out. For men like that, we have to think of the stiffer punishments of up to half a season's suspension."

Determining the proper amount of punishment for such crimes is clearly difficult. It seems likely that the probability of an individual's committing assault and battery late in the evening in a bar would depend upon a number of variables. One may be how much he had to drink, another the strength of his emotions at the time, and a third would be the probable consequences of the action. Considering the latter, which is the only variable we have available for social control, we could probably not totally prevent such assaults without extraordinarily cruel punishment. It is likely that if all bars were equipped with two husky policemen who would immediately pounce upon any individual engaging in any kind of violence and pop him into a kettle of boiling oil, acts of violence would not occur (at least not in bars). Furthermore, people who thought they might succumb to temptation to commit acts of violence would stay out of bars. Needless to say, I do not propose this method.

The fact that we can imagine ourselves committing such crimes is, perhaps, relevant. We would like to minimize the total suffering that might be imposed upon us through being victims of such crimes and also through being severely penalized for a possible loss of control of our emotions. In any event, the exact amount of punishment that should be handed out in such cases is a very difficult problem. I suspect that we would find a rather slow pay-off to increases in the amount of punishment. That is, if we experimented by gradually raising the punishment for attacking a man in a bar from a fine of $25 to life imprisonment, we would find a relatively slow reduction in the number of assaults that were committed as the penalty was being raised. All that can be done in the present state of knowledge is to make some kind of rough-and-ready approximation of the correct penalty.

The lack of calculation in this type of crime is, of course, its distinguishing characteristic. Nevertheless, I think that we would be unwise to draw too firm a line of division between crimes of this sort and crimes such as theft or embezzlement. There, also, a lack of calculation may sometimes turn up; there, also, we have a spectrum from crimes that are carefully thought out to those crimes that in many ways result from the impulse of the moment. The so-called thoughtless act of violence also represents a somewhat similar spectrum, although probably the degree of advance thought is much less than in embezzlement, and the difficulty in deterring this type of crime by threat of imprisonment is correspondingly greater.

Thus far, I have deferred discussion of one very large category of crime; namely, sex crimes. This category is actually composed of two quite different types of acts. In the first group (prostitution, homosexuality, and a number of so-called deviations in which all the persons involved in the act give their consent) no one is directly injured. Laws against crimes of this sort, and statistically they are almost certainly among the commonest, are expression of moral disapprobation and not an example of the type of reasoning used thus far in this book. I may, perhaps, be annoyed by the musical review *Oh, Calcutta*. If this were so, there is an externality involved and I am, in a sense, injured. But in this case, the externality and my injury come, in essence, from my moral feelings; this is something of which we have avoided discussion thus far. Thus, this type of behavior falls outside the scope of this book. The most significant legal reforms in English history —associated with the name of Bentham—included the legalization of prostitution that is still perfectly legal in England. There are, however, restrictions on the efficient economic organization of prostitution in England. Pimping is certainly a nasty occupation in the view of most people, but there is no obvious, nonmoral, reason why it should be illegal.

The professional criminal operating in an area where no one concerned in the crime is likely to complain to the police has found it a profitable and not particularly dangerous field of crime. Furthermore, the police have tended to feel that there is very little wrong with the activity and, hence, have been willing to accept bribes to permit it to continue. Thus, the repeal of laws against this type of activity (also gambling) would probably work a very great change in the structure of our criminal community.

There remains, however, a minority of sex crimes in which it cannot be said that all parties consent. Rape, of course, is an obvious example. It is probable, however, that the commonest example is exposure. Regardless of the details, in each case some person (usually a woman) is subjected to some kind of sexual behavior to which he or she objects. In many of the cases, it is very hard to explain the behavior of the person committing the crime except on grounds of mental derangement. It would appear still to be so, however, that the principal instrument of social control is the use of punishment as a deterrent, and these matters would not differ theoretically from assault committed in a bar. In this class of crimes, as indeed for most sex crimes, we should hope for medical progress that may eventually solve the problem. Meanwhile, we must continue to use the ordinary penal methods.

In some ways, the chapter we are now concluding is most unsatisfactory. To a very large extent, it deals with crimes that are undertaken for reasons that do not really lend themselves to careful calculation, either by potential criminals or students. We cannot hope to have as simple a system for dealing with these crimes as for such obvious crimes of calculation as straightforward burglary. It is, nevertheless, true that these crimes are undertaken in order to maximize the preference function of the criminal and that by putting a penalty on the commission of the crime, we will affect behavior. The mother who punishes a child for having a tantrum is not behaving irrationally. Similarly, punishing someone for losing his temper and killing in a drunken rage is also not irrational. Unfortunately, it is unlikely to be as effective as similar punishment for burglary.

PART IV

ETHICS

14

Ethics

Traditional legal theory started with an ethical foundation and built a legal structure upon it. Thus far, we have largely avoided ethics and have used only utilitarian considerations. It is true that such words as "unjust" have occasionally occurred in the text, but primarily as a result of the limitations of the English language. If a law is enacted that provides for punishment for committing assault and battery, then it is clumsy to say, when the court procedure miscarries, that the outcome was contrary to the intent of the persons who drafted the law. The use of the phrase "unjust" in such a case seems to be an excusable simplification.

In this chapter, we finally turn to ethical considerations. Our approach, however, will be opposite to that of the usual legal treatise. We shall argue not that the law should be ethically correct but that our ethics should be in accord with the law. In a sense, our argument will be based on the work of John Wesley, the founder of Methodism. When discussing his preaching with the upper classes, Wesley always pointed out that his missionary activities reduced the crime rate, which in turn resulted in a reduction in the expenditures for such things as police and prisons. It is clear that this is a valid argument. The prevention of crime and enforcement of contracts by use of courts and police may be effective, but making this our sole reliance is probably not the least expensive way of dealing with these problems. One part of all educational systems is the indoctrination of children in a particular ethical code. If children are indoctrinated in this way and if the indoctrination is continued while they are adults, it is likely that it will be somewhat easier to enforce the law. This indoctrination will, however, make it harder to change the law when that seems desirable.

Perhaps my own interest in this aspect of the matter is greater than that of the average person because I spent some time in China. The Chinese approach to the law has been very largely an exercise in propaganda. Among the major duties of the state was propagandizing the law and fairly large expenditures of resources were made to this end; much more, proportionately, than we use for similar activity.

A number of the equations that we have used to deal with specific crimes have contained the term C_o or "cost of conscience." When I first introduced this terminology, I apologized for its use as it clearly carried ethical overtones. It is now time to discuss these ethical overtones. If we can (by the indoctrination of children or of adults) put a sizable C_o into the utility function of all individuals in society, then violation of the laws will become rare or indeed nonexistent. The question, of course, is whether this is a lower-cost method of reducing the crime rate than the use of policemen and prisons. This is an empirical problem on which no real research has been done. It would seem likely, however, that at least some resources should be employed in such indoctrination.

There is another part of our basic equation in which indoctrination may be helpful. The likelihood of detection L_d and the likelihood of conviction L_c are actually quite low in our society. If we could convince potential criminals that they were high, this would change their probability calculus and, hence, make their commission of crimes less likely. It is notable that this particular type of propaganda is a major part of the current approach to crime. Such phrases as "Murder will out" or "There is no perfect crime" are repeated endlessly. Their objective is to convince the average man that the danger in committing a crime is vastly higher than it actually is. Surely this must mean that our crime rate is lower than it would be if potential criminals had a more accurate view of the risks involved.[1]

These considerations are not entirely left out of the standard approach to law and ethics. One of the purposes of education is to give moral indoctrination to the children. Furthermore, a good deal of similar indoctrination is given to adults. It is no accident that on television criminals never succeed in the long run. In real life, of course, they do; but it is likely that the continuous repetition of crime stories in which the criminal eventually gets caught discourages crime. Last, but not least, the highly ethical content of a great deal of our literature probably leads people to a somewhat more ethical approach to many problems. All of these things should reduce the cost of enforcing the law. Note, however, that they simply reduce the cost; they do not mean that we can abandon the courts and the police. Our appropriations for courts and police may be lower with an active system of indoctrination than they would have to be without it, but they will still be positive.

Furthermore, reliance on indoctrination has the unfortunate characteristic that it gives the badly indoctrinated people a distinct advantage over the well-indoctrinated. If we reduce our police activity, we reduce the real risk that individuals will be punished for their crimes. Many people are poorly indoctrinated either because they are resistant to indoctrination or because there is some failure in the process. For them, this is a net advantage. If we relied solely on indoctrination, we could end up with a situation in which those people who are systematic violators of the social norms have a very great advantage over those who are not. Needless to say, this is only a theoretical possibility. No society has ever put its total reliance on indoctrination.

If we consider the source of our ethics, we will find that, to a large extent, they are simply something we were taught when we were children; possibly there has been some change since we became adults. Furthermore, in different countries and in different cultures, the ethical principles that are taught to children differ. For those who do not believe in the natural law, there is no

[1] No book that I have written has sold more than 10,000 copies. In view of these considerations, this is perhaps very fortunate.

reason why we would anticipate that ethics would be similar in different areas. For those who do believe in the natural law, and I suppose it will not escape the reader that the author of this book is not one of them, a uniform ethical code for the world as a whole would be expected. Among those friends of mine who do believe in the natural law, I find that this expectation has been formed and they will allege that such a worldwide ethical code does in fact exist.

In order to avoid the empirical problems into which this view would lead them, they sometimes deny that people in foreign countries have somewhat different ethics than they themselves do. More commonly, they will not deny that foreign countries have different ethics than we, but will allege that, at the fundamental level, all ethical codes are identical and that the differences are superficial and not important. This is not the way that I read the anthropological literature. As far as I know, for example, the people who ran Stalin's concentration camps were not subject to any particular qualms of conscience. They honestly thought that disposing of the "enemies of the people" in a painful way was a desirable thing to do. In this case, the ethical indoctrination to which they were responding had been given them after they were adults, but cannibals normally receive their ethical training as children.

In any event, this book has been based upon the assumption that ethics are something we learn. If ethics are learned, then we can inquire what would be the best ethics to teach. Clearly, this would involve the ability to compare different ethical systems. An ethical system that led to efficient behavior in society would presumably be superior to those that led to inefficient behavior. The considerations that we have developed in this book with respect to the law would apply also to ethics. Thus, in a sense, what I am recommending in this book is that we first work out the most efficient legal system and we, then, enforce it by use of the courts and police forces. But we should also indoctrinate a similar ethical code.

Under this system (which many readers will, no doubt, think paradoxical), the ethical system becomes subordinated to the law rather than *vice versa*. People who have been indoctrinated into a given ethical system differing from the system of law that we have developed in this book would normally regard my proposal as being very wicked, and, indeed, it would be in terms of the particular ethical code that they happen to believe in. If, however, we cannot change ethical systems, clearly we are stuck with a nonprogressive part of our society. It seems to me that progress might be made. The traditional methods of "research" in ethics have had very little success. It is not at all obvious that we are more knowledgeable in this field than were Aristotle or Epictetus. Under the circumstances, a radical change in research strategy would seem advisable. This book has been based upon such a radical revision. It may be the wrong type of radicalism, but I hope that it will be judged on its merits rather than condemned simply because it proposes drastic changes in a very conservative field of study.

APPENDIX A

Exceptions to the Social Contract

In Chapter 2, I promised to demonstrate in this Appendix that a society could include a certain number of people who had rather odd preferences without the general principles of the book being inapplicable. Since these preference orderings are unlikely, the demonstration is basically of little importance. It may, however, permit us to make a slight improvement in our society. It may be that a rearranging of our laws to provide for these unusual preference orderings would be an improvement in our polity. This improvement would come partly from those very rare people who actually did have these peculiar preference orderings finding their preference better fitted, but more importantly from the fact that a great many people would be given an open choice between accepting or rejecting certain institutions. A certain element of irrational discontent would thus be eliminated.

I have never met a person with a preference pattern in which being robbed had a high value, although I have met some anarchists who would argue that there should be no laws against robbery. Thus, to repeat, our demonstration is not about a matter of much importance. There are, however, some groups of people who are quite disenchanted with our present system of law. It might be desirable to permit these people to find out, by experience, whether their view of the world is correct. The most important of these groups are the pacifists, and I would like to proceed now to a modest proposal to change our institutional structure so as to make it possible for the pacifists to eschew all use of force and violence.

Pacifism has always posed a serious problem, both to the pacifist and to the nonpacifist. The nonpacifist, feeling "a pacifist is either a slave or a parasite on someone who will fight for his freedom," tends to resent being a host. The pacifist, on the other hand, does not wish to use force or to have it used for him by others. In a recent case, some pacifists who were pushed around by some drunken teen-agers refused to prefer charges because they were not willing to even indirectly apply force. Having the police and courts use force or the threat of force on your behalf is as much a violation of nonviolence as using force directly. Furthermore, some pacifists not only object to the use of force by those parts of the social organization (police, courts, and the armed forces), which are built upon the premise that the use of force is necessary, but they also object to the very existence of these institutions of organized violence and would rather not pay taxes for their support. They will refuse to serve if drafted, which means that their share of the burden of military service is shifted to nonpacifists. Since the number of pacifists is small, this is, of course, a minor effect.

It would seem sensible to search for an institutional improvement—a change that from the standpoint of the pacifist and from the standpoint of the nonpacifist will appear to be desirable.[1] In part, this agreement would result from the somewhat different views of the nature of the world and of human nature held by the pacifist and the nonpacifist, and the enactment of the necessary changes would, in a sense, be an experiment of finding out which view of the world is correct. The scientific value of the experiment would be a further argument for the change.

The proposal, stated in the simplest terms, is to permit the pacifist to put his principles into practice by arranging to let him

---

[1] Some of the people who call themselves pacifists are actually simply trying to evade the draft by lying. These people would not be benefited by the proposed changes.

stop paying taxes to support the police and army, and, at the same time, see to it that these agencies do not use force to protect him.[2] Pacifists can be roughly divided into two classes: those who object to the use of force or the threat of force to protect them from foreign enemies, and those who object to the use of force or threats to protect them both from foreign and domestic enemies. The first group does not object to police forces, only to armies, and are much more numerous than the second. For simplicity, however, let us begin our discussion with the second group—those who also object to the use of force by the police.

The institutional arrangements would be fairly simple. Anyone who formally declared himself a pacifist of this sort would be immediately excused from paying that share of *future* taxes that went to support the organs of force and violence, the police and armed forces. He would be compelled, however, to wear a conspicuous symbol of his pacifism and display a similar symbol on all of his property.[3] This would leave him with all of his rights as a citizen except the right to call on the organizations of force and violence to protect him, and would resemble the situation in some small towns where fire protection is provided only for those who pay subscriptions to the volunteer fire department.

If, for example, someone occupied the pacifist's house, he could go to court and get a judgment against the occupier that he could then display to the person wrongfully living in his house or put on a picket sign, but the sheriff would not remove the occupier. Similarly, if the occupier, tiring of the pacifist's picketing his house, came out with a club and inflicted severe injury upon him, this would be an illegal act, but the police would not use force to confine the assaulter or to stop him. It would be open to anyone,

[2] Pacifists do not necessarily object to all of the activities of the police and armed forces. The police direct traffic and return lost children, and the army engineers engage in public works. The pacifist presumably would wish to continue paying that part of his taxes that supports these non-coercive activities and continue to benefit from them.

[3] The converse possibility, having everyone except the pacifists wear and display a symbol of nonpacifism, would be more trouble in view of the disproportionate numbers involved, but there would be no other objection. In practice, keeping up-to-date lists of the pacifists and their property and making them available to anyone interested would, no doubt, be sufficient even without the symbols.

including, of course, the police, to expostulate with the illegal occupier of the pacifist's house and to point out to him the wicked
nature of his activity, but no force or threat of any sort would be
used to coerce him into the paths of virtue.[4]

The possibility of a private citizen's using force to protect pacifists would require special arrangements. Suppose, for example,
Miss Smith, a registered pacifist is being raped by an evil-doer.
Jones, passing by, attacks the rapist. Clearly, Jones is violating
the wishes both of Miss Smith who does not want force used to
protect her and the rapist who wishes to be undisturbed. Strictly
speaking, he is committing an assault on the rapist. It would, however, not be necessary to arrest Jones in order to insure Miss
Smith against forcible protection. Jones could have the situation
explained to him by the police and, if necessary, they could re-
strain him while the rape proceeded.[5]

Another complication would arise if one of the registered pacifists used force to defend himself. Richard Roe, for example,
approaches pacifist Doe with the objective of taking his wallet
and car key. Doe tries to prevent this by hitting or threatening to
hit Roe. There are three possible explanations for his behavior.
The first, that Doe is not really a pacifist, but only a man trying
to fraudulently reduce his tax liabilities, raises no particular difficulties. He can be sent to prison for tax fraud. The second, that
Doe has changed his mind and wishes to cease to be a registered
pacifist, also raises no particular difficulties. The rule should be
that he can cease to be a pacifist at any time, subject only to the
requirement that he proceed forthwith to the tax office in order
to make arrangements to be put back on the tax rolls. If, however, Roe had got hold of the wallet before Doe ceased to be a

[4] Since policemen normally wear a uniform that suggests the use of
force in such situations, if they chose to chide the unlawful occupier, it
would be advisable for them to make the situation clear to him in order
to avoid his misunderstanding their words as containing a threat of force.
Some form of words such as: "Your victim is a registered pacifist and,
therefore, we police will not use any form of force or threat of force to
stop you from beating him or to put you in prison or collect a fine from
you, but I think what you are doing is wrong," would be suitable.
[5] If Jones were the hot-tempered type, it might be wise to put him
under peace bond in order to insure that he does not assault the rapist the
next time he sees him.

pacifist, Doe would not be permitted to use force to reclaim it because that would be the use of force to protect a registered pacifist even though retroactively. It might also be wise to put Doe under a peace bond to make sure that he did not take his abandonment of pacifism too far.

The third possibility, that Doe is still a pacifist but has temporarily lost control of himself, raises more difficult problems. Clearly he has violated his own standards of morality and presumably wishes to be punished for his dereliction. He has also violated the law by using force to protect a pacifist—legally, he is assaulting Roe. It would seem clear that he should be imprisoned, but here it may be wiser to be merciful. After he has recovered himself, Roe could be allowed to proceed. If Doe has any doubt of his ability to stay true to his principles, the police could help him by, say, handcuffing him so that he will not be able to interfere with Roe even if he once again loses control.

So much for the total pacifists. The pacifists who object to the use of force against foreigners but not against domestic criminals can be dealt with in a very similar manner. They would be excused only that share of their taxes that went to the support of the armed forces and would receive normal police protection against depredation by their fellow citizens. If a citizen or agency of a foreign country, however, takes a pacifist's car or kidnaps him in order to put him to work in a slave labor camp, no force would be used to protect him. Presumably there would be a certain time lag between the institution of this special status for pacifists and the establishment by foreign businesses and governments of the necessary organizations to take advantage of the opportunity. With time, however, it would be fair to assume that various alien individuals, companies, and governments would establish offices in the United States for the purpose of exploiting the situation. The underdeveloped countries with their shortage of technically qualified personnel would probably be particularly active in acquiring selected pacifists. If the present king of Saudi Arabia is not successful in suppressing the slave trade in that kingdom, it should provide a ready market, particularly for young women.

The basic idea could be expanded to deal with other groups.

In recent years there has been an upsurge of anarchism, and providing the anarchists with the right to refuse to pay all taxes in return for their agreement that they will receive no governmental services might be practical. In my own opinion, both the people who call themselves anarchists and those who claim pacifism would, if presented with the opportunity of putting their principles into practice, refuse. Furthermore, those who at first chose to abandon the protection of the organized use of violence by special organs of society would, I think, rapidly change their minds on experiencing the results.[6] But this is only my opinion. Making the institutional change I suggest would not only increase freedom by making a set of alternatives that is now barred open, it would also provide experimental evidence on what is now a debated point of social theory.

Pacifism and anarchism, however, are general social philosophies. The purpose of this book has been to deal with a large number of detailed problems of social policy. It is true that the use of force to compel people to carry out the policies decided upon has been implicit, and, hence, the argument is relevant. But, basically, we have been concerned with such mundane matters as whether theft and robbery would be illegal. The reasoning can be applied in many of these areas, as well. The social contract is not necessarily without exceptions. Let us suppose that Smith objects to laws against theft. There is no reason why we could not provide a modification of the law so that he is free to steal the property of his neighbors (subject, of course, to possible reaction on their part) and is not protected against theft of his own property. If a great many people took this option, it might cause serious economic difficulties; but if only a few did, there is no reason why it should raise any difficult problems.

Furthermore, it is highly probable that in practice no one would take advantage of the "privilege"; if a few people did, they would very rapidly decide to retract. We can think of a number of other parts of our law in which this is also true, the law against murder,

---

[6] Einstein, during his early life, was an active pacifist. During the later period of his life, he was an active proponent of preparedness and war. His experience with the Nazis was the cause of his remarkably rapid conversion.

the law against assault and battery, and the law against robbery. We could not, of course, permit people to suddenly move out from under the law of murder and then move back in again a few minutes later.

There are certain parts of the law where this option could not be offered because the "criminal" activity is not reciprocal. Rape is the obvious case, but automobile offenses are probably much more important. In general, the individual who decides he does not wish to obey the speed limit would be endangering his own life and would be endangering other people's lives as well, but there is no way in which his desire not to obey the speed limit can directly react back on him in the same way as would his withdrawal from the law against theft. Thus, it would not be possible in this case to permit individuals to opt out.

Still, there does not seem any basic reason why we should not give individuals the right to opt out of a number of particular portions of the law. This, it must be admitted, would have very little practical effect; since it would be a complication, we might object to it on those grounds. Its principal advantages would be in making the mutually beneficial aspects of the law more obvious. If individuals were permitted to step outside some particular portion of the law any time they wished, they would then be prevented from arguing that this law worked to their disadvantage. This is, however, a very modest advantage and this whole Appendix is, in my opinion, a matter of very little importance. That, in fact, is the reason it is an Appendix instead of part of the text of the book.

APPENDIX B

GENERAL TABLE OF SYMBOLS[1]

B	$=$	Benefit expected to be derived by potential liar from the action being urged
B_{b_1}	$=$	Benefit obtained by Party 1 from successfully breaching the contract
B_{b_2}	$=$	Benefit obtained by Party 2 from successfully breaching the contract
B_{c_1}	$=$	Benefit derived by Party 1 from the completion of the contract
B_{c_2}	$=$	Benefit derived by Party 2 from the completion of the contract
C_1	$=$	Cost of lying (conscience cost)
C_{b_1}	$=$	Cost to Party 1 of successful breach of contract by Party 2
C_{b_2}	$=$	Cost to Party 2 of successful breach of contract by Party 1
C_c	$=$	Total court costs to parties
C_{c_1}	$=$	Cost to Party 1 of court proceedings
C_{c_2}	$=$	Cost to Party 2 of court proceedings
C_{in}	$=$	Cost of information
C_o	$=$	Conscience cost
C_p	$=$	(Chap. 8) Private cost of enforcement (includes cost of incorrect tax penalties)
		(Chap. 12) Costs of punishment
C_r	$=$	(Chap. 11) Crime rate, likelihood individual will be victim of crime
		(Chap. 12) Injury to reputation through others' knowledge that an individual has lied

[1] In some cases, the same symbol has been used to represent different things in different chapters.

C_R = (Chap. 8) Cost of Revenue Protection Service
C_t = Cost of being victim of crime
D_c = Disgrace resulting from confession
D_t = (Chap. 9) Disgrace resulting from conviction at trial
(Chap. 11) Direct profit of crime
E = Evidence
I = (Chap. 4) Insurance payment
(Chap. 8) Income
I' = Some part of income
I_c = Cost to individual of investigation by authorities of crimes that he did not commit
I_l = Injury suffered by victim from carrying out action urged by liar
L = Likelihood that the lie will be believed
L_{b_1} = Likelihood Party 1 will attempt to breach the contract

L_{b_2} = Likelihood Party 2 will attempt to breach the contract

L_C = Likelihood of compliance
L_c = Likelihood of conviction
L_d = Likelihood of detection of evasion
L_e = Likelihood that court will make erroneous decision
L_{fc} = Likelihood individual will be falsely convicted for crime he did not commit
L_{ns_1} = Likelihood that if Party 1 breaches the contract, Party 2 will refrain from suing him
L_{ns_2} = Likelihood that if Party 2 breaches the contract, Party 1 will refrain from suing him
L_p = Likelihood of punishment if lie is not believed
L_r = Likelihood that injury to the reputation will occur if lie is not believed
L_s = Likelihood individual will commit crime
N = Social return on tax (excess burden not subtracted)
P = (Chap. 4) Procedural function
(Chap. 8) Penal rate for detected noncompliers
(Chap. 11) Payoff (may be negative)
(Chap. 12) Persuasive effect of the lie: probability that the lie, if believed, will bring about the desired action
P_1 = Payoff of contract to Party 1
P_2 = Payoff of contract to Party 2
P_{b_1} = Payoff to 1 of breaching the contract

P_{b_2} = Payoff to 2 of breaching the contract

P_c = (Chap. 9) Punishment resulting from confession
(Chap. 11) Cost of maintaining police, prisons, courts
P_n = Persuasive effect of the lie: probability that the lie, if believed, will bring about the desired action.
P_r = Private cost of protection against theft. Includes nonproduction
P_t = Punishment resulting from conviction at trial
P_u = (Chap. 9) Publicity case has received
(Chap. 11) Punishment

Q_d = Quality of defense
Q_j = Quality of trial system
R = (Chap. 8) Tax rate
      (Chap. 9) Risk aversion factor
R' = Prosecutor's aversion to low conviction ratio
T_r = Tax revenue (net of direct enforcement costs)

Index